After '89

series editors
MARIA M. DELGADO
MAGGIE B. GALE
PETER LICHTENFELS

advisory board
Michael Billington, Mark Ravenhill, Janelle Reinelt, Peter Sellars, Joanne Tompkins

This series will offer a space for those people who practice theatre to have a dialogue with those who think and write about it.

The series has a flexible format that refocuses the analysis and documentation of performance. It provides, presents and represents material which is written by those who make or create performance history, and offers access to theatre documents, different methodologies and approaches to the art of making theatre.

The books in the series are aimed at students, scholars, practitioners and theatre-visiting readers. They encourage reassessments of periods, companies and figures in twentieth-century and twenty-first-century theatre history, and provoke and take up discussions of cultural strategies and legacies that recognize the heterogeneity of performance studies.

also available

Directing scenes and senses: The thinking of Regie
PETER M. BOENISCH

The Paris Jigsaw: Internationalism and the city's stages
DAVID BRADBY AND MARIA M. DELGADO (EDS)

Theatre in crisis? Performance manifestos for a new century
MARIA M. DELGADO AND CARIDAD SVICH (EDS)

World stages, local audiences: Essays on performance, place, and politics
PETER DICKINSON

Performing presence: Between the live and the simulated
GABRIELLA GIANNACHI AND NICK KAYE

Performance in a time of terror: Critical mimesis and the age of uncertainty
JENNY HUGHES

South African performance and the archive of memory
YVETTE HUTCHISON

Jean Genet and the politics of theatre: Spaces of revolution
CARL LAVERY

Not magic but work: An ethnographic account of a rehearsal process
GAY MCAULEY

'Love me or kill me': Sarah Kane and the theatre of extremes
GRAHAM SAUNDERS

Trans-global readings: Crossing theatrical boundaries
CARIDAD SVICH

Negotiating cultures: Eugenio Barba and the intercultural debate
IAN WATSON (ED.)

After '89
Polish theatre and the political

BRYCE LEASE

Manchester University Press

Copyright © Bryce Lease 2016

The right of Bryce Lease to be identified as the author of this work has been asserted by him in accordance with the Copyright, Designs and Patents Act 1988.

Published by Manchester University Press
Altrincham Street, Manchester M1 7JA, UK
www.manchesteruniversitypress.co.uk

British Library Cataloguing-in-Publication Data is available

ISBN 978 1 7849 9295 8 *hardback*
ISBN 978 1 5261 3954 2 *paperback*

First published by Manchester University Press in hardback 2016

This edition first published 2019

The publisher has no responsibility for the persistence or accuracy of URLs for any external or third-party internet websites referred to in this book, and does not guarantee that any content on such websites is, or will remain, accurate or appropriate.

CONTENTS

List of figures	*page* vi
Acknowledgments	vii
Note on the text	ix
Introduction: really existing democracy	1
1 The move to neoliberalism	29
2 No more heroes	53
3 Beyond a *teatr kobiecy*	83
4 Gay emancipation and queer counterpublics	110
5 Rethinking Polish/Jewish relations	138
6 Equivalencies of exclusion	174
Conclusion	198
Bibliography	205
Index	216

FIGURES

1 *Cokolwiek się zdarzy, kocham cię* (*Whatever Happens, I Love You*), directed by Przemysław Wojcieszek. Roma Gąsiorowska as Sugar and Agnieszka Podsiadlik as Magda. Photo by Stefan Okolowicz, © TR Warszawa page 118
2 *Anioły w Ameryce* (*Angels in America*), directed by Krzysztof Warlikowski. Jacek Poniedziałek as Louis Ironson and Tomasz Tyndyk as Prior Walter. Photo by Stefan Okolowicz, © TR Warszawa 124
3 *Kabaret Warszawksi* (*Warsaw Cabaret*), directed by Krzysztof Warlikowski. Magdalena Cielecka in an ecstatic dance routine as Sally Bowles. Photo by Magda Hueckel, © Nowy Teatr 128
4 *(A)pollonia*, directed by Krzysztof Warlikowski. Andrzej Chyra as Hercules. Photo by Magda Hueckel, © Nowy Teatr 168
5 Equivalencies of exclusion, drag and black face in *Opowieści afrykańskie według Szekspira* (*The African Tales by Shakespeare*), directed by Krzysztof Warlikowski. Photo by Magda Hueckel, © Nowy Teatr 188

ACKNOWLEDGMENTS

There are too many people to thank in such a short space. I am extremely grateful to Paul Allain, who supervised my PhD thesis and has been an encouraging mentor, an insightful editor and a generous colleague. In his inimitable style, Michal Kobialka offered a provocation to a panel I was chairing on postcommunism and performance at the Performance Studies international conference to reconsider Western-centric understandings and theorizations of 1989. This was the beginning of a conversation that has not found its end, and I am thankful for the courage of Michal's thinking and his determination to probe into cultural taboos and commonplaces. I would like to acknowledge the support of the British Academy, which made my attendance at that conference possible. Chapter 5 would not exist without Richard Schechner's insistent questions and careful editing. Conversations with Roman Pawłowski, Elwira Grossman and Bartek Frąckowiak have been illuminating and hugely beneficial. I am very excited about the culture of political experimentation that Bartek is implementing at Teatr Polski Bydgoszcz, which can act as a healthy model of coalitional, democratic theatre practice I speak to in the book. Thanks to Piotr Gruszczyński for sending me scripts when I needed them, and to Nowy Teatr and TR Warszawa for generously sharing production photographs. Discussions on gay and queer culture in Poland with Robert Kulpa and Błażej Warkocki were invaluable. Thanks to Ursula Phillips for organizing an excellent conference at University College London in 2011, where I had crucial dialogues with

Izabela Filipiak and Grzegorz Niziołek. I am still grateful for dinners with Małgorzata Sugiera and Mateusz Borowski during my initial research trips to Kraków. The archivists at the Zbigniew Raszewski Theatre Institute were patient and informative: without the extensive archives at the Institute, this project would frankly not have been possible. My Polish teacher Julia Krynke, who is also a very talented actor, has spent countless hours offering suggestions and adding nuance to my translations. Her detailed knowledge of Polish grammar – and theatre – has been of inestimable help. If there are any remaining weaknesses in the translations, I take full responsibility. Unless otherwise stated, translations are my own.

Segments of Chapter 5 appeared in my 2012 article 'Ethnic Identity and Anti-Semitism: Tadeusz Słobodzianek Stages the Polish Taboo,' *TDR/The Drama Review*, 56(2), 81–101, © 2012 New York University and the Massachusetts Institute of Technology. One section from Chapter 4 appeared in 'In Warsaw's New York: Krzysztof Warlikowski's Queer Interventions,' a book chapter in Alyson Campbell and Stephen Farrier (eds), *Queer Instruments: Local Practices and Global Queernesses* (2015), reproduced with permission of Palgrave Macmillan.

The European Theatre Research Network at the University of Kent was of tremendous value, and I want to acknowledge Peter Boenisch, Frank Camilleri and Duška Radosavljevic for their discussions on critical theory and contemporary European theatre. Simon Jones, Katja Krebs, Pam Tait and Martin White at University of Bristol were very supportive during the early stages of this work, and all of my brilliant former colleagues at University of Exeter need to be acknowledged. This was a hugely supportive environment, which helped me to find my way with this project. My current colleagues at Royal Holloway, University of London have been welcoming and generous. Melissa Blanco-Borrelli, Helen Nicholson and Dan Rebellato deserve specific acknowledgment in relation to this project. I am grateful to the editors of this series, and to Maria Delgado in particular, who read the entirety of the manuscript. Maria has been an encouraging and perceptive editor, and I am extremely thankful for her support and insights. I would also like to acknowledge the invaluable assistance from Matthew Frost at Manchester University Press. Many friends have cheered me on from the sidelines over the years – thank you to Anna Harpin, Catherine O'Gorman, Lucy Tollman, Lorenzo Anastasio, Zoe Belton and Christine Evans. To my parents for their tireless support of my scholarly endeavors and travels. Thanks to our dachshund Gretchen, who took me for walks when I needed a break from a long bout of writing or a difficult translation. And finally, all my love to Martin, who patiently endured my research trips abroad, and my books, notes and coffee cups cluttering our dining-room table. You are in this book more than you know.

NOTE ON THE TEXT

All Polish production titles are accompanied by an English translation. Where there is an existing official translation, the title is in italics. Where I have been unable to source this, I have translated the title and given it in roman. The Polish title comes before the translation except in cases where the original text was written in English.

Introduction: really existing democracy

What was to be the function of political theatre in Poland after 1989? Following four decades of Soviet-enforced communism, which included mass censorship, anti-democratic bureaucratization, systemic corruption, imperialist militarization and the brutal disciplining of political dissidents, this question formed a vital part of the ten-year anniversary celebration in 2013 of Warsaw's Instytut Teatralne (Theatre Institute). This cultural institution houses the largest physical and digital archives of contemporary theatre in Poland and is intended to support research and education and prompt public debate. *Teatr*, one of the country's leading journals, devoted a special issue to mark the anniversary, including a number of interviews and articles considering the Institute's role in the formation, analysis and documentation of contemporary and historical Polish theatre. *Teatr*'s chief editor, Jacek Kopciński, criticized the Institute's director, Maciej Nowak, for instigating 'a permanent cultural revolution' in his unconventional programming and commissioning of publications, seminars and workshops. By this, Kopciński meant that theatre studies at the Institute has been defined since its inception primarily on the grounds of feminist, gender and queer theory, which was exemplified in the Institute's flagship publication series *Inna Scena* (Another Scene). Kopciński suggested that such strands of philosophy, theory, activism and criticism were too restricted and that the Institute should also refer to mainstream modes of thinking about the theatre and the world that are 'less eccentric and, for many, less ideologised' (2013: 8).

In this argumentation, Kopciński articulates popular anxieties around Polish cultural and national identity through an exclusionary process of community formation that implies an 'authentic' audience that represents a general population who do not face matters relating to gender and sexuality as central to their experiences of social marginalization. Subjects such as gender inequality and alternative sexual identities are marginal rather than marginalized, peripheral rather than fundamental, and not the central concern of the political, public sphere. While thematically feminism, gender and sexuality might deserve attention, they are not a principal cultural focal point. Kopciński lamented that *Inna Scena* undeservedly preceded a more basic series on theatre history that has yet to come to light, which might have included biographies of canonical male theatre directors of the late twentieth century such as Gustaw Holoubek or Kazimierz Dejmek. While what is needed is a 'proper history' of the Polish theatre that is still woefully full of lacunae, Kopciński argues, the Institute has only invested in debating its alternative versions, which he opines as 'extravagant.' Disappointingly, Nowak, who championed an alternative theatre practice over the past two decades, capitulated to Kopciński's view, claiming that he was simply offering a 'complement' to traditional narratives.

In *After '89*, I will take the opposite view of both Kopciński's claim to the primacy of mainstream national and historical narratives and to Nowak's defense of the vanguardist representation of marginalized subject positions as significant only in their correlation or complementarity to normative majority positions.[1] I argue that it is the role of political theatre to activate precisely such a 'permanent cultural revolution' that does not find closure through adherence to a particular and substantive cultural identity that obscures precisely the exclusive demarcations on which it is grounded. In this way, my methodology and conceptual framework have implications for the discipline that resonate and have implications beyond the direct cultural focus of this study. Not only is the notion of a 'cultural revolution' significant in its diagnostic undermining of a stable construction of culture, 'permanent' is equally crucial in its temporal durability. I will suggest that a radical democratic pluralism is only tenable through the systematic destabilization of such attempts to close ranks and essentialize Polishness through a focus on the development of new theatre practices that have responded to the growth of pluralism and that interrogate the rise of nationalism in the move to democracy after 1989. While nationalism under communism had particular social functions, some (although not all) of which held subversive potentials, in a liberal democracy, nationalism often attests to the needs of conservative factions that foreclose contestation, counter the conditions for free individual self-development, mobilize popular anxieties and perpetuate domination by constructing the national as an omnipotent apparatus that manages and reduces difference through assimilatory and disciplinary strategies.

As I will argue in this introduction, I am wary of theatre practice that motivates unwavering adherence to particular social formations and classifies community as a site of normative values and fetishized cultural identities. The relationships I develop between theatre *and* pluralist democracy and theatre *as* a political act have wider implications for theatre and performance studies. Opposing a nationalistic theatre as a nexus for community spirit that constructs democratically defined difference as a threat to or a violation of the rights of an originary ethnic, national population, I will propose and corroborate a political theatre that encourages dissensus, and that is constitutively disruptive and skeptical of communities that are not heterogeneous and coalitional.

Poland is celebrated internationally for its rich and varied performance traditions. Throughout its history, theatres in the country have been treated as sacred institutions where Poles have fought against censorship and occupation, constructed viable cultural bonds and affirmed social cohesion. Studies in English that considered Polish theatre before 1989 generally placed an emphasis on political resistance or actor training, and the innovations of Tadeusz Kantor and Jerzy Grotowski. While Kantor and Grotowski both hold a particular (and not unproblematic) place in Western discourses and imaginaries, this project will take as its subject the dynamic new range of aesthetics, conventions and practices that have been developed since the demise of communism in the flourishing theatrical landscape of Poland, which I have not restricted to Warsaw, Kraków and Wrocław. I document how Poznań, Gdańsk, Szczeczin, Wałbrzych, Lublin, Bydgoszcz, Opole and Łódź all vie for their status as artistic centers. Since 1989, changes to political structures, governance, religious faith, community building, national and ethnic identity, and attitudes towards gender and sexuality have had a profound effect on Polish society. The theatre has retained its historical role as the crucial space for debating and interrogating cultural and political identities and this has been attended by a proliferation of criticism. For this reason, I also spend time evaluating and engaging with the dynamic and often tense debates posed by and through the Polish critical establishment. Providing access to scholarship and journalism not readily accessible to an English-speaking readership, this study will survey the rebirth of the theatre as a site of public intervention and social critique since the establishment of democracy and the proliferation of theatre-makers that have flaunted cultural commonplaces and begged new questions of Polish culture.

Political names

The title of this introduction is clearly a play on 'really existing socialism,' which is intended to draw attention first to the mode in which democracy has been too often subsumed under the banner of 'really existing capitalism,' thus eclipsing democratic conventions for the dynamics of the free market, and second, to the failures of a democracy grounded in neoliberalism, which was conceived of as the unchallenged political structure of transformation founded on the four primary concepts of privatization, liberalization, stabilization and internationalization. In *After '89*, I have been very attentive to the use of terminology that shores up conceptions of communism and life in the Polska Rzeczpospolita Ludowa (PRL, People's Republic of Poland) as they were fetishized and derided in the West. I do not use the designation Eastern Bloc, for example, which offers an impression of homogeneity, obscuring a large and diverse geographical terrain. Václav Havel observed that such an indiscriminate determination rendered the barriers between the 'Bloc' countries as inconspicuous to the West (cited in Reading, 1992: 12). 'Central Europe' replaced 'Eastern Bloc' in an effort to align postcommunist countries, particularly Poland, Czech Republic, Slovakia and Hungary, with Western European values, cultural norms and forms of Christianity and to provide distance from the proximity, both cultural and ideological, of the East, which implied Russia in particular. Historian Larry Wolf has been equally wary of Winston Churchill's coinage 'Iron Curtain,' which produced an ideological bisection of Europe during the years of the Cold War. Wolf is critical of the shadow cast by this 'curtain' on the eastern regions of the continent, which 'made it possible to imagine vaguely whatever was unhappy or unpleasant, unsettling or alarming, and yet it was also possible not to look too closely, permitted even to look away – for who could look through an iron curtain and discern the shapes enveloped in shadow?' (1994: 1). Before 1989, Western media mostly framed defection as unidirectional, escaping the terrifying East for the safety and freedom of the West, and the turn to democracy, the so-called Springtime of Nations, served to reinforce the idea of the dominance and supremacy of the West's political order, wherein the only choice politically was liberal democracy and, economically, free-market capitalism. As the political scholar Graeme Gill (2002: 178) has noted, the collapse of communism was equivalent to a 'return to Europe,' which, somewhat paradoxically, encompassed both a return to European ideals and a reassertion of traditional Polish values, often at odds with one another.[2] Within Poland, the PRL is largely seen as a period in which the country was divided from the progressive development of European history, and is expressed as an interregnum. The 1990s were then largely construed as a time for Poland to catch up with Western modernity; an entirely one-sided binary in which the country needed to regain normality after the certain and inevitable failure of the communist experiment. Poland was not seen as a cultural space that offered anything new, valuable or constructive for the West. Western tourism to postcommunist countries was constructed as the uncritical enjoyment of cheap prices and the fix of witnessing the faded kitsch of the 'second world' free from the anxieties, perceived dangers and political risks of visits under communist rule. These reductive East–West binaries do not shed light on the innumerable ways in which populations, economies and cultures have been interdependent and mutually supporting both across the continent and globally.

Some scholars have chosen to use the term 'state-imposed socialism' as opposed to 'communism' as it more clearly represents the reality of the PRL. I choose to use 'communism' although the political project was never fully realized, partly because of the way in which the goals, beliefs and strictures of the ideals of communism were nevertheless crucial to the formation of culture, and partly because, while English-language scholarship sides with 'socialism,' researchers in Poland tend to use 'communism,' and I have chosen to follow their lead. Nevertheless, the failure to establish actual communism is inherent to my usage of the term and its application to Polish culture. There was equally a temptation to employ the now popular term 'postcommunism' in the title of this book, but I have resisted this given that it too quickly restricts understandings of contemporary Poland by focusing directly on a particular moment in its history. I chose '1989' instead, as it is devised of associations around transition, transformation, vulnerability, hope and instability that I intend to unpack and critique.[3] Political theorist Michał Kozłowski warns that terms such as 'postcommunism' and 'transition' are both overly elastic and unclear, 'applied as they are to countries as disparate as Slovenia and Mongolia'; these terms are constantly redefined and exploited in the Polish political realm. Kozłowski (2008) puts pressure on postcommunism in particular, which he contends functions as a 'catch-all' for the post-1989 era that classifies what is legitimate and reasonable. The lack of any unity or coherence in this conception does not hinder its performance. On the contrary, while to designate a country as 'postcommunist' appears to be an act of benign description, in practice this assignation actively manipulates, limits and contains according to Kozłowski. Postcommunism is seen as a pejorative term that links Poland and other former communist-ruled countries to their (traumatic) past, which begs the question of the longevity and applicability of this term. There are two standard answers to this. When the 'ideals, ideologies and practices of socialism are perceived to provide a meaningful (albeit increasingly mythical) reference point for understanding people's present condition' (Hann, 2002: 11), the term will begin to lose traction and, moreover, when the generations raised under communism disappear then the category will consequently dissolve. I employ the term 'postcommunism' when I am articulating cultural identity or political configurations in either direct or perceived relation to the ongoing legacies and decipherable traces of Poland's communist past in the present. I do this with the awareness that the term 'postcommunism' is not a neutral designation, nor is it a singular narrative that encompasses a fixed set of national norms, but is rather a discourse in flux. I find 'post-transition' fails to act as a productive replacement as it too easily implies Francis Fukuyama's 'end of history,' that is, a stable and effective end of politics that finds its ultimate resolution in the particular horizons of free-market capitalism and liberal democracy. Fukuyama (1992) famously argued that liberal democracy was, in effect, the embodiment of the Hegelian stage of the end of ideological evolution and, with the collapse of communism, this political system had no legitimate opponent. Therefore, free from inherent contradiction and at the conclusion of the struggle of ideas, liberal democracy was equivalent to the 'end of history.' Ultimately, quite the opposite has been apparent. Over the past quarter of a century, it has become apparent how liberty and equality are not mutually inclusive principles in neoliberalist democracies, liberal societies are not free from internal contradiction and the principle of equality cannot be fully actualized in capitalism.

Transformations of the political

Kathleen Cioffi (1996) and Elżbieta Matynia (2009) have both championed the political impact of the alternative theatre scene in Poland under communist rule. Cioffi pointed out the particular funding systems that not only allowed for but promulgated subversive theatre practice in distinction to the professional theatres, which as primary cultural institutions were subject to strict censorship, and the ancillary institutions such as amateur theatres, particularly student groups who worked under the protection of university sponsorship, that were allowed to produce work at particular moments in the 1950s, 60s and 70s with less restrictive oversight and control. The administration of censorship mechanisms fluctuated throughout the communist period, particularly relaxed during the 'thaw' that followed the death of Joseph Stalin and the decade of the 1970s during Edward Gierek's alleged economic miracle that resulted in economic disaster, and then acutely stringent during Stalinism, the aftermath of the 1968 events in Poland and Czechoslovakia that confirmed there could be no 'socialism with a human face,' and the induction of Martial Law in the 1980s. In *Alternative Theatre in Poland, 1954–1989*, Cioffi celebrated the work of Warsaw's Studencki Teatr Satyryków (STS, Student Satirist's Theatre), who attempted to directly portray the grim communist reality rather than rely on the metaphors and allegories of the professional system; the popular avant-garde of Bim-Bom, the 'socialist romantics' who marshaled the subversive value of mirth and whimsy; Taduesz Kantor's Cricot 2, not only distinguished for the director's formal experimentation with autonomous theatre and his excavations of cultural and individual memory, but also for the company's unique position of existing outside of the state system of subsidy; the dynamic combination of physical expressivity and political daring of the Teatr Ósmego Dnia (Theatre of the Eighth Day); and the stunning visual theatres of Scena Plastyczna and Akademia Ruchu, who produced their own innovative sign systems. The closure of theatres in Warsaw on December 13, 1981 at the commencement of Martial Law signified a major crisis in Poland for resistance-oriented theatre practice. In this tense political climate, the director Jerzy Jarocki disregarded authorities and placed himself in real danger by staging T.S. Eliot's *Murder in the Cathedral*. The production was quickly put together over the Christmas period and opened in the Archikatedra św. Jana (St. John's Archcathedral) in Warsaw in 1982 with the acting ensemble from the Teatr Dramatyczny (Dramatic Theatre). Theatre in churches boomed in this period precisely because state censorship did not extend to private performances of a religious character on Church property, which made them a unique place for political critique. This was particularly significant as two major artistic directors, Adam Hanuszkiewicz at the Teatr Narodowy (National Theatre) and Gustaw Holoubek at the most politically subversive theatre in Warsaw, the Teatr Dramatyczny, both lost their tenures in the 1980s. While official state-funded theatres were highly restricted as sites of social criticism, as Maciej Karpiński noted, the Church supported many independent cultural projects and theatre productions that had become included under the rubric of 'unofficial culture,' previously restricted to literary readings (1989: 110). Similarly, Andrzej Wajda staged Ernest Bryll's religious dramatic poem *Easter Vigil* at the Kościół Miłosierdzia Bożego (Church of the Lord's Mercy) in Warsaw in 1985, starring Krystyna Janda.[4] Wajda's simple staging in the church drew an audience of more than 6,000 spectators in just 12 performances, which relied solely on word-of-mouth as publicity. Jarocki and Wajda's performances were political manifestations as much as theatrical events, drawing on the Church as a traditional space for collective gathering, the articulation of independent culture and implied protest against the communist regime. While the political thrust of the work of these directors and companies was immediately apparent before 1989, the political transformation that followed generated a radically new understanding of resistant artistic practice, as well as the role of the Catholic Church in the political organization of Polish society.

This book both picks up from Cioffi's work and goes in a radically different direction. I examine the way in which social norms are contested in the theatre, how such contestations register as political acts, and the way in which publics are differently formed after 1989. This is not a survey of Polish theatre over the past 25 years. I consciously choose examples from within and from without the construction of the contemporary canon, which is itself a concern of many public debates. If Cioffi looked at alternative theatre that worked outside of the officially funded and carefully censored professional system in order to trace the politically subversive potential of Polish theatre, I am more concerned with the professional system itself, which in good old-fashioned capitalist style has been able to assimilate precisely the norms that challenge contemporary morality, but that all too often do not present any actual challenge to the political and ideological structures underpinning that morality. This is of course one of the defining differences between communism and capitalism. In the PRL, the communist regime did not support political or social critique, which led to the often violent suppression of the intelligentsia, political dissidents and ideological critics, while conversely capitalism thrives on the assimilation – and sterilization – of criticism. The production of communities in distinction to the communist regime, which sought to collapse the boundaries between the public sphere and the state, can be seen as a political act, even if these communities were tied to particular conceptions of what the

Polish nation is (in the minds of its people) and should be (in practice). Within the horizon of democracy, however, the political, as theorized by the French political philosopher Claude Lefort, is conceived of as the moment in which there is a hole opened up in the social fabric that has not yet been filled with positive content; that is, with a definitive and singular ideological system, and therefore demands alternative forms of resistance and subversion. The change in political theatre practice after 1989 has therefore been from one that opposes the state while championing Polish nationalism to a more pluralistic practice that engages with marginalized identities purposefully left out of the rhetoric of freedom and independence. I will theorize those performances that extend the discursive limits of Polish national and cultural identity as part of a wider democratic project of implementing pluralism, paying heed to the socially marginalized, producing visibility and new subject positions, and making of public concern that which has been relegated to the private sphere and, as a consequence, considered politically irrelevant.

The Polish theatre critic Tomasz Plata maintains that the notion of political theatre under communism took two particular routes (2006: 218–19). First was the use of allusion to thwart censorship, in which stage signs had to be decoded by spectators to render their subversive, hidden meanings. The second mode, employed by Konrad Swinarski, Andrzej Wajda and Jerzy Jarocki, was the focus on the defenseless individual at odds with society, caught within an existential battle that highlighted the absurdity and precariousness of history and historical progress. In the latter case, the focus was not on individualism, but rather on the functional metaphor of the individual as representative of the national community. Considering how a wave of productions of Chekhov replaced the abandonment of grand narratives after 1989, Erika Fischer-Lichte counters Plata's claim that the focus on the 'private' discourses at work within Chekhov signaled an escapist tendency in the Polish theatre that moved from the 'here and now' to the 'always and everywhere' and consequently neglected social and public affairs (2014: 138–9). While I would argue that this shift in focus was part of the larger transcendental turn that could be seen in the work of Jarocki, Lupa and Grzegorzewski, Fischer-Lichte contends that Chekhov was the appropriate playwright to stage in this decade given his historical insights into eras of great political upheaval and social transformation. Writing in *Teatr*, Andrzej Wanat (1993) observed the similarities between the transitional eras in which Chekhov was writing in pre-revolutionary Russia and post-independence Poland, both of which were defined by generational conflict, the collapse of traditional values and practices, a denial of authority and a loss of stable categories of meaning. Breaking with the naturalistic tradition of GITIS and the Moscow Arts Theatre, Jarocki in his 1993 interpretation of *Płatonow* (Platanov) at the Teatr Polski in Wrocław mined a new approach to the play that led the critic Jacek Sieradzki (1993) to compare this production with Grzegorzewski's contemporaneous staging of *Uncle Vanya* at the Studio Teatr in Warsaw, concluding that both directors expressed ambivalent attitudes to their protagonists. Deemphasizing the empathy one normally finds with Chekhov's characters allowed for the more bitter and ironic aspects of the playwright's comedic lines to emerge, which lampooned the audience's normally reverent reception of the Russian playwright. What's more, portraying the excessive declarations of melancholy and existential angst as false, melodramatic and ultimately the result of social privilege chimed perfectly with the economic chaos of the early 1990s. By the end of the decade, however, the work of political theatre abandoned the emphasis on both allusion and the portrayal of the isolated individual forsaken by history, and took a new turn.

In *Strategie publiczne, strategie prywatne: Teatr polski 1990–2005* (*Public Strategies, Private Strategies: Polish Theatre 1990–2005*), Plata pointed to 1997 as a crucial year for a radical change in Polish theatre (2006: 227). It was in this year that Jerzy Grzegorzewski took over as artistic director of the newly reopened Teatr Narodowy (National Theatre) in Warsaw. While social alienation, temporal disunity, spiritual apathy and existential disorientation and displacement were the dominant themes in Jarocki and Lupa's productions, Grzegorzewski's highly anticipated premiere at the Teatr Narodowy moved in an entirely new direction. As I will explore in Chapter 2, what had been crucial in Grzegorzewski's directorial interventions into canonical texts in the latter part of the twentieth century was a profound break with the inherited covenant between stage and audience that formally unties the theatre as the locus of community spirit, which explains why his work is inhabited by a defamiliarizing effect. Grzegorzewski distinguished himself as a director more interested in the theatre's formalistic potentials rather than its moralizing and ideological function, and the dominating themes of his work have been the condition of the artist, particularly their pursuit of excellence, struggles with moral weakness and the limitations of the physical world. Having trained as a painter, his primary concentration was often on theatre as a visual and plastic art rather than on pictorial mimesis or psychological realism. Throughout his career, Grzegorzewski faced sharp condemnation from Polish critics due to his liberal adaptations of canonical texts, often flaunting authorial intention and stable narrative structure. Given the director's trajectory of deconstructing sacred national mythologies, it is significant that Grzegorzewski was selected to head the National Theatre, suggesting that this theatre was a place for the vital critique of Polish cultural and national identity rather than a patriotic stronghold for its inscription or reification. Stanisław Wyspiański's *Noc listopadowa* (*November Night*, 1904) was selected for the premiere. The play, which some critics refer to as effectively the fourth part of Adam Mickiewicz's paradigmatic Polish Romantic text *Dziady* (*Forefathers' Eve*), uses the 1830-31 Uprising as a nodal point to frame the tragedy of failed rebellions in the nineteenth century that fundamentally shaped Polish political consciousness in the twentieth century. The critic Roman Pawłowski (2007) noted that for two centuries the Polish intelligentsia shared the fate of their National Theatre, which held the responsibility of defending national identity, guarding cultural traditions and teaching patriotism. Grzegorzewski's National Theatre, however, was a mirror for the Polish sociopolitical reality at the turn of the millennium rather than a monument to a sublimated past or messianic future.

The year 1997 was equally significant in marking the emergence of two major new Polish artists, one in the visual arts, Paweł Althamer, and the other in the theatre, Krzysztof Warlikowski. These artists established a new set of questions, expectations and conventions that in turn produced new publics. By posing relevant questions about social marginalization that moved away from the standard constructions of Polishness as white, Catholic, heterosexual and, very often, male, they critiqued Polish society as a depository of insular values and exclusionary moral interests. Through his installations Althamer opened up the artistic spaces previously reserved for the intellectual and economic elite to the socially marginalized and expanded the field of cultural reference outside of Polish contexts in the shaping and contesting of cultural identity. Krzysztof Warlikowski, a member of the first generation to work exclusively in a 'free' Poland, has undoubtedly had the greatest impact on Polish theatre since the late 1990s. Kopciński (2000) argues that Krystian Lupa introduced Warlikowski to subjects that would come to shape his work, such as cultural dispossession, spiritual atrophy, a deficiency of collective identity, internal chaos and immaturity. Warlikowski eschewed texts and directing styles that rely on assimilationist or exclusionary cultural strategies, which attempt to essentialize Polish history or embody the essence of the Polish nation. Warlikowski's theatre has disrupted accepted historiography, broken down traditional gender roles, frustrated dominant cultural discourses and commentaries, reconsidered synchronic notions of time, favored the individual over the collective and interrogated sexuality in place of nationality.

Grzegorz Jarzyna was only 29 years old when he took over management of the Teatr Rozmaitości, making him the youngest artistic director in the country at the time. In this theatre on Warsaw's trendy Marszałkowska Street, Warlikowski directed many of his early seminal productions of Shakespeare, Euripides and Sarah Kane. Fearing that Warsaw had become a cultural desert in the 1990s, Jarzyna wished to open a venue for the production of avant-garde theatre similar to those in neighboring Germany, such as the Kulturbrauerei in Berlin and the Kampnagel in Hamburg (cited in Wyżyńska 2005). Fueled by substantial media attention, the Rozmaitości was soon known as the 'fastest theatre in town.' Many critics remarked on the immense enthusiasm, even impatience, mounting in audiences that matched the energy of the productions. After asking Warlikowski to join forces in 1999, the two young directors were indelibly linked, treated for some time as Siamese twins, according to Kopciński (2000), who spoke with one voice the manifesto of a new generation. The situation, however, was far more complicated in reality. Rumors of the large riffs over creative control that shaped much of their artistic cooperation, which only served to increase their popularity and notoriety, ended with Warlikowski's departure to start his own company Nowy Teatr (New Theatre) in 2010.

Despite their creative differences, these directors were responsible for drawing a new younger audience who had been put off by the transcendental 'high art' theatre of their parents' generation. Performances frequently sold out at the stylishly rebranded TR Warszawa, where an innovative brand of aesthetics borrowed from pop music and culture, street slang, uses of English and German adopted into contemporary Polish vernacular and quotations from art-house cinema (Pasolini, Dogma 95, Lynch, van Sant, Godard and Hitchcock in particular). Representing Poland at major theatre festivals around the world, including Edinburgh, Avignon, New York, Hong Kong and Moscow's Golden Mask, the pair have stood as ambassadors for contemporary Polish theatre and the TR Warszawa became the most identifiable Polish brand for theatre overseas. Fischer-Lichte contends that Althamer and Warlikowski, to which I would add Jarzyna, 'followed paths that connected Polish art and theatre with that of Western European countries,' which 'opened up the possibility of a dialogue with other European cultures, emphasizing what Polish culture shared with them instead of highlighting its otherness' (2014: 144),[5] and the extent of their influence led one critic to claim that 'the history of contemporary Polish theatre can be divided in pre- and post-Jarzyna/Warlikowski' (Nyc, 2007).

Throughout *After '89*, I give particular attention to Warlikowski's interventions into historical narratives and normative identities. Having explored the limits of cultural taboos through his feminist and postcolonial reworkings of Shakespeare, the performativity and elasticity of gender in Sarah Kane, and the decline in religious faith in Euripides, Warlikowski's later work dealt directly with Polish/Jewish relations, contested legacies of the Holocaust, Polish anti-Semitism, gay rights and AIDS, queer identities and alternative sexualities. Warlikowski's work in the 1990s and 2000s signaled a widespread move away from a focus in much Polish theatre on the 'human soul' and a preoccupation with transcendental spirituality, which has been replaced by a corporeal turn, a concentrated focus on material bodies, gender roles and sexuality.

Defining the political theatre

In 'Political Fictions and Fictionalisations: History as Material for Postdramatic Theatre,' Mateusz Borowski and Małgorzata Sugiera consider the political potential of Hans-Thies Lehmann's oft-cited study *Postdramatic Theater* (1999; English translation 2006). One of the primary concerns for the establishment of political theatre practice today, they observe vis-à-vis Lehmann, is that the diffusion of authority, power and governance in the contemporary globalized world results in both the obscuring of social and economic processes and their expansion across national borders that makes it impossible to grasp motivations for crises and conflicts in their entirety (Borowski and Sugiera, 2013: 67). Consequently, it is no longer reasonable to assume that Brechtian forms of epic theatre will lay bare the underlying structures of oppression engendered through capitalist production and social relations in a transparent and straightforward manner. Borowski and Sugiera are particularly sensitive to Lehmann's argument that political theatre today must subvert the very foundational categories of the political in order to probe the assumptions underwriting popular political discourse and to make room for spectators to reflect on the ethics, efficacy and limitations of current forms of political involvement, many of which are deeply complicit with the dynamics of late capitalism. Equally, audiences engage with theatres as institutions in particular historical moments in relation to their 'current interests, frame of mind, cognitive capacities and dominant convictions' (*ibid.*: 72). Actively shaping audiences and producing particular, and I would argue temporally bound, counterpublics to hegemonic discourses is therefore one of the primary political tasks of the theatre.[6] Michael Warner has defined *counterpublics* as a public 'structured by alternative discourses or protocols, making different assumptions about what can be said or what goes without saying,' whose 'exchanges remain distinct from authority and can have a critical relation to power' (2002: 56).

Borowski and Sugiera are invested in the notion of the 'sensible' elaborated in Jacques Rancière's *The Politics of Aesthetics* (2004), wherein the author posits a theory of art and politics as an historically contingent means of social ordering and communication that are responsible for the 'distribution of the sensible.' Art then only becomes political 'the moment it confirms the existing order or introduces a new pattern of distribution of the material and symbolic space, and shifts the borderline between that which in the public domain is either visible or invisible, excluded, and deprived of representation and autonomous voice' (Borowski and Sugiera, 2013: 73). The onus of the political then becomes the register of representation rather than the deliberate amplification of politics, social conflicts or identity-based concerns. Following from this incentive, in the performance examples I examine I am as concerned with the political register of representations, both their aesthetic and social conventions and effects, as I am with offering semiotic-based performance analysis. While I agree with Borowski and Sugiera that art does not need to take up the concerns of politics to be political, I differ from their choice of terminology when they assert that 'politics lies at the core of establishing communities based on a set of shared values, beliefs and principles of conduct' (*ibid.*: 73). Far from producing harmonious collectives organized around common belief systems or shared values, I side with gender and economic theorist Miranda Joseph, who suggested the abandonment of the notion of 'community' altogether in her seminal study *Against the Romance of Community* (2002). Joseph is suspicious of the connotations of 'community' and particularly attentive to the modes in which it can shut down rather than mobilize collective action. While community might suggest 'cherished ideals of cooperation, equality and communion,' Joseph demonstrates how communities can also be 'disciplining and exclusionary' (2002: vi–vii). Of necessity is the way in which racism, sexism and violence have been central to the establishment of nations and liberal states as communities, and critics' fetishization of community as a predetermined good obscures 'the enactment of domination and exploitation' predicated on the constitution and organization of society as community. Benedict Anderson (2006) has also focused on the narrative function of conceiving of nationhood through the evocation of a mythic trauma that is continuously recirculated and repurposed in the construction of nation as an organic community. Seeking the organic over the constructed element of community seems to me to be particularly treacherous in the post-1989 political universe.

The assertion of Polish homogeneity by the conservative right functions like philosopher Slavoj Žižek's conception of a 'sublime object' that disguises a social antagonism and promises social unity through its eradication. Siding with Žižek, I argue that national identity is not correlative to the category of truth. Žižek's notion stems from Immanuel Kant's reflection on ethnic roots, which 'engage in a *private use of reason*, constrained by contingent dogmatic presuppositions' (Žižek, 2006: 9, emphasis in original). Adherence to ethnic identity should therefore be directly contrasted to the dimension of universal reason. Particular reason (national identity), an equivalent term to 'private use of reason,' is not the exact obverse of the universal, which follows an entirely different logic. What particular reason fails to take into account in its xenophobic aspect is that social antagonism is not the direct opposition between 'self-identical' social groups, but rather an inherent feature of social identity; that is to say, antagonism always-already splits any self-identical group itself. One must reject adherence to national identity insofar as it functions as a displacement of social antagonism onto a foreign, ethnic or religious other. Identity politics have been crucial in left-wing theatre in Poland precisely because the implementation of this democratic discourse requires that structural forms of oppression are highlighted, contested and subverted. It is not enough to simply offer token representations of sexism, misogyny, racism, anti-Semitism and homophobia, none of which can be completely divorced from class relations, unless the social relations on which they are structurally compounded are interrogated.

While it was crucial to signify dissonance through the particular assertion of 'Polishness' against the communist regime, which was often framed as a foreign invader, the next step was to create counternarratives for those excluded from this particularity. Supposed Polish homogeneity, which was already mythical and largely inaccurate, functioned not only as a category for the exclusion of minority identities, it also was a category that disguised the social desire *for* homogeneity that re-emerged in the 1990s. Rather than forming a community around shared values, which I see as the effort to produce unity through the universalization of identity and the reduction of difference, I am invested in an understanding of political theatre as predicated on dissensus, which Rancière defines as 'an activity that cuts across forms of cultural and identity belonging and hierarchies between discourses and genres, working to introduce new subjects and heterogeneous objects into the field of perception' (in Corcoran, 2010: 2). Dissensus is not simply the opposite of consensus, but is rather the 'reorienting of general perceptual space' that unsettles forms of belonging grounded through consensus, and is an act or demonstration of impropriety that unfixes the assumed indivisibility between a fact and its interpretation, legal status and the declaration of rights, or between a subject and her 'proper' place in the social hierarchy that makes it possible for new subjects and heterogeneous objects to come to light.

Although operative in creating effective bonds of solidarity between citizenry, Jürgen Habermas warns against the affective or emotional identification of citizens to a community that are produced through attempts to define the nation through ethnicity (2002: 115). I side against conceiving of a 'national people' that presupposes hereditary membership to the nation through kinship and shared ethnicity, and instead conceive of nation after 1989 as equal citizens in a legal membership. Economic instability, among other political factors such as social alienation, has led to the rise in Poland and across East and Central Europe of nationalistic-oriented rhetoric that attempts to renew social solidarity through the revivification of a national consciousness, the 'thick' citizenship that Habermas sees as regressive in *The Inclusion of the Other* (1996, 2002); he further argues for citizens to identify with the principles of democracy and to acknowledge the equal worth of others. With regards to these concerns, I spend time in Chapters 2–4 analyzing the nationalist and exclusionary orientation of Lech and Jarosław Kaczyński's Law and Justice Party (*Prawo i Sprawiedliwość*), which met with huge popularity in the first decade of the twenty-first century. The point is that one has to move away from an essentialized notion of community and nationality across the political spectrum, from a socialist-oriented conception of the social body to the ultra-conservative Catholic-inflected national body. In eras of political upheaval and stratification, it is one thing to situate history and traditions within a pluralistic society to find an anchor for cultural identity; it is quite another to attempt to constitute a nation around a homogenous set of cultural values that absolutely excludes others based on race, ethnicity, gender or sexual orientation. The pluralistic approach of contemporary theatre practice is crucial in this de-essentialization.

Scholars such as Michal Kobialka have considered the ongoing effects of 1989 as a spatial and temporal category that resonates with the neoliberal imaginary of new materialist conditions. Moving beyond a limited focus on narrative and aesthetics, Kobialka calls for new models in the consideration of the problems and failures resulting from the 'emancipatory endeavors prompted by the Western idea of liberal democracy' and the 'recurring utopian dream that it will still be possible to construct a rational order of things' (2009a: 79). It is in the nature of political theatre to change shape, form, context and framework as part of a process of discarding stale political identities and obsolete national, cultural and social configurations. As I outline in Chapter 1, in Krystian Lupa's work we see a move away from cultural essentialism after the 1990s, where the spiritual condition of the nation is represented through Dostoyevsky and other European novelists, to the focus on celebrity, media and alternative sexualities in the 2000s. While these have significant relations to neoliberalism, they are not confined to the concerns of a particular or essentialized cultural position. This move sums up a more widespread trend in democratic Poland to open up the exclusionary category of Polishness. While national identity may remain a unifying signifier for the political designation of a civic body, the civic body must remain open and un-signified. Once the positive content of this signifier is firmly and finally established, it loses its political potential and instead begins to function as the site of exclusionary discourse that results in domination and marginalization.

The political theatre can be a shared social space in which citizens come to know their human rights, what Claude Lefort refers to as the 'generative principles of democracy' (1988: 260), and take part in the dissemination of a radical democratic discourse in which normalized forms of subjugation are graspable. This is crucial in shifting experiences of subordination that do not allow the subject to grasp that her identity is overpowered by an agent that blocks the full realization of her identity, to a self-conscious understanding of oppression. As political theorist Anna Marie Smith explains, this shift requires that a subject must have tools to allow her first 'to envision a world that lies beyond subordination and to imagine what she could become in that alternative space, second, to analyze the ways in which she has become caught up in and thwarted by the relation of subordination, and third, to grasp the possibilities for collective struggle to overthrow the entire subordinating structure' (1998: 8). The demand for equality within the horizons of liberal democracies, therefore, may only occur if there is a shift in perspective from one of subordination to one of oppression. The political work of the theatre functions along similar lines that often begins with imagining a new, alternative world that requires the spectator's analysis, which has liberatory implications both for an individual's personal life choices and expressions of identity as well as her participation within a collective struggle. While I will demonstrate in Chapters 3–5 how these have been more productive for women, gays and lesbians and Polish/Jewish relations, I will focus in Chapter 6 on the less successful construction of political critique with regards to race and racial discrimination.

The question is how to deploy or instrumentalize a radical democratic pluralist imaginary, and how the theatre in particular plays a role in its formation and distribution. If politics is 'a positively determined sub-system of social relations in interaction with other sub-systems (economy, forms of culture)' (Žižek, 2002: 193), the political (Claude Lefort's *le Politique*) is a moment of openness or undecidability in which the structuring principle of society is called into question. For this reason, as political theorist Chantal Mouffe argues, it cannot be 'restricted to a certain type of institution, or envisaged as constituting a specific sphere or level of society,' but rather 'must be conceived as a dimension that is inherent to every human society and determines our very ontological condition' (1993: 3). The Lacanian political theorist Yannis Stavrakakis argues that in defining politics as the space of 'political institutions, such as parties, etc.,' we lose the dimension of the political itself (1999: 72). For this reason, the political engenders social transformation without being correlative to a new social fantasy or a 'political' project's institutionalization. For Lefort,

> The political is thus revealed, not in what we call political activity, but in the double movement whereby the mode of institution of society appears and is obscured. It appears in the sense that the process whereby society is ordered and unified across its divisions becomes visible. It is obscured in the sense that the *locus* of politics (the *locus* in which parties compete and in which a general agency of power takes shape and is reproduced) becomes defined as particular, while the principle which generates the overall configuration is concealed. (Lefort, 1988: 11)

This is in line with Rancière's positing of the political as 'that [which] simultaneously denies every foundation on which it might come to form the positivity of a sphere or a purity' (in Corcoran, 2010: 3). Taking up Lefort's postulation of the political, Mouffe and Ernesto Laclau have theorized a radical democratic pluralist imaginary that challenges and delegitimizes normalized forms of subjection, thus opening up the possibility of envisaging an end to subjugation. The shift to liberal democracy and free-market capitalism after 1989 resulted in the reduction of women's rights and a documented rise in homophobia, racism, anti-Semitism, xenophobia, ethnic exclusionism and chauvinist nationalism across the postcommunist landscape. Such forms of prejudice either were not officially accounted for in the PRL, or were buried for political purposes.

Therefore, it is perhaps not enough to simply say that there was a sharp rise in these forms of prejudice after 1989, but rather that the occurrence of such beliefs in Polish culture came to light. In opposition to these developments, Laclau and Mouffe dispute Habermas' emphasis on public consensus, instead offering a vision of radical pluralist democracy that is reliant on an infinite series of political contestations that are never fully resolved, in which those who exercise public authority can never become self-identical with the position of power, and in which shared values, cultural identity and common goals never find a substantive and undeviating articulation. In opposition to an authoritarian hegemony that seeks the greatest disciplining of difference and which strictly regulates spaces of dispute, radical democratic pluralism multiplies the points of contestation and defends the plurality and autonomy of public space created by democratic struggles.

Further to dissensus, in conceiving of a counterpublic produced through political theatre, I side with Nancy Fraser's critique of Habermas' conception of the public sphere, which the German philosopher confines to a singular conception of the public that is dependent upon the normative limitations of the white, male bourgeoisie. Distancing herself from Fukuyama's premature proclamation of the demise of Soviet communism as synonymous with capitalism's world domination that signified the 'end of history,' and which Derrida critiqued in *Specters of Marx* (1994) as a fundamental misunderstanding of liberal democracy as a contemporary process of exploitation and subjugation, Fraser is invested in theorizing the limits of late-capitalist societies and the ongoing discursive and ethical work involved in the development of liberal democracies. It is well-known that communist regimes failed to fully appreciate the necessary critical distance required between the state and civil society, which requires unrestricted public arenas for the circulation of discourse and analysis and the formation and articulation of public opinions, which, in the long run, support the preservation of a stable society. Fraser uses Soviet-style communism as an example to reinforce the value of Habermas' championing of the public sphere and its political significance and impact, arguing that the conflation of state apparatuses with the public sphere in East and Central Europe resulted not in a participatory form of socialism but rather in the authoritarian repression of the socialist citizenry (Fraser, 1992: 110). The public sphere for Habermas, Fraser maintains, 'designates a *theater* in modern societies in which political participation is enacted through the medium of talk' that produces a 'space in which citizens deliberate about their common affairs, and hence an institutionalized arena for public discursive interaction' (*ibid.*, emphasis added). The public sphere and the state must therefore be separated in order to nurture and ensure a site for the production and circulation of discourses that are capable of criticizing that state. In capitalism, the public sphere must also be separated from determinate market relations. Reiterating the stage metaphor, Fraser suggests the public sphere is 'a *theater* for debating and deliberating rather than buying and selling' (*ibid.*: 111, emphasis added). Fraser is particularly critical, however, of Habermas' assertion that the public sphere requires a bracketing of social inequalities between citizens for the unrestrained and democratic interaction of competing discourses. The problem is that Habermas presumes that the systemic exercise of power can be temporarily neutralized in order for social inequalities to be temporally bracketed to enable the free circulation of democratic discourse. However, the public sphere is determined through gender, largely masculinity, ethnic privilege and education. While the theatre allows for silenced voices to be heard and marginalized bodies to be visible, I argue that political theatre, as a site of public debate, does not propose to bracket inequalities, but rather to emphasize them, thus challenging the very social prejudices that are disavowed, and thus confirmed, by their ostensible neutralization or temporary banishment. This process of un-bracketing makes space for the *political* work of the theatre, as Rancière articulates the aesthetics of politics, by making visible that which was unknown or invisible, producing subject positions on the part of those with no part.

In the Polish context, the problem is the mode in which the political transformation resulted in a particular claim to the role of the public by the groups that were suppressed under communism. After 1989, the very same repressed and marginalized public returns in its obverse form, as the exclusive community (ethnically Polish, heterosexual, Catholic, male-dominated) that legitimates its own interests and articulations of nationhood and nationality, thus naturalizing such national formations. What's more, the assertion of a singular public constitutes culture as autonomous in time and space, rather than porous, open to change and multivalent. What we see in the political theatre, quite vehemently by the nascent years of the twenty-first century, is the emergence of rival publics and counterpublics that challenge the assertion of a singular Polish public and the understanding of Polish culture as predetermined and intransigent. I follow Michael Warner's differentiation between public and counterpublic. The former is a 'space of discourse organized by nothing other than discourse itself' that exists 'by virtue of being addressed.' In other words, 'an addressable object is conjured into being in order to enable the very discourse that gives it existence' (Warner,

2002: 67). A public is self-organized and independent from the state, and is addressed to strangers as public discourse, and not only reserved for known members of a group or community. Given that a public is formed through the medium of its address, it can be differentiated from a nation not only because membership is free and voluntary but precisely for the reason that its members must be active and attentive. Indeed, attentiveness is precisely the 'sorting category' of a public, rather than national or communal identity (*ibid.*: 87). Although a counterpublic is generated by the same features, it is distinguishable from a public in a number of ways. First, it remains conscious of its status as subordinate to dominant publics and a 'hierarchy of stigma is the assumed background of practice' (*ibid.*: 121). This impacts its modes of address, its use of speech and its discursive articulation of bodies and identities, placing emphasis on transformative rather than replicative discourse. Crucially, for political theatre and the circulation of discourse that produces publics and counterpublics, address must be extended impersonally and be available for co-membership based on attention and not on bounded or restricted and exclusive notions of identity.

Across the chapters of this book, we find examples of political theatres producing both publics and counterpublics, which have been able to contest the exclusionary norms legitimized through a singular articulation of a Polish public and the realization of collective social knowledge resistant to change, which in the theatre has been reliant on fresh approaches to directing, the abandonment or rewriting of canonical texts, the staging of emergent subject positions, the employment of daring new aesthetics and innovative experiments with modern technologies. As these theatres are publicly funded institutions not working independently of the state I do not see them as what Fraser has coined 'weak publics,' those publics whose 'deliberative practice consists exclusively in opinion formation and [do] not also encompass decision making' (1992: 134). I agree with performance theorist Shannon Jackson that designating certain publics as 'weak' is normative (2011: 9), and I also share her attentiveness to the implications and significance of the state funding critical art practices. Unlike the theatre counterpublics that contested the official and appropriated civic society under communism and that were determined by shared moral values, developing publics and counterpublics elaborate alternative norms, generate dissensus and conceive of the public sphere as constituted by difference rather than unity. This shift in the nature of the public sphere in the 1990s denoted a move from a repressive mode of domination to a hegemonic one, that is 'from rule based primarily on acquiescence to superior force to rule based primarily on consent supplemented with some measure of repression' (Fraser, 1992: 117). The public sphere today then is no longer something one may simply resist or withstand; as the site of the construction of majority consent, it can therefore either directly be linked to hegemonic modes of domination or it can act as a resistant site of antagonization, provocation, contestation and conflict. The public sphere is *both* a stage for the formation of discursive opinion and an arena for the formation and enactment of social identities, which for theatre and performance scholars is of acute significance.

Where Fraser diverges from Habermas is in the latter's assumption that the propagation of competing counterpublics is a move away from greater democracy and that deliberation about the common (public) good is of more value than individual (personal) interests. If there were the kind of singular, overarching public sphere that Habermas articulates in his seminal *The Structural Transformation of the Public Sphere* (1962, 1991), then 'members of subordinated groups would have no arenas for deliberation among themselves about their needs, objectives and strategies' (Fraser, 1992: 123). Theatre as a significant location for the inaction of the public sphere in Poland – a space that any person has the right, if not always the means, to attend – makes it a crucial site of political activity, particularly for the expression of repressed histories and curtailed, marginalized or heretofore unimagined identities. As I will demonstrate throughout the book, oppositional theatre publics and counterpublics have been crucial in articulating the thoughts and voices of those left out of the official discourse on Polishness by *un*bracketing inequalities and overtly thematizing them. Not only then does the theatre substantiate 'interpublic relations,' provoking dialogue between publics with conflicting views or competing political agendas, it also enables 'intrapublic relations,' safe spaces for the discursive interaction and strategizing of a marginalized public who are connected by a common history, political affiliation or identity. Fraser calls these 'subaltern counterpublics' that are 'parallel discursive arenas where members of a subordinated social groups invent and circulate counterdiscourses to formulate oppositional interpretations of their identities, interests and needs' (1992: 123). What was relegated as an individual and personal matter, and thereby not of interest to the public sphere, is recuperated and enunciated as a public and political concern through the work of these counterpublics that widens the discursive space of cultural and national identity and the political. The point is that such understandings of counterpublics, which have both a contestatory *and* a publicist function, present one possible solution to the kind of separatism that the communist usurpation of the public sphere produced. Whereas subversive political performance intended to undermine communist society, the publics and counterpublics I analyze help to stabilize stratified pluralist society through their formation, enactment of a democratic participatory parity and performances of contestation.

Overview

Analyzing these publics and counterpublics, I consider the political and aesthetic tenants of Polish Romanticism, which was traditionally understood to fortify the ideals of a 'nationless' Poland during Partitions and occupations, inclusive of Soviet-enforced communism, by placing emphasis on the metaphysical and rebellious nature of a national hero. In Chapter 1, first conceiving of the modes in which this tradition translates directly into both patterns of thought and national identity in the 1990s and its subsequent dismantlement in the 2000s, I then frame this discussion with a focus on the contested and disavowed legacies of the Solidarity movement, a politically charged referent that remains open-ended and thus easily instrumentalized in cultural debates in Chapter 2. I argue that the legacy of the Polish Romantic hero is a figure that must be extremely sensitive to changes in specific historical situations, political constellations and ongoing social metamorphoses, which I assert is not so much a death of tradition, as is laboriously hypothesized, as its realignment. Spending time over Jerzy Grzegorzewski's grapplings with Romantic paradigms and Tadeusz Kantor's resistance to nationalist essentialism, I consider a subsequent generation of directors such as Jan Klata, Monika Strzępka, Paweł Demirski, Paweł Wodziński and Michał Zadara, who have adapted Romantic texts in an effort to redraw boundaries of national consciousness and community formation that were seen as absolute and unassailable. Ultimately, I contend that the crucial understanding of pluralistic democracy requires the inclusion of identities that have been traditionally excluded from the restrictive notion of the 'Romantic community' that is built on complex lines of racial, ethnic, national and sexual division.

In Chapters 3 and 4, I turn my focus towards developments in feminist and queer thinking in the theatre. In examining feminist new writing and reworkings of the Polish canon, I assert that it is imperative to amend the habit of interpreting the political transformation as lacking gender components and to stop codifying women's experiences as uniform or homogenous. As both the civic and the social spheres have become increasingly sexualized, the radical right continues to reinforce conceptions of nationhood through gender binaries. The performances by Krystian Lupa, Krzysztof Warlikowski, Andrzej Wajda, Anna Augustynowicz and Maja Kleczewska I concentrate on in Chapter 3 seek to disrupt the ongoing solidification of binary tropes that position women as either eroticized victims and sexualized objects or asexual martyrs that safeguard conservative national narratives and restore traditional hierarchies in a return to a Polish 'normality' that is antithetical to communism. I argue that the primary objectives of staging gender in political theatre over the past two decades has been to repudiate a perceived 'proper' femininity, to advocate and contest legacies of feminism, to represent innovative and lateral forms of kinship and intimacy, to disrupt the reinforcement of heterosexuality as originary and natural and to attend to the insights offered by trans bodies, identities and experiences.

Given that vanguardist approaches to theatre-making privilege the culturally excluded, I maintain in Chapter 4 that queer theory does not merely *illustrate* formal innovations, but rather provides a uniquely appropriate vocabulary for the theatre to articulate its own aims to itself. Queer theory is both before and between, rather than descriptive and after.[7] In conservative public discourses, gays and lesbians are still framed in conservative rhetoric as a threat to the family, a concomitant symbol of the collapse of society, demonized figures produced through sin and perversion and a pathologized body in need of medical treatment and prayer. Homophobia continues to mark the boundaries of normative masculinity in public discourse. I invest considerable space to theatre that has staged alternative paradigms, tested the limits of political activism through new conceptions of alternative sexualities, championed gay rights, constructed queer counterpublics and enacted queer worlds.

Conceptualizing the Polish other has been complicated by the composite concurrence of the country's colonial histories, rebellions and attendant narratives of Polish suffering, marytrdom and victimhood alongside an identification with Western Europe that produces a sense of cultural elitism that distinguishes Poland from Russia. In the final chapters, I chart the most paradigmatic interventions into 'exclusive communities' that attempt to yoke national identity to Polish ethnicity and practice decisive omissions from the construction of critical histories. In the twentieth century, the anti-Semitism either directed at Jews in Poland or that was more broadly at work within ideological systems was largely disavowed, deployed for political point-scoring or simply prohibited from critique in public discourse. In Chapter 5, my focus on Polish/Jewish relations gives particular attention to the public debate provoked by the publication of the historian Jan T. Gross' *Neighbors: The Destruction of the Jewish Community in Jedwabne, Poland* (2001), which attributes guilt for the 1941 Jedwabne pogrom to ethnic Poles rather than the German National Socialists. The publication of Gross' monograph caused mass outrage, provoking Joanna Michlic (2002) to identify the debate around the pogrom as the most important and longstanding in postcommunist Poland. A large number of productions by artists such as Krzysztof Warlikowski, Jan Klata, Tadeusz Słobodzianek, Małgorzata Sikorska-Miszczuk, Artur Pałyga and Marcin Liber appeared within an environment of public outrage and recriminations over culpability for anti-Semitic violence in Poland over the course of the last century that gave voice to alternative and often-repressed histories, Jewish lives and experiences, and that mark a haunting and acutely felt absence of Jewish populations after the Holocaust and the purges of 1968.

Furthering this discussion, the staging of non-ethnic Polish others and attendant questions around the status of Poland as a postcolonial space form the basis of Chapter 6. While a number of scholars have detected an overlap between the colonizing experiences of language, political economies, labor, resistance and emancipation between postcolonial nations in the Global South and countries formerly governed by or under Russia and later the Soviet Union, the performances I examine both undermine and disrupt the assimilation of Poland under the referent of postcolonial by drawing attention to a concomitant capacity in the country to reproduce colonial discourses. Although a number of progressive directors such as Krzysztof Warlikowski and Bartek Frąckowiak and writers like Weronika Szczawińska and Dorota Masłowska have felt empowered to articulate a discerning appraisal of Polish values through the lens of race and ethnicity, I articulate an apprehension about the coupling of a critique of ethnic nationalism purely and singularly to the ethnically Polish body. Despite artists' attempts to disarticulate biology from culturally constructed notions of racial character, they do not purport to resolve social contradictions in the confrontations they stage between ethnically Polish bodies and other cultures and races. Throughout Chapter 6, I challenge the equivalencies of exclusion that move across the political spectrum on race and ethnicity but that fall short of generating dissensus, demonstrating that the universalization of exclusivity as a category fails to take into account the particularities of oppression that are systemically linked to the prerogative of Polish whiteness, as well as the postcolonial imperative to allow for a speaking position that does not render the other invisible or silenced.

First attempting to theorize a shift towards neoliberalism and a subversion of the Polish-Romantic paradigms that were so crucial for expressions of public resistance to the communist regime, the chapters that follow look towards the particular subjects and bodies that have been excluded from understandings of national identity and, as a result, the public sphere. Acknowledging the legitimacy of genuine democratic differences, I hope to uncover the obfuscated desires at work in the founding of the political with a positive content, asking whether theatres function as a symptom of social antagonism or if they, instead, reinforce the fantasy of consistent cultural self-identity. If the proliferation of sites of contestation is a sign of the health of a pluralistic democracy, then the establishment and multiplication of political theatres are one of its significant expressions. Political theatre, as I posit it, does not offer substantive, concrete or universalist solutions to hegemony but provides a space for the enacting of political demands that bring to light social exclusions, working against the closure strategies that jeopardize democratic principles. I invest time in productions that fully attempt to account for dominance, upholding difference in identity, exposing and putting at risk hegemonic social relations, activating effectual alliances, offering alternative understandings of the law and its transgression, and strengthening bonds of reciprocity in the work of building pluralistic democracy in Poland after 1989.

Notes

1 Here I choose the term 'subject positions,' by which I mean identities that perform interpretive and mediating roles in the provocation or encouragement of certain practices at particular historical moments, as opposed to the *subject*, which in psychoanalysis is associated with lack and the 'impossibility of identity.' While subject positions are also unstable, imperfect and incomplete, this term focuses on the political effects and mobilizations of identities over their coherent or stable production. For more on subject positions, see Norval (1996: 64).

2 Jerzy Szacki argues that in the PRL the only serious Western tradition Poland retained was the strong tie to the Roman Catholic Church. The 'freedom' that one finds in postcommunist political rhetoric is attached to a much older notion of the Polish nobility and not to modern liberalism (1995: 45–7). This signals some of the obstacles in the transition period. If Poland's experience of liberalism was strictly limited to the struggle against

communism, then it follows on that the country did not have a positive political program to revert back to after 1989. This accounts for the apparent absence of a solid or stable liberal doctrine that safeguarded personal liberty, freedom of choice and the protection of individual rights through society. This led Szacki to query whether any other kind of liberalism in Poland existed beyond economic liberalism (*ibid.*: 173). No one would deny the legacy of hostility between the Catholic Church and proponents of liberalism in Poland. The essential problem revolves around the appearance of these ideologies as incompatible and in direct competition, wherein liberalism is positioned as militantly atheistic and anti-clerical and the Church as fundamentalist and closed (*ibid.*: 201). There needs to be a change in the very discourse that sets up this binary opposition if there is to be constructive discussion between groups.

3   The defining image of the collapse of communism was the fall of the Berlin Wall. This was a tangible image of mass protest to which the success of democracy and liberty over the evil of communism could be attributed. What was missing from this picture was the communists themselves. If one was to overthrow them, where were they? This peculiar absence in most CEE countries, with the obvious exception of Nicolae Ceauşescu's execution in Romania, led to a period of transition that was at times difficult to define. Because the memory of this collapse failed to unite citizens in a cohesive national identity, many politicians sought in reinscribe the events of 1989 with their own ideological significance (Mark, 2010: 2).

4   Bryll was a particularly controversial figure at the time. Having been one of the writers officially extolled by the state, the poet-playwright changed his political alignment as a result of the Solidarity movement and became a dissident writer. Given Bryll's abandonment of his earlier literary conformism, the censor would not allow a poem by the author to be produced at a state theatre.

5   Warlikowski and Jarzyna's work in international festivals can be seen as new mode of intercultural interaction that stands in opposition to Richard Demarco's obscurantist othering of Polish theatre at the 1992 Edinburgh Festival where he claimed that, 'Western Europe needs Poland, because alone it is spiritually bankrupt. The only important energy in art is the energy of the spirit. I hope that you [Poland] realize how heavily the responsibility regarding Europe weighs on you' (cited in Cioffi, 1996: 227). Interestingly, Demarco's claim fully coalesces with the Polish Romantic paradigm, in which the resurrection of Poland acts as the salvationary function for the European continent, while also wholly reinscribing the East–West binary into Polish–UK interactions that purports to emphasize and privilege Poland's unique position in Europe, while in actuality marginalizing and obscuring the imaginary 'East.' It is the same logic with which the category of 'woman' is sublated in Polish Romanticism in a mode that alleges to empower her while, in fact, it diminishes her agency.

6 This is in line with Jacques Rancière's concept of the 'emancipated spectator,' who realizes the mode in which ideologies are experienced as naturalized, as opposed to the natural experience of ideology. Rancière suggests that the emancipated spectator is produced through aesthetic and formal challenges to the passivity imposed by mimetic theatre practices within the proscenium-arch stage that produce a clash of 'senses' rather than the development of arguments established by conflicting views in a play's diegesis. See Rancière (2014).

7 Across the chapters, I adapt contemporary theoretical paradigms within Polish culture and assert that given my sensitivity to local and national contexts, this is not a case of intellectual colonization or a generic mapping of Western theory. While I oppose any blanket use of critical theory that is inattentive to cultural specificity, I am also wary of the East–West binary that a wholesale resistance to the application of Western theory in non-Western spaces shores up. What's more, many of the theorists that I employ, such as Judith Butler, Slavoj Žižek and Nancy Fraser, are already deeply embedded within the circulation of contemporary thought in Poland.

1

The move to neoliberalism

The collapse of communist regimes in Eastern and Central Europe, the so-called 'velvet revolution,' unfolded quickly and superseded the political dreams of most dissidents. In 1989, General Jaruzelski initiated the famous Round Table Talks that resulted in the first partially free elections in Poland since the interwar period in the 1930s. Jaruzelski's motivation for these talks was a response to growing social unrest and workers' strikes. When Solidarity, which became a legal and legitimate political party after the Round Table Agreement, agreed to the snap elections in June 1989 Jaruzelski hoped they would shoulder the burden of the economic disaster. Although the elections were only partially free – Solidarity was only allowed to contest 35 percent of the seats in the lower house of Parliament – the electorate overwhelmingly sided with Solidarity with most of the Communists losing their seats. With the governing authority in disarray and the Solidarity party refusing to join forces with a Communist coalition, Solidarity found itself leading the government of Poland in September 1989. The rapid and intoxicating success of this political transformation left many theatre artists feeling disorientated and bewildered. On the one hand, many artists had built their practice around the explicit or implied critique of the communist regime, largely restricted to the alternative theatre scenes, while others, who had worked within the professional sphere, were subordinated to the communist authorities and the censorship of the state. Across this deeply complex spectrum from dissidence to conformity, the situation for theatre artists working within free-market capitalism changed drastically and suddenly. Many theatres struggled to maintain their former structures, despite a loss in prestige and funding. Eleanora Udalska pinpointed an attendant transformation in audience demographics. The disappearance of the so-called 'artificial' spectator, who was introduced to the theatre through her trade union, was accompanied by the undermining of the 'real' spectator, those who chose to attend for their own personal or political convictions, largely because theatre performances in the PRL constituted a significant place to stay in touch with free thought (Udalska, 1997: 167). Intellectualism was and remains today a key referent in discussing spectatorship in Poland. Audiences are often concerned with they perceive as 'intellectual spectating,' which the director and dramaturge Bartosz Frąckowiak sees as a 'cognitive integrity, a curiosity about the world that is not overly concerned with superficial, everyday observations' (cited in Gruszczyński, 2012). Losing its unique mission to speak on behalf of society and express its ideals, the theatre no longer appeared to be a 'stronghold of freedom' (Udalska, 1997: 168). There was indeed a moment of profound hesitation in response to the unfixing of values and the monumental changes occurring in politics, the economy, culture and society that followed political transformation. It took nearly a decade to reconstitute the theatre as a bastion for democracy and pluralism, which required the abandonment and mourning of precisely such a singular articulation of society that was crucial to experiences of spectating before 1989.

The first few years of the 1990s were defined by cultural dislocation and disequilibrium. State-funded theatres quickly lost audiences to cinema and television, VCRs and, for the wealthy elite, a burgeoning restaurant culture and travel industry that quickly exploited previously closed borders. Theatre in Poland before independence was suffused with a relentlessly political agenda where audiences found crucial relevance in decoding theatrical allusions to oppression and marginalization entrenched in director-led productions, where stage semiotics often frustrated state censorship. In the early part of the 1990s, cultural life unhampered by political subjugation also had a detrimental impact on audience attendance, given the theatre's former role as the locus of national identification, collective gathering and critique of the communist regime. Following Western models, many theatres changed their repertoires to more commercially viable, entertainment-oriented fare. Independence made such a dramatic shift in the cultural landscape that it took several years for the professional theatres to develop an appropriate language to address the new reality.

Shock therapy

In the 1990s, the 'shock therapy' of the transformation to neoliberalism resulted in economic devastation, the rise of mass unemployment, growth in social inequality and severe cuts in state expenditure. No meaningful alternative to this political system has been presented and, as political economist Stuart Shields has argued, 'both opposition and former state-socialist social forces have been co-opted into reproducing neoliberalism' (2007: 161). Buttressing this system against critique, successive Polish governments denigrated cultures of labor and the working classes, which Michael Fleming suggests is the 'flip side of the promotion of discourses of individualism and responsibilization' (2012: 489). This position is further sharpened by the pejorative ideological associations of the working classes with the former communist regimes. The result of this has been the representation of Polish workers in mainstream media and politics as parochial, unchanging, old-fashioned and, perhaps even worse, incapable of garnering the skills necessary for labor in a market-focused economy. The West's belief that the invention of neoliberalism would easily accommodate political transition in postcommunist countries was reliant on a simplistic formulation in which the free exchange of commodities would logically provoke individual self-interest that would ultimately produce a middle class who would demand civil rights and vote for governments that facilitate 'trade, prosperity, freedom and growth' (Don Kalb cited in Hann, 2002: 321). This prescription also neglects the particular ways in which vulnerable postcommunist countries were quickly manipulated by Western capitalist investment.

Geographers Michael J. Bradshaw and Alison Stenning observe two primary modes in which this was a misguided belief. First, there is not a singular articulation of capitalism. The relation between capital and labor is culturally bounded and regulated through a broad set of social relations, and, second, really existing capitalism is historically contingent and resistance to its ascendancy is culturally inflected by the terms of its historical evolution (2004: 3–23). In short, just like communism, capitalism is not self-evident nor is it straightforward; unlike communism, its success is dependent upon the marginalization of the working classes. Neoliberalism can be broadly defined as the 'mobilization of state power in the contradictory extension and reproduction of market(-like) rule,' which indicates that there is no 'pure' neoliberalism but rather 'geographically specific manifestations of neoliberalization-in-process' (Tickell and Peck, 2003: 163, 168). Conceiving of neoliberalism in these terms helps to break the longstanding temporal injunction against East and Central Europe to 'catch up' with the West, reconfiguring this label for economic liberalism as diverse and diachronic rather than singular and simultaneous.

Historian Michael Fleming has argued that the 'non-intentional structural violence of the market [has replaced] the intentional structural violence of the state as the dominant form of violence' after 1989 (2012: 483). Fleming differentiates between disparate forms of violence in order to theorize the shift in focus from communist regimes to postcommunist societies. Under communism, 'as a consequence of power transparency and the relatively automatic organizing of social anger against the Party,' Fleming argues, 'it [was] absolutely essential that the Party [found or created] alternative targets for the expression of negative emotions and passions to inhibit challenges to its rule,' which in Poland were frequently minority communities (*ibid.*: 487–8). Using political historian David Ost's point that the transparency of political power is particular to communist societies whereas capitalism diffuses the 'face of evil,' displacing the social frustration and anger that was directed towards the Party in communism. Precisely because the execution of power in postcommunist countries is more enigmatical, it became crucial in the 1990s to find an alternative scapegoat, which was, once again, minorities and former Communists who had retained their positions of political power. In order to garner support within a country that was by majority anti-Communist, the PRL consistently espoused a rhetoric of national homogeneity, which it used to justify the so-called Ziemie Odzyskane (Recovered or Regained Territories or Lands), which were formerly part of Germany, and to displace social anger away from the Party. In the 1990s, the 'shock therapy,' economic devastation that followed regime change, led to a problematic process of lustration that sought to purge former Communists from positions of authority in the political sphere.

This same shift in forms of violence also meant that the theatre as a locus of community spirit and a hotbed of political resistance also had to transform its practices and methods, the very nature of its being. While on the one hand, companies such as Teatr Ósmego Dnia (Theatre of the Eighth Day) were able to explicitly engage in political critique directly after political transition, there was no longer an obvious foe to target when venting social frustrations. While past forms of repression, propaganda and censorship at work under communism were dismantled, it took time to discover the precise modes in which these were reworked through neoliberalism; that is, the unintentional violence inflicted on the population through the establishment of the primacy of the market and the neoconservative attempts to redefine Polishness through prescriptive and exclusionary strategies. One of the key issues to arise in the 1990s is the shift in focus from communism to neoliberalism that entailed a new paradigm for cultural identities that relied on old forms of marginalization of non-ethnic Poles, women, gays and lesbians and other minority communities. As Fleming notes, the 'narrative that Poles were victims of assorted national other in the socialist period has been reused to account for difficulties after 1989,' and therefore re-creating capitalist social relations after a several decade hiatus has demanded higher levels of representational violence than in Western countries (*ibid.*: 490). By 'representational violence,' Fleming means the damaging and hegemonic stereotypes around gender, sexuality and ethnicity that are embedded in language and discourses that underpin wider social relations.

Corporeal readings

Productions at Kraków's Stary Teatr had some of the most profound influence on the shaping of culture in this decade. In 1991, the Stary Teatr was given the exclusive title 'The National' – the Teatr Narodowy (National Theatre) in Warsaw had been destroyed by a fire in 1985 and would not reopen until 1997 – a recognition of its significant status in Polish culture as the venue for serious discussion of national identity. Jerzy Got contends that the Stary Teatr, in contrast to Warsaw's National Theatre's association with the aristocracy, was the first to be born out of a civil initiative that was middle-class and democratically oriented (cited in Burzyńska, 2012: 48). This honor placed an increased pressure on the theatre to commit to Poland's future and show guidance in the new capitalist reality. One of the theatre productions that is now considered to be paradigmatic of the 1990s was Jerzy Jarocki's restaging of Witold Gombrowicz's *Ślub* (*The Marriage*) in 1991.[1] Celebrated for his rejection of communal, national or patriotic values in favor of the rights of the individual, Gombrowicz was perhaps the most appropriate writer for the early 1990s in the immediate collapse of communism. In a moment of profound culture shock, the habit in Polish theatre was to seek out and emphasize obvious political and spiritual connotations in the new reality. However, mainstream theatre's responses to the social field failed, for the most part, to entice audiences. Jarocki's use of Gombrowicz was particularly noteworthy precisely because of the director's refusal to introduce external meanings into a play that 'contains no political journalism or discourse, carries no political message, incites to nothing and does not speak out in favour of anything' (Baniewicz, 1992: 98).

Ślub takes place in an oneiric world somewhere between sleeping and wakefulness, in which reality cannot be easily distinguished from a dream or merely attributed to consciousness. In this way, Gombrowicz's play calls attention to the artificiality of the theatre itself as a location that is both real and imagined. A sharp and often grotesque depiction of the moral chaos that followed the Second World War, the play follows Henryk, a soldier who faces a moral war staged as a debate between individualism and collectivism, authoritarianism and anarchy, honor and ambition. Cherished by theatre directors and audiences alike in the late 1970s and early 1980s, Gombrowicz was no longer seen as scandalous or entirely relevant when Jarocki chose to stage the play for the final time.[2] Nevertheless, Jarocki's ability to highlight the dizzying sense of social disorientation and the widely felt pessimism that accompanied the introduction of liberal capitalism added to its monumental success.

Often referred to as 'intellectual' by the Polish theatre critical establishment, Jarocki's productions were known for their cold precision, mathematical specificity, emotional restraint and careful stage design. Anna R. Burzyńska (2012) argued that Jarocki created performances for skeptics, doubters or rationalists who longed to experience significance in the theatre without recourse to cheap sentiment or gaudy grandeur. Ślub epitomized the director's style in an unparalleled fashion. The opening scene revealed the blackness of the theatre space at the Stary Teatr, with the actor Jerzy Radziwiłowicz emerging from a dark void that could only be filled in by his imaginative constructions. Having crossed the liminal threshold of the stage space before fully assuming the role of Henryk, this initial image, which would be inverted at the end of the performance when Radziwiłowicz turned his back to the audience to face the black screen of the once-again emptied stage with hands raised in a gesture of humble supplication, was hailed by critics as radically embodying the historical moment of moral vacuity that accompanied the demise of the totalitarian regime. As Henryk's thoughts and desires fluctuated in this indistinct and blurred universe, the scenery followed suit. Using precise lighting and simple stage machinery, props and furniture appeared and then evaporated with the fluidity and fleetingness of an actual dream.

In Jarocki's staging, Henryk's parents appear as spectral figures from an indistinguishable past, a reminder of nationhood, obedience and education. Jerzy Trela's performance as the father, too shaky and physically fragile to be sublimated to the level of a majestic or epic hero, highlighted the instable category of traditional Polish virtues. Emerging from the power games played between father and son, the narrative turns towards patricide. The death of the father figure as ultimate arbiter of moral order was popular in a number of postcommunist countries in this period, Lithuania in particular. A Drunkard appears as a foil to the Father, promising a revolution in which man will replace God in his ability to construct his own universe. After deposing the King-*cum*-Father, Henryk's resolve to stage a wedding functions as an attempt to re-establish civic and moral order; however, Henryk's victory simultaneously signals his downfall and the incursion of total chaos. Having triumphed as the ultimate vanquisher and constructor of reality, both meaning and the 'natural order' of the world collapse, signaling the experience of what Adam Michnik famously termed 'grey democracy' in the immediate years following political transformation.

Two major productions by Krystian Lupa in the early 1990s at the Stary Teatr have been cited by nearly every major critic as the most powerful and accomplished stagings of that decade in Poland. The first was the 1990 adaptation of *Bracia Karamazow* (*The Brothers Karamazov*), Dostoyevsky's classic tale of sin and redemption. Although audiences of the Stary Teatr were familiar with the Russian author – three of Dostoyevsky's novels were staged in the theatre between 1971 and 1984 – Lupa's nearly nine-hour production was unlike any of its predecessors. The production was characterized by extended periods of almost complete inactivity on stage that tested the patience of most audiences to the extreme. Theatre scholar and critic Grzegorz Niziołek defended Lupa, arguing that the director successfully explored the burden of time, and while his performances delight and torment the spectator in equal measure, the multiplicity and diversity of ways of experiencing time – swelling and shrinking, jumps and turns, flows and blocks – is the key to the success of his performance (Niziołek, 1990: 27–8). In many ways Dostoyevsky's portrayal of a period of radical modernization in Russia, accompanied by a crisis of spiritual values, perfectly mirrored the period of transition at the end of communism in which Lupa was working.

The next and perhaps best realized of Lupa's adaptations was Thomas Bernhard's *Kalkwerk* (*The Lime Works*), first staged in 1992. Ruthlessly rejecting sentimentality, the production was seen as a shocking account of man's metaphysical search for meaning in a world composed of outmoded routines and hollow rituals. Fittingly, in the same year *Kalkwerk* premiered, Halina Filipowicz wrote in the pages of *The Drama Review*, 'For the Polish theatre, the present is a time of disorientation and traumatic discontinuity. The old certainties have disappeared: visions of the future are plagued with doubt' (1992: 76). The novel is loosely based on a formerly affluent married couple, Konrad and Konradowa, who have moved to a deserted lime works in the Austrian countryside in order for Konrad to finish his major academic study on hearing. Set up as a murder mystery, Konradowa's corpse is discovered on the premises of the lime works at the outset of the performance. The scene opened with the testimony of three unreliable narrators incapable of finding agreement on the basic facts of the case. While it was clear that Konrad was guilty of the murder, the events – experienced as diachronic flashbacks – leading up to the crime were conflicted and circulatory. The theatrical time of the performance, like that of the subconscious mind, bore no relationship to synchronic lived experience, and the natural laws of cause and effect were disrupted in a series of scenes that did not develop a progressive narrative. Lupa's aesthetic chimed with Bernhard's writing style, characterized by a lack of action and a verbal avalanche of anxiety, misguided or preposterous conceptualizations and suppressed desires. Substituting stable characterization for an emphasis on intersubjectivity and a physicalization of individual neuroses, the scenes never took the form of realism, although the relationships between the actors remained entirely believable. As one critic pointed out, in *Marzyciele* (The Dreamers), Lupa's first adaptation of Robert Musil in 1988, the dialogue did not consist of discussions but rather functioned as a series of short monologues in which individual sentences sound like philosophical aphorisms (Konic, 1989: 7). Despite Lupa's sharp focus on interpersonal relationships, characters rarely manage to actually communicate with one another and the act of listening becomes an intolerable burden. There is an oppositional logic to the virtuoso performances of Lupa's actors, which involves a very nuanced tension between total exposure of their interior world and a certain retention of their privacy, a side of the actor that remains hidden or purposively obscured, that Piotr Bogusław Jędrzejczak (1986: 7) sees as a clear influence from Konrad Swinarski. Rather than focusing directly on politics, Lupa portrayed the 'peculiar mechanisms of social interaction in an epoch of transition' (Miłkowski, 2012: 15), which profoundly resonated with audiences in the early 1990s.

In his 1995–98 two-part staging of *Lunatycy* (*The Sleepwalkers*), Hermann Broch's twentieth-century classic, Lupa returned to themes he had explored in Dostoyevsky – disintegrating social values, changing gender relations and the erosion of religious identity – but what is most striking about this choice of text at the end of the decade was the move from the sublimated figure of the artist that had preoccupied Lupa for so many years to the depiction of a relatively unexciting and mediocre 'everyman'. The other break from previous stagings was a step away from the standard concentration on the web of interrelationships between actors to a fast-paced run-through of events composed of more than 50 scenes in each production. The rather banal events of the protagonist's life were captured in excessive detail, which provoked Piotr Gruszczyński (1995) to compare the style with New Objectivity, the post-expressionist art movement in the Weimar Republic that was intended to reflect the world in a more pragmatic or objective manner. The anarchy in the title of the first part, *Esch, czyli Anarchia* (Esch, so Anarchy, 1995) refers to the protagonist's battle with Romantic optimism and blind faith, responding to an era of widespread disillusionment in Poland in the mid-1990s and a concomitant experience of political disorientation and powerlessness. By 1997, the country had seen nine successive prime ministers, whose politics had swung violently across the political spectrum from neoliberal and anti-Communist to reformed socialist. In the transitional era, both Jarocki and Lupa created worlds devoid of pathos, in which the hero functions as an absurd although not unlikable figure, and where formerly decipherable concepts of struggle and fortitude, good and evil, power and subjugation are obscured.

Emerging from the 1990s, Lupa was at first reticent to put aside his focus on the lonely genius who inhabits darkened and shabby spaces littered with the detritus of European history. Having had a rather belated Warsaw debut in 1999 at the Teatr Dramatyczny with a production of Stanisław Wyspiański's *Powrót Odysa* (*Return of Odysseus*), Lupa accepted a second invitation from the theatre's then artistic director Piotr Cieślak. Returning for the penultimate time to Bernhard, Lupa chose the novelist's most difficult composition for his newest project. Working from his own translation, Lupa described *Auslöschung/Wymazywanie* (*Erasure*) as 'an unbridled torrent of words' in which Bernhard had abandoned any pursuit of linguistic beauty (cited in Wyżyńska, 2001b). Indeed, the performance was dominated by the protagonist's long, meandering, erratic and often comical monologues. Grieving the death of his parents, who were represented as large mannequins in coffins, the mournful tone of the performance was dramatically underscored by Verdi's *Lacrimosa*.

Played in a tour-de-force performance by Piotr Skiba, who had also become Lupa's frequent assistant stage designer, the central character, Franz Josef Murau, is an intellectual who has fled his homeland of Austria for its hypocrisy, xenophobia, parochialism and religious (Catholic) double standards. Lupa decided to keep the German title both because the term *wymazywanie* is rarely used in Polish, and because the original *Auslöschung* indicates the double signification of erasure and extinction. While mourning, Franz Josef contemplates his family's collusion with the Nazis and the pilfering of Jewish property. These themes had strong associations with Jan T. Gross' recently published *Neighbors*, a historical account of Polish anti-Semitism that led to a pogrom in the village of Jedwabne in northeastern Poland during the Second World War that I discuss in detail in Chapter 5. Gross' publication caused public outrage and debate on an unprecedented scale and was critically divisive for Poles who wanted to deny the accusations and those who wished to honor the past and seek forgiveness. Fittingly, the publication of Bernhard's novel in 1986 coincided with the 'Waldheim Affair,' which resulted in a long overdue admission of Austria's own culpability for Nazi crimes. Lupa has often been accused of escapism; that is, avoiding any directly political content in his largely abstract and allegorical productions. In fact, the cultural discourses that govern the reception of Lupa's work have come to rely on such a distancing activating critics and scholars in their attempt to decode his dense, metaphorical material. Franz Josef's monologues are governed by precisely this need to confess and take responsibility and the seemingly paradoxical wish to erase the past. One might say it was the refusal to directly identify with the Jedwabne debate that leant the performance such power and allowed audiences to be guided by their own critical responses. As usual, Lupa did not see the theatre as a medium for pedagogy or moralizing, nor as a nursery for national education, but as a crucial space for reflection and introspection.

When asked why he had not turned to Polish writers since his lauded stagings of Witkacy in the 1980s, Lupa replied that he had learned more about the complexity of the new Polish reality from foreign literature. Returning to the Stary Teatr in 2002, Lupa adapted Mikhail Bulgakov's *Mistrz i Małgorzata* (*The Master and Margarita*), a much-loved classic in Poland that was ranked as the most popular book of the twentieth century in a poll taken by the magazine *Rzeczpospolita* in 1995. Some of the novel's appeal is undoubtedly due to the author's biting criticism of Soviet communism, but it also draws directors because of its freewheeling irreverence, metatheatricality and the refusal to establish a clear boundary between reality and fantasy. Rather than emphasizing a defiance of

Soviet communism, as Oskaras Koršunovas did in his Lithuanian production mounted in 2000 at the Vilnius City Theatre, Lupa instead used the central setting, a psychiatric hospital, as a respite for those who were unable to adapt quickly enough to the demands of the postcommunist world. The production divided audiences, and for the first time praise for Lupa's direction was matched by disapproval. Many reviewers complained that Lupa was too willing to treat perpetrators of communism with the same sympathy afforded to their victims. This controversy only increased ticket sales and the run of the show, again eight hours over two evenings, sold out in a single day. One critic in *Gazeta Wyborcza* commented that while the sense of emptiness in *Lunatycy* still had a noble quality, in *Mistrz i Małgorzata* randomness and destruction prevailed (Targoń, 2002). A deft soundtrack of increasingly intense vocal shrieks and groans was supplanted by Lupa's own voice and the banging of his small drum, elements that simultaneously dominated and interfered with the rhythm of the onstage action. Lupa's depiction of Christ, played by Andrzej Hudziak, broke with the sublimated and adored image familiar to Polish audiences from those productions that dominated in the twentieth century. In direct challenge to Gustaw Holoubek's renowned performance in 1988 as a proud and strong Woland, the most legendary staging of Bulgakov prior to Lupa's, the Devil suffers from arthritis and lies in bed all day. Woland is not the ruler of hell or a victim of political oppression, but is merely a psychiatric patient. Unlike Frank Castorf's updated, highly colorful and fast-paced adaption of the novel that premiered in the same year at the Berlin Volksbühne, Lupa's setting was radically minimalist, composed of black curtains, degraded doors and windows and some metal scaffolding. Both productions, however, criticized the emergence of the market of Western goods in the postcommunist landscape, modern consumption and the exploitation that accompanies capitalist luxury.

In 2004, Lupa travelled to Greece to stage *Zaratustra* (*Zarathustra*), a major co-production between the Stary Teatr and the Odeon of Herodes Atticus, the stone theatre on the southern slope of the Acropolis in Athens, as part of the Hellenic Festival. This production more closely resembled his earlier adaptations. Lupa revisited his obsession for the life work of the philosopher-artist, combining text from Friedrich Nietzsche's *Thus Spoke Zarathustra* (1883) and Einar Schleef's semi-biographical play *Nietszche-Trilogie* (2002). The first half of the performance was punctuated by male nudity and heightened scenes of homoeroticism, both of which remained noticeable features of Lupa's theatre in years to come. Emphasizing Zarathustra's passionate desire for new forms of governance, spirituality and community, one particular image showed the pope slumped forward on a papal throne discussing the death of God, connected through a series of blood-filled tubes to a ravaged man floating in an aquarium. Roman Pawłowski remarked that this contentious stage picture could be read as a symbol of the sickness and frailty of modern man's faith. A related iconoclasm prevailed throughout this merciless dissection of contemporary experiences of freedom in a world that had recently lost its religious leader. This irritated a number of conservative reviewers, who felt that the association with John Paul II was in bad taste, particularly given that the Polish Pope had only died a month prior to the Kraków premiere, and the city was still in the grip of mass mourning for one of the most exalted men in Polish history.

Tracing Lupa's productions over the past two decades also offers a dynamic overview of the corporeal turn that has generated differently displayed and authored bodies. This turn was the focus of Krystyna Duniec's *Ciało w teatrze* (The Body in the Theatre), which considers theoretical categories of the body in contemporary theatre through the interpenetration of theatre anthropology, the cultural consequences of the functioning of the body of the actor in the stage space, and semiology, the analysis of the spectacle as a dense structure of the character, in the production of stage signs (Duniec, 2012: 10–12). Duniec's analysis is far-ranging, taking into account the iconic signs in Artaud's theatre of cruelty, the ideograms of Jerzy Grotowski's Laboratory Theatre, Tadeusz Kantor's reduction of bodies to ready-made objects, Jozef Szajna's treatment of actors as mannequins, the category of the dreaming body in Krystian Lupa's psychoanalytic theatre, and gender as a sign of equality in Warlikowski's productions. Duniec also praises Gardzienice and Teatr Pieśń Kozła (Song of the Goat Theatre) for producing forms of actor training that harness the radical, subversive potential of the body, which she claims is not fixed in a system of psychological impulses, but rather employs anti-realist gestures and instinctual and irrational body dynamics. These theatre practices resonate alongside the work of contemporary Polish visual artists such as Alicja Żebrowska, Katarzyna Kozyra, Anna Baumgart, Artur Żmijewski, Grzegorz Klaman and Zbigniew Libera, who have revised and reanimated understandings of the body through their representations of oppressive sexualities and gender binaries, the public depiction of genitalia and a critical interrogation of conceptions of ugliness, suffering or disability that eschew normative standards of beauty and 'normality.'

While the transcendental bodies of Lupa's male protagonists dominated his dreamlike visions of the 1990s, the director's production of *Factory 2* – constructed from biographies, films, interviews and scholarship around The Factory, Andy Warhol's studio from 1962 to 1984 – at the Stary Teatr shocked critics and audiences alike in 2008. Despite the fact that the role of the artist had dominated his productions since the 1980s, this champion of the American pop-art scene was heralded as a significant move away from Lupa's traditional focus on the 'high art' of European philosophy and literature, marking a turning point in the director's taste that appealed to a new generation of spectators. Lupa commented that it was refreshing to have this meeting with the non-European personality, a highly intuitive creator that was the polar opposite of Moritz Meister's excessive self-commentary and intellectualization that held sway in his 2006 adaptation of Thomas Bernhard's *Na szczytach panuje cisza* (*Over All the Mountain Tops*) (cited in Derkaczew, 2008). Depictions of the exposed male body in *Factory 2* were substantial, including Piotr Skiba as Warhol purposelessly meandering naked around the studio and, most memorably, Piotr Polak performing a long improvised monologue in the nude in front of a camera, hinting that publicity is more crucial than talent in a world dominated by indulgence, celebrity and self-infatuation. This signified a radical departure from traditions of Polish theatre that yoked the exposure of the actor's body to psychical and spiritual revelation. In Lupa's later work, from Andy Warhol to Marilyn Monroe and Simone Weil in his *Persona* series, the naked body was resignified as yet another surface, the uncovering of which brings one no closer to the authentic personality or to an understanding of human mystery, which breaks entirely with his previous Jungian-inflected stagings that require 'deep' readings of a buried or repressed subconscious and prompt penetrating interpretations of nuanced subtext, which was the long-held habit of Polish audiences both under and emerging from communism. As opposed to Lupa's earlier careful renderings of intimate human relationships in Dostoyevsky, Bernhard and Broch, his recent productions portray a secular universe – following the death of God announced in his *Zaratustra* – 'free love' stripped of eroticism, sexual relationships defined by puerile attention-seeking behavior, and seduction as a metonym for a general lack of real affection, relationships and familial bonds.

Here the sublime transcendental bodies of the Romantic hero have been exchanged for the materiality of the actor who fails to take up the moral burden of messianic expectations and to embody the national spirit – a substitution that marks the end of the Romantic paradigm as the key referent of nationhood and community. A pluralistic approach of contemporary theatre practice has been vital in the de-essentialization of community across the political spectrum, from a left-wing socialist-oriented conception of the social body to the ultra-conservative Catholic-inflected national body. In Lupa, this is evident in the move from the 1990s – where the spiritual condition of the nation is represented through Doysoyevksy and other novels – to the focus on celebrity, media and alternative sexualities. Responding to neoliberalism, they are not confined to the concerns of a particular or essentialized cultural position. This move sums up a more widespread trend in postcommunist Poland to stage pluralism, tolerance and to open up the category of Polishness to new bodies.

Teatr na lewo

In order to occupy a position that supports radical democratic pluralism, political theatre in Poland has had to reassess the possibility of recuperating socialism as a viable political option, while making discursive space for the inclusion of alternative minority subject positions that counters such forms of representational violence. As theatre scholars Krystyna Duniec and Joanna Krakowska (2006) have observed, mainstream theatre in Poland has rarely been on the left (*na lewo*). Before the Second World War, while the director Leon Schiller was vocally supportive of a workers' theatre, his revolution in theatre-making was also 'aesthetic rather than social, emotional rather than ethical, spiritual and not materialistic' (Tymon Terlecki cited in Duniec and Krakowska, 2006). In the PRL, there was an ideological demand to produce theatre for the proletariat, but this was instrumentalized by the government rather than the proletariat themselves. Those who wished to produce theatre with socialist-leaning values after 1989 were often condemned as nostalgic communist sympathizers. It is not surprising then that so many directors eschewed social problems, dealing instead with parables, the production of plays banned under communism, popular boulevard-style musicals and comedies and a keen interest in mysticism and spirituality. New directors who came of age in the postcommunist landscape were interested in liberal or pluralistic notions of culture. This resulted in a reinterpretation of Polish cultural myths, representation of alternative sexuality, the influence of international cinema, third-wave feminism and anti-capitalism movements. Of particular note, Poland's forced inclusion by the US in the war in Iraq galvanized the younger generation to rethink the fetishized and unbalanced relationship between Poland and their Western allies.

Kozłowski (2008) argues that the 'constitutive moment for the political discourse on postcommunism is establishing a continuity between postcommunism and communism itself, which requires an epistemological shift that cannot 'be grasped at the level of social phenomena'; namely, the criminalization and/or vilification of Poland's heritage of 'real socialism.' By the end of the 1990s there was rift in the assessment of the PRL that began to define distinct generations around socialism that insinuated what Polish scholars and critics refer to as an emerging new left, and the reworking of a leftist position has, in part, required the reassessment of representations and competing conceptualizations of 'really existing socialism.' The critic Łukasz Drewniak (2007) voiced his concern that theatre productions reflecting on the Polish experience of communism tended to consider the PRL as a singular or isolated example without parallel in the Soviet or European contexts. A primary example of this is Jerzy Jarocki's large-scale production *Historia PRL według Mrożka* (History of the PRL According to Mrożek, 1998) at the Teatr Polski in Wrocław, which provided an expansive overview of the PRL. The action of the performance moved between the immediate postwar Poland of the 1940s and an internment camp during the period of Martial Law in 1981, and memories of servitude and subjugation were foregrounded over a linear history of the PRL. To unpack the not yet fully evolved history or tested myth of the PRL, Jarocki used excerpts from five of Sławomir Mrożek's plays (*Pieszo, Portret, Zabawa, Alfa, Emigranci*), historical documents from internment camps and popular songs from the 1950s in praise of socialism, such as Konstanty Ildefons Gałczyński's panegyric 'Umarł Stalin' (Stalin is Dead). While the collision of these sources was dynamically intertextual, evoking new conceptual frameworks through which to interpret their contexts, the production was heavily criticized by a younger generation of reviewers who either did not recognize their own histories within the patchwork performance text or were disappointed by the lack of analytical distance from the subject matter. Overlapping images from Mickiewicz with Mrożek were seen by critics as lazy, outdated or clichéd rather than transformative, indicating that Jarocki was still stuck on aesthetic norms and moral values prescribed by Romanticism that lost their critical traction in the 1990s. Piotr Gruszczyński (1999) bemoaned the production as 'a national shrine dedicated to the martyrs of the Polish People's Republic,' pronouncing it 'inert and dead.' This was surprising largely because Gruszczyński had commended Jarocki for his previous erudite treatments of Polish history and his iconic productions of Mrożek, a playwright known for his highly allegorical renderings of history. At the production's conclusion, a father, freed from internment, turns directly to the audience to explain why his generation, unable to shed grief and trauma, felt a profound disappointment as a result of their earlier immense hope, precisely reflecting the perspective of the Jarocki/Mrożek generation who had built the PRL from scratch. What is particularly significant in this production is the mode in which audience reception, nearly a decade after the end of communism, had fundamentally changed. *Historia* was as much a collage of Jarocki's own directorial catalog as it was of Mrożek's literary canon, and this was perhaps its greatest flaw. The main criticism underlying the skepticism in the reviews indicated that the director had failed to keep pace with the times, simply reaffirming what was already known rather than confronting Poland's troubled and contested past. As an alternative to Jarocki's approach, Gruszczyński looked specifically to the German theatre as a healthy model for reflecting without nostalgia, hypocrisy or falsehood on painful national histories, a tendency that would become stronger in Poland in the following decade.

In the 1990s, the national motto might have been 'the market is always right.' This was promulgated by the emergence of economically conservative factions that, largely uncritically, supported the introduction of capitalism. Socialist-leaning thought was seen as a relic of communism and was widely excluded from public discourse. One of the most visible missions of the political theatre has been to tackle Polish patriotism and neoconservative articulations of identity by recuperating a culturally liberal orientation sympathetic to socialist values, which had lost credibility through its pejorative associations with Soviet-style communism and the lived oppressions of the PRL. One of the primary resistances to the rehabilitation of socialism in the political sphere was the disappointment still acutely felt by those who had already attempted to revise communism in a less repressive form before 1989. The intellectual elite, who had been bullied, intimidated and oppressed during the initial postwar Stalinist period were again marginalized when Władysław Gomułka failed to fulfil his promises of reform in the wake of October 1956. As Cioffi (1996: 145) has contended, the events of March 1968 had a radical impact on intellectuals' socialist leanings, who revised their loyalties and political alliances, and any traces of Marxist thought as a 'third way' through the impasse of communism and capitalism in the Solidarity movement were obliterated by the imposition of Martial Law. As a result, no considerations of socialism or Marxist political thought were taken into consideration as part of the political transition to capitalism. The disappointments of 1956, 1968 and 1980–81 produced a deep cynicism about the promises of socialism that were still acutely felt in the 1990s and early 2000s, which produced tensions between the older and younger generations that had grown up in capitalist Poland and desired some elements of a welfare state.

Political analyst Rafał Pankowski (2010) has interrogated the rapid rise of what he calls 'radical right parties' (RRP) that culminated in the election of the Kaczyńskis' Law and Justice Party in 2005. This had a profound impact in mobilizing resistance in theatres. The appeal of the 'radical right' has been construed first as a 'consequence of the widespread discontent that has accompanied the transformation of state-led economies to market economies' and, second, as part of a re-emergence of shared culture that is reliant on the ingrained perception of the social realm as existing prior to and taking priority over the individual (De Lange and Guerra, 2009: 528). What developed in the 1990s was an antagonistic split between two opposing and opposed ideologies, the sublimation of Poland before communism, perceived as a 'natural order' organized around native values, and a push towards modernization. Kozłowski (2008) observes with great nuance the implicit identification with the US, who successfully yoked these ostensibly conflicting beliefs (an affirmation of natural values intertwined with the imperative of constant capitalist modernization), as opposed to the more welfare-oriented European Union (EU). An analysis of a left/right distinction is complicated in Poland and does not map seamlessly onto the political spectrum in the US or UK. Political scientists Sarah De Lange and Simona Guerra interpret the Polish left in terms of 'a positive attitude towards the communist past, liberal social values, secularism and opposition to a significant public role for the church,' whereas the right actively promotes decommunization, conservative social values, religiosity and the active role of the Catholic Church in public life (2009: 534). The fundamental distinction between these factions rests on the relationship between modernization and the process of decommunization. The left tends to believe that the former will lead to the latter, while RRPs insist the modernization of the market is impossible without first ridding the government of both post-Communists and those legislative practices that have carried over from the former regime. Former President Aleksander Kwaśniewski, for example, embraced the notion of 'memory politics' that had been employed by nationalist factions. Kwaśniewski purported to represent Poland's future, asserting that anti-Communists were caught up in now obsolete battles against irrelevant foes from the country's past (Mark, 2010: 17). Memory politics, or what is known in Poland as *polityka historyczna* (historical politics), was assimilated by the radical right in the 2004 campaign. Lech and Jarosław Kaczyński rearticulated this debate 'stressing the country's need for uniting values,' which should be found in the national history, which was 'treated exclusively as a storage of patriotism' (Górny, 2007: 131).[3] The conservative anti-Communist right, who played a major role in opposing Poland's ascension to the European Union, expressed their anti-EU campaigns as a defense of Poland's ability to self-govern, a fundamental condition of political transition, claiming the erosion of its powers were dangerously reminiscent of previous occupations. In 2001, the Kaczyńskis asserted that they could complete the unfinished revolution of 1989, working hard to revive the memory of resistance to communism (Mark, 2010: 3). It is no coincidence, of course, that leaders of radical right parties are former dissidents from the communist era, and their position is framed as a resistance to the corrupt communist elite who struggle to remain in power; this mode of thinking is a leftover of former Polish intellectual thought that candidly divided the country between those who colluded with the system and those who remained morally astute and patriotic. It is a commonplace of radical right parties to side with the ongoing reservations about political parties in general – stemming from the generally felt misgivings about the Party – through the endorsement of anti-party discourse and the contention that Poland's Third Republic was corrupt, immoral and anti-nationalist (Mark, 2010: 15). The Fourth Republic they promised, which placed the Catholic Church at the heart of society and reawakened a sense of national dignity, prompted an explosive period of political theatre that critiqued nationalism in its many articulations.

Duniec and Krakowska have argued that artistic movements through their social and educational engagement have an opportunity to transform public discourse, undermine stereotypes and treat social phobias. Following Antonio Gramsci, Duniec and Krakowska (2006) contend that promoting the consciousness for social change is a political struggle for cultural hegemony. If there is no viable left-wing, they argue, it is because Poland has no 'leftist' media; as opposed to journalism and politics, it is only in the theatre that the new articulations of socialist left has a chance to appear as a viable and realistic alternative. This notion of the left (*na lewo*), which I adhere to in my own use of the term here, indicates an emphasis on the increase in social equality and social welfare and the concomitant move to secularization in the political sphere. One of the most significant attempts to recuperate the socialist left in the theatre was Maciej Nowak's programming at the Teatr Wybrzeże (Coast Theatre) in Gdańsk, which carried considerable weight with critics across the country. During his tenure at the Teatr Wybrzeże (2000–06), Nowak championed the career of a number of emerging theatre-makers, such as Grażyna Kania, Agnieszka Olsten, Wojciech Klemm, Grzegorz Wiśniewski and Michał Zadara. In 2006, local politicians sacked Nowak from his directorship, sparking huge controversy and a public outcry from the country's theatre elite. If anything, this drastic move revealed the ideological tug-of-war that continues to be fought between modern politicians and theatre-makers viewed as defiant or subversive. What this also called up was the particular taboo around the direct engagement of theatre artists with politics, which made critics accuse artists of politicking, practicing journalism and producing shallow work. As Paweł Mościcki has observed, Polish artists have been discouraged from assuming clear political attitudes, thus producing the specter of propagandist theatre that is a misappropriation of artistic ideals. Such open political engagement is therefore seen as a moral problem as well as an aesthetic one (Mościcki, 2008: 9).

Paweł Demirski worked as literary manager under Nowak at the Teatr Wybrzeże where he composed plays with huge sociopolitical resonance that broadcast his radically leftist position as a staunch member of the 'Krytyka Polityczna' (KP, Political Critique), a movement of Polish left-wing intellectuals, artists and activists founded in 2002 by Sławomir Sierakowski, who has been particularly scathing about the radical right's domination of the public sphere in the culture war that has been raging in Poland since 1989 between secular forces and the Roman Catholic Church. Nowak produced a number of Demirski's early plays, whose widely varied topics included a biopic of the Solidarity leader Lech Wałęsa, a caustic depiction of Polish migration on a mass scale and a scathing attack on the violation of the country's labor rights, based on a real-life case in Łódź where a factory worker was decapitated due to lax healthy and safety controls. Demirski joined forces with the director Monika Strzępka in 2007. Together they cultivated a number of international influences from European political theatre, including German director René Pollesch and German-speaking playwrights such as Thomas Bernhard, Heiner Müller, Werner Schwab and Peter Turrini. Using post-dramatic, ludic or parodic forms based on these sources, Demirski was also influenced by British playwright David Hare's tackling of contemporary social problems in his dramatic texts. In 2007, Pollesch made his first professional visit to Poland, collaborating with Grzegorz Jarzyna at the TR Warszawa. Renowned for his fairground aesthetics, destabilization of character, direct audience address, lyrical monologues, chaotic stage action and carefully articulated expressionist stage design, there are certainly a number of indicative overlaps with Demirski's writing and Strzępka's direction, particularly with what Demirski has coined his 'political tabloid' theatre, constructed from political incorrectness, circus athleticism and ready-made propaganda. As Rafał Węgrzyniak (2011) observed, at least some of the ideas, themes and solutions appearing in

Strzępka and Demirski's productions were adapted from modern theatre practices commonly associated with the historical pre-war radical left in Poland, and not only from British and German-speaking theatre traditions.[4] At the same time, thoroughly resistant to the stranglehold of time-honored theatre traditions in Poland that sublimate essentialist culture, the pair have used Polish Romantic texts as a springboard for blazing critiques of Polish society and politics. For Strzępka and Demirski, the theatre is not a spiritual or ritualistic space in which to honor culture through convenient and celebrated modes of describing the world, but a dissecting table where the audience must face ugly truths frequently ignored or disavowed.

At the Teatr Wybrzeże, Nowak also supported the burgeoning career of the *enfant terrible* of the Polish theatre scene, Jan Klata, whose uniform of rosary beads, Swiss Army fatigues and Mohawk make him easily identifiable at any theatre event. Klata has offered a high level of critical insight into internal conflicts in Polish identity founded on established religion and counterculture. Although Klata generously cites his former mentor Krystian Lupa as one of his major influences, his recent creative efforts do not necessarily match Lupa's choice of texts nor his highly distinctive visual language. Klata's use of pop music, documentary theatre and Romantic texts has led to fierce debates around Polish Catholicism – he is one of the few theatre directors who openly discusses his religious faith – and articulations of freedom in the Third Republic. 'Poland is a kind of polygon,' Klata claimed. '"New" here takes the most radical and wild forms. Freedom is always problematic' (cited in Janowska and Mucharski, 2006). In another interview, Klata argued that the 'theatre is a catalyst for [him] to talk beyond the discourse set by the media and political parties' (cited in Cieślak, 2005a). The ephemerality of the theatre allows Klata to practice social critiques that are site- and time-specific, and, crucially, not interrupted or framed by advertisements as in cinema and television. At first an outcast of the cliquish Warsaw theatre circles, Klata became increasingly focused on work that responded to more provincial areas of Poland neglected by artists working in Warsaw and Kraków. Wałbrzych, Gdańsk and Wrocław became fecund ground for his often nihilistic visions of the disappointments and complications of life outside the economic bubble of the capital city.

Having critiqued the reverberations of Edward Gierek's political and economic policies in the PRL of the 1970s in his staging of *The Government Inspector* (2003) in Wałbrzych, a post-industrial city with one of the highest rates of unemployment in Poland, Klata turned his attention to *Fantazy* (Teatr Wybrzeże, 2005), Juliusz Słowacki's satire of Romanticism and its excesses in an effort to critique the marginalization of the working classes in the development of neoliberalism after communism. The replacement of a dollar sign for a 'z' (*Fanta$y*) presciently reflected a change in national values in a new era when 'Poles [were] ruled by money' (Cieślak, 2005a). An émigré poet whose work became more nationalist in tone after the failed November Insurrection of 1830–31 against Imperialist Russia, Słowacki was strongly influenced by Andrzej Towiański, a Messianic philosopher and mystic who led a group called 'The Circle of God's Cause,' which believed in the progression of the spirit through history to reach a Supreme Good. This group was dedicated to the cause of fighting for a free and autonomous Poland. Although Słowacki had broken from Towiański's circle by 1844, he continued to be interested in mysticism for the rest of his life and he was responsible for one of the most celebrated Romantic dramas, *Kordian* (1834), and poems, such as *The Slavic Pope* (1848), seen by many as a foretelling of Polish Pope John Paul II's papacy, earning him the title of national prophet. *Fantazy*, however, is unlike any other play in the Polish Romantic oeuvre, and is not the type of drama one would expect to encounter from a Polish émigré. Published posthumously in 1866, *Fantazy* is a parody of the overblown mannerisms and values of Polish Romanticism in which Słowacki, having adopted positivism as his *weltanschauung*, satirized the disavowed elitist affectations of the crumbling upper classes, their fixation on the pastoral, the façades of tragedy and the idealization of the artistic sublime. By the 1840s, Słowacki's view of Romanticism was so tainted with cynicism and the 'exalted word' and the excessive notions of ideal love seemed so repulsive to him that comedy was the only appropriate form to embody them (Segel, 1977: 61).

Fantazy's plot follows the Respekts, members of the Polish gentry, now penniless as a result of the sociopolitical circumstances of post-Partition Poland in the mid-nineteenth century, who have to 'sell' their daughter Diana into a marriage with the wealthy count Fantazy for half a million Polish zloty in order to save themselves from financial ruin. In this way, Słowacki juxtaposes the social-climbing couple, the Respekts, with the equally ridiculous Count Fantazy and Countess Idalia, who represent the frivolousness and narcissistic posturing of Romanticism. Positing this as an unfinished tragedy, Klata commented that its form was decidedly contemporary, and able to conjure the fragmented, unhinged reality of today's Poland (cited in Antoniewicz, 2005). Social stratification and the exclusion of class analysis from mainstream theatre was at the heart of

Klata's adaptation. Moving the play from the era of the Polish Partitions to the present day, Klata set the piece in a Gdańsk communist-era concrete apartment block in place of the crumbling country estate in picturesque Podolia. Money is the dominant signifier in this world, indicated by the national lottery – the only means the underprivileged tenants have of liberating themselves from lifelong deprivation – and a pawnshop. Constantly threatened by hooligans and local mafia, Respekt loses several of his fingers to a chainsaw when he is unable to pay his debts. No longer aristocracy, the Respekts are rendered as members of a now-ruined intellectual elite. The family's famous English garden is reduced to a narrow strip of dead lawn bordered by two thirsty trees and a grimy barbecue. Much of the explosive comedy emerged from the glaring disparity between the indignity of the surroundings and the Respekts' pretence that they continue to inhabit a sophisticated estate. 'The clash of comic and tragic conventions,' Klata explained, 'allowed the poet in a fantastic way to describe the gap between high ambitions and reality, which is brutal and degenerate' (cited in Cieślak, 2005b). The text was tightly edited and the incipient erosion of the Respekts' aristocratic world was shown through a provocative collision between the elegance of Słowacki's language and a crude use of working-class lingo.

Referencing the war in Iraq – the tall concrete block would re-emerge in Grzegorz Jarzyna's Iraq War-focused adaptation of *Macbeth* in 2007 – this production also offered a frightening comic take on Poland's involvement in George W. Bush's globalized 'War on Terror.' In Słowacki's text, eastern Poland is the victim of Russia's prolonged occupation and repeated military invasions. Klata deftly inverted this position of victimhood, portraying Poland as an *ally* of the US and other Western occupying forces. In one particularly memorable scene, wounded soldiers who have returned from battle perform a mock ballet in wheelchairs, displaying their maimed or severed limbs in a coquettish and stylized dance routine. Shifting imperial relations from East to West, Klata also showed through musical selections and costumes the degree to which American popular culture has become the insidious form of social domination today. Madonna's 'Material World' provides an acoustic background to carefully enunciated lines of verse, signifying a postmodern pastiche that does not favor high over low culture, or pop singers over Romantic poetry. Klata observed that although he saw the difference between Russia as a hostile, sadistic colonizer and a 'smiling, instructive Uncle Sam,' the problem remains that Poland is a nation that requires an 'older brother' who, in turn, demands obedience (cited in Cieślak, 2005b). Tempted by high wages, Jan, the protagonist forced into exile in

Siberia in the original text, voluntarily signs up to fight in Iraq. The only viable career options open to him are determined by legal (the military, police) or illicit (a local gang, the mafia) forms of aggression and violence. Given the range of problems tackled in *Fanta$y*, I would take issue with Jacek Cieślak's (2005b) argument that Klata was 'probably the only young director for whom issues such as Poland and patriotism are more important than the Western imported problems of violence, sex, drugs and sexual minorities.' Klata reveals the extent to which it is no longer possible to entirely single out Poland's economic crises or cultural values from those of the West. Indeed, when asked to whom this performance was addressed, Klata showed customary resistance to defining a localized demographic.[5]

By 2005, Klata had become such essential viewing that the Instytut Teatralny organized Klata. Fest in Wrocław and Warsaw to showcase five of the director's most celebrated works. It is true that many younger directors have steered clear of Polish Romantic texts – they are untouched at the TR Warszawa – but Klata has used Romantic legacies to confront a culture that he maintains is founded upon victimhood.[6] At the basis of his work one particular question resonates: 'What are we to do with all this messianism, with this layer of chains, with the themes of slavery?' (cited in Baran, 2005). Klata's revolutionary attack on bourgeois nationalism, spiritual and religious hypocrisy and lazy politics has come to be the hallmark of a new generation of Polish directors. In keeping in line with the national role of Kraków's Stary Teatr, Klata, whose directing oeuvre testifies to his mature and insightful interrogation of Polish culture, dogma and ideology, was made the prestigious theatre's artistic director. While his approach to theatre-making is radically different from former artistic directors, such as Zygmunt Hübner (1960s), Stanisław Radwan (1980s), Tadeusz Bradecki (1990s) and Mikołaj Grabowski (2000s), Klata is as fundamental to the national theatre scene as his predecessors were in their own historical moments. As Anna R. Burzyńska (2012) pointed out, acts of 'desecration' – that is, the desecration of sacred texts, myths and beliefs – in the Stary Teatr have always existed, although they appear within a certain framework: not as blind, aggressive or cynical acts, but rather as important examinations of the viability of a Polish 'community.' As I shall discuss in the next chapter, although their risk-taking is not always successful, Klata, Zadara, Strzępka and Demirski have breathed fresh life into the theatre, pushing hard against the carefully defined boundaries of what it means to be Polish today that challenge the increasingly defunct Romantic *communitas*, and their work has been at the heart of a new theatre practice *na lewo*.

Notes

1 In 1959, Jerzy Jarocki helped inaugurate Student Theatre (Teatr STG) at the Silesian University of Technology in Gliwice where he directed the world premiere of *Ślub* in 1960. STG was a critical site of resistance against communist censorship and authority, which was reflected in the decision to mount Gombrowicz's banned play. Predictably, the production was shut down after only four performances by the authorities.
2 For a critique of previous stagings of *Ślub*, see Sieradzki (1991).
3 Solidarity is a defining movement against which to define a political stance. For post-Communists, it is important to frame Solidarity as the Communists' downfall from power, which evidences their ideological conversion. This also allowed '1989' to stand for the actualization of the original aim of the movement in 1980. Obversely, for the anti-Communists, Solidarity 'embodied the failure to forge a new moral, Catholic, anti-Communist Poland; its memory could not therefore become the basis for post-Communist national commemoration' (Mark, 2010: 17).
4 For a comprehensive analysis of the connections between Strzępka and Demirski and twentieth-century leftist theatre practice in Poland see Węgrzyniak (2011).
5 This production was followed by Przemysław Wojcieszek's *Made in Poland* (2004), staged as a site-specific performance in a low-income housing project in Wałbrzych, which also directly responded to the city's economic deprivation and concomitant social problems.
6 Klata adapted Witkacy's *Szewcy* (The Shoemakers) with Sławomir Sierakowski, leader of Krytyka Polityczna, for the TR Warszawa in 2007. The title, *The Shoemakers at the Gates* was intended to reflect Slavoj Žižek's *Revolution at the Gates* (2002, Polish translation 2006). Sierakowski was interested in Žižek's theorization of political lost causes and his investment in the reemergence of the radical left in the contemporary world. Although it attracted close attention from the media, the overtly political production was universally recognized as too didactic and uninteresting.

2

No more heroes

On April 10, 2010, a Polish Air-Force Tupolev Tu-154M aircraft crashed in a field near Smolensk, Russia, killing 96 members of an official Polish delegation scheduled to visit the site of a former atrocity known as the Katyń massacre, *the* emblematic space of twentieth-century Polish martyrology, and the mass graves of Polish officers who had been the victims of executions ordered by Joseph Stalin in 1940. The horrifying coincidence of this air disaster and the memorialization of the Katyń massacre became a significant factor in the public discourse that framed the tragedy and led to a mode of mourning that is haunted by nineteenth-century Polish Romantic thought and, as performance theorist Dariusz Kosiński (2011) has argued, Adam Mickiewicz's canonical text of the period *Dziady* (*Forefathers' Eve*, completed 1832) in particular. Among the dead were Polish President Lech Kaczyński and his wife Maria, former President Ryszard Kaczorowski, the chief of the Polish General Staff, senior Polish military officers, the president of the National Bank of Poland, the deputy foreign minister, members of the Polish parliament, senior members of the Polish clergy, as well as relatives of victims of the Katyń massacre. The title of Mickiewicz's *Dziady* refers to the pagan ancestor commemoration enacted by Slavic and Baltic peoples on All Souls' Day. The apotheosis of the play's action is centered around the ritual transformation of the ghost of the lover Gustaw into Konrad, a mystical Romantic hero who must fulfill the political mission of saving the lost nation. In the aftermath of the Smolensk disaster, crowds gathered to mourn in front of the Presidential Palace in Warsaw. When the dead president's identical twin brother, Jarosław Kaczyński, emerged in front of the grieving masses, the enthusiasm with which he was greeted blotted out the fact that the Kaczyński twins' ultra-conservative Law and Justice Party had significantly lost its popularity by the spring of 2010. Following the same logic we find in *Dziady*, in which Gustaw's rebirth as Konrad is mirrored by the uncanny appearance of Jarosław *qua* the dead Lech, the brother came to stand in for the lost leader and therefore to fulfill his unfinished mission. This seemingly miraculous resurrection could be construed as an invocation of Polish Messianism, 'which stresses the Christ-like attitude of the individual Pole engaged in the "salvic" mission of his country's struggle for independence' and 'other enslaved nations of Europe' (Kraszewski, 1998: 10–11) and, furthermore, as a conservative backlash of xenophobic and Catholic politics that reasserts the primacy of the nation over globalized or pan-European and EU politics right at the moment the left was gaining popularity in Poland. Kosiński claims that this evocation of *Dziady* in the public sphere should not be read as an archaic cultural conception but as an active political and ideological tool in Poland today.

In traditional scholarship, the foremost contribution of Polish Romanticism is seen to be its ability to fortify the ideals of a 'nationless' nation, one that should have been annihilated by the Partitions of the Polish-Lithuanian Commonwealth, the eradication of sovereign Poland for a period of 123 years beginning in the second half of the eighteenth century, by placing emphasis on the metaphysical and on the rebellious nature of a national hero (see, for example, Czerwinski, 1988). In his famous 'Lectures on Slavic Literature' given at the Collège de France in the early 1840s, Mickiewicz set out the role of a national drama, specifying that each new era require a genius to set it in motion. Art has a duty to call upon all of its resources, from architecture to dance and music, in its quest to animate the masses, who would otherwise remain inert and submissive (Mickiewicz, 1986 [1844]: 93). Although Maria Janion argued in 1975 that 'even up to the present time there can hardly be any utterance or dialogue outside of Romanticism, outside of the languages of social understanding it has created' (1975: 7), in her celebrated 2000 study *Do Europy tak, ale razem z naszymi umarłymi* (*To Europe: Yes, but Together with our Dead*), the feminist literary theorist and historian declared these very values were irretrievably eroded in Polish culture in the decade following political transformation (2000: 248–58). Tadeusz Bodio (1999: 10), on the other hand, sees a change in the sociopolitical climate, wherein the dynamism of Romantic ideals gave way to pragmatism after

1989. The political transition in the last decade of the twentieth century was so fast that many intellectuals have struggled to found a critical platform with which to theorize the shifts in cultural values, which has resulted in resistance to political and economic transition. This has had profound repercussions with regard to Poland's accession into the EU. It is no coincidence, for example, that a statue of Adam Mickiewicz was raised in Kraków to celebrate the bicentenary of his birth in 1998 as a benchmark, but also a reminder of a longstanding cultural identity that perceives nationhood under threat, which ultra-conservative parties such as the Kaczyńskis' Law and Justice Party associate with the incursive mandates of EU legislation.

Romanticism is more than a genre in Poland; it signifies a commitment to community-building, collective belonging, self-assertion and a defense of independence but also, and perhaps more importantly, Romanticism offered a social critique, identifying truths that are uncomfortable for the nation to hear (see Karpiński, 1989: 117–19). Throughout the twentieth century, *Dziady* was staged at moments of political and social crisis, demonstrating Polish solidarity and moral superiority over Russian and later Soviet colonizers. The most notorious example was Kazimierz Dejmek's 1967 staging at the National Theatre in Warsaw, which communist authorities closed down, eventuating the infamous student riots of 1968. When considering theatre history in the intermediary period from communism to liberal democracy a careful reflection on Polish Romanticism is necessary to understand the conventions of spectatorship and authorship that were embedded through this movement and genre in order to produce a fuller picture of the experience of transition in ideological and aesthetic terms. This chapter will concentrate on the incremental shift in theatre productions of Polish Romantic texts and themes, from their appropriation to their deconstruction, which defined the covenant between stage and audience in postcommunist Polish theatre and offered new platforms for national and social critique.

Eschewing patriotism

Long before 1989, two Polish directors had already begun to challenge the patriotic tenants of Polish Romanticism. The first of these is one of the most globally acclaimed artists of theatrical innovation in the twentieth century, Tadeusz Kantor. Although Kantor displayed a profound fascination with Polish Romanticism and neo-Romanticism as a young man, his productions form a crucial break from the Romantic covenant between stage and audience. One of Kantor's earliest productions was Juliusz Słowacki's *Balladyna* in 1943 with his Independent Theatre, in which the eponymous character was an abstracted figure represented with masks. Jerzy Merunowicz, director of the underground One-Act Theatre, observed that certain 'patriotic circles' had sent him to warn Kantor that his production of *Balladyna* 'was a provocation against the Polish nation, against tradition' (cited in Pleśniarowicz, 2004: 39). As Krzysztof Pleśniarowicz maintains, Kantor was also accused by Jerzy Kujawksi, on the opposing camp, that a legitimate avant-garde artist must jettison all Romanticism and national sentimentality. However, Kantor's relationship to Romanticism should not be determined in purely nationalist terms; the artist was often accused of being unpatriotic, and in his last essay, 'From the Beginning, in My Credo Was...' (1990), written in the midst of his final performance, *Today is My Birthday*, Kantor explicitly advocates freedom in art, discouraging patriotism. In the *Milano Lessons* (1986), the only example of theatre pedagogy in Kantor's writings, the artist supports the work of the Dadaists in their attempt to question the social values that had been in place in Europe up until the First World War, to make a sacrilege of all the old cultural shrines, to denounce a system where 'nationalism turned out to be nothing more than a base primitive instinct' (Kobialka, 1993: 258).

Polish (Romantic) history plays a major role in the Theatre of Death trilogy (1975–85), with the significant events such as the 1830–31 Polish insurrection and characters such as Marshal Józef Piłsudski represented. As Michal Kobialka argues, *Umarła klasa* (*The Dead Class*, 1975) refuses to sentimentalize the past, to provide nostalgic material for consolation or pleasure (2009b: 83) – a habit of spectating that one finds in standard stagings of Romantic texts in the twentieth century – which portrays 'fissures in a traditional construction of the meanings and symbols associated with national life and staged as a utopian configuration' (*ibid.*: 90). In *The Silent Night* (1990), the Inn of Memory is a space 'which departs from all sacred conventions, moral codes and idealizing procedures' (Kantor cited in *ibid.*: 443). This reflects the acutely political slant to Kantor's work, wherein the theatre space is made autonomous from nationalist desire, and the practice of identity formation is reconceived as fluid and not stuck to the signifier, a practice that should be directly opposed to the substance of Romantic national identification.

The second Polish director to significantly rework Polish Romantic plays after Konrad Swinarski's expressionistic treatments in the 1960s–70s was Jerzy Grzegorzewski, who faced sharp condemnation from Polish critics due to his liberal adaptations of canonical texts, often flaunting authorial intention and stable narrative structure, and, purportedly, obfuscating intelligibility. Time as a linear concept is often invoked in his productions only to be systematically undermined. Grzegorzewski wholly rejected the concept of 'historical time as an ordered line of causes and effects' (Morawiec, 1984: 78) and preferred to think about memory as a disorientating force, out of time and linked to the individual psyche, a motif that has also been instrumental in the work of Krystian Lupa. One could base Grzegorzewski's oeuvre in modernism, particularly his attempt to uncover 'dormant meaning in everyday objects and interiors' (*ibid.*: 82). Grzegorzewski's habit of reconfiguring canonical dramatic texts in new and original patterns or collages led Jacek Sieradzki (1985) to probe the modern usage of terms such as *reżyser* (the humble director who, following the preserve of nineteenth-century theatre, seeks only to serve the demands of the written drama) versus *inscenizator*, the director as *auteur*. Sieradzki further argued that in what he termed Grzegorzewski's 'theatre of variations' – named after the director's 1977 production that combined the writings of Thomas Mann, Witold Gombrowicz, Fyodor Dostoyevsky, Anton Chekhov, August Strindberg and Antonin Artaud among others into a *inscenizator*-authored text for theatre – the choice of subject matter was subordinated to the form of staging.

Extracted from standard causality, the world Grzegorzewski presented was subjective, internalized and dreamlike, not unlike the familiar Romantic universe that was constructed exclusively through the lens of an individual ego. Conversely, Elżbieta Morawiec claimed that while Konrad Swinarski was a Romantic of postwar theatre, Grzegorzewski, insofar as his art is a quest for a 'Paradise Lost,' frames him as a neo-Romantic (1984: 87). This contention derives specifically from Grzegorzewski's work with tragedy, such as Tadeusz Różewicz's *Śmierć w starych dekoracjach* (*Death in the Old Decorations*, 1978), a play that interrogates metaphysical determinism as it affects humanity at large rather than the fate of isolated individuals. Grzegorzewski returned to works of the Romantic poets as well as Wyspiański, Witkiewicz, Chekhov, Genet and Różewicz throughout his life, and although he was largely considered apolitical, especially in contrast to Andrzej Wajda and Jerzy Jarocki, two of his productions – *Wesele* (*The Wedding*, 1977) and *Nie-Boska komedia* (*Un-Divine Comedy*, 1979) – bestrode the Romantic and the avant-garde in the activation of the spectator through their immersion 'w podwójnym czasie' ('in double time') (Morawiec, 1977), the proliferation of memories of past productions produced through the plural potentialities engendered by the 'open' text of Grzegorzewski's vision. The rousing incitement of the audience through the activation of a 'free' imagination against prevailing forms of censorship was precisely the political goal of the Romantic drama. Configuring the artist as a fallen demiurge, one of the fundamental appeals of Grzegorzewski's work for Polish critics was the constitutive appeal to an authoritative divine force that reinforced a stable, Catholic moral order. Whereas Swinarski attempted to shock in order to reveal, using alienation and distancing techniques influenced by his assistantship with Bertolt Brecht at the Berliner Ensemble in the mid-1950s, Grzegorzewski's theatre became associated by his detractors with a dull seriousness and a sluggish pace that many members of the public – that is, those excluded from the elite circle who were able to either find his work intelligible or to accept its unintelligibility as a productive condition of its reception – found tedious or impossibly obscure. Maria Janion (1979) became a proponent of the director after watching his *Nie-Boska komedia*, claiming that, due to his move away from acting techniques reliant on declamatory rhetoric in favor of indistinct and subdued voices and his ability to exceed a singular stage time through the open and non-linear form that reflected the Romantic dramas themselves, Grzegorzewski was the only theatre artist capable of rendering the Romantic imagination on stage, a feat previously accomplished only in the cinema.

However, frequent motifs in Grzegorzewski's productions counter the conceptualization of his work as Romantic, as does his reliance on modernist and, from the 1990s onward, postmodernist staging techniques. Between 1995 and 1996, Grzegorzewski directed three plays that clearly marked a break with the Romantic aims of national myth-building. Despite his attempts to undermine the focus on martyrology in Romantic texts and to place himself at an ironic distance from the concepts that traditionally supported the Polish intelligentsia, Elżbieta Baniewicz is right to point out that Grzegorzewski did not successfully free himself of Romantic paradigms altogether. Baniewicz argued that in the mid-1990s there were certain topics, remembered images and obsessions that governed the Polish collective consciousness that no one had yet replaced or filled in (1996: 475). Of the three performances of the 1995–96 season that created a direct polemic with Romanticism – *La Bohème* (based on Stanisław Wyspiański's texts *The Wedding* and *Liberation*), *Dziady – dwanaście improwizacji* (*Forefathers' Eve – Twelve Improvisations*) and Molière's *Don Juan* – it is perhaps not surprising that the *Dziady* adaptation has been cited by a number of Polish theatre scholars as one of the most important productions after 1989, given its direct confrontation with Mickiewicz and the affirmation of a national collective conscious.

Grzegorzewski participates in a long line of directors in the twentieth century who have attempted to stage Mickiewicz's *Dziady*. Tadeusz Kornaś (1996) suggests that any staging of the canonical poetic drama compels a director to give a declaration of their ideological intentions. The staging of spirits in particular is crucial for a director's determination of an extra-rational world and the role of a divine presence in contemporary reality. In Wyspiański's seminal 1901 production, one sees an equation between materiality and the spiritual, an unintentional mix between worlds, while in Swinarski's mounting of *Dziady*, the ancestors deliberately leave the stage and assemble in the lobby of the theatre on the same level as the audience. For Grzegorzewski, on the other hand, the theatrical artifice is primary. One does not believe in his ghosts as such. Jan Kłossowicz commented shortly after Swinarski's production of the play in the Stary Teatr in 1973 that a director must either destroy Mickiewicz's text or break the theatre (cited in Majchrowski, 1998). According to Zbigniew Majchrowski (1998), Swinarski accomplished the latter with his disturbance of the traditional performance space, while Grzegorzewski's *Dziady - dwanaście improwizacji* destroyed the text altogether. Unlike Maciej Prus' 1979 production at the Teatr Wybrzeże in Gdańsk, which subjected the text to the Aristotelian unities of action, place and time, Grzegorzewski built upon its fragmentation. These approaches fit with the two models Majchrowski suggests for structuring a performance of *Dziady*: linear or biographical, what one might call the 'pilgrimage' approach (Wyspiański, Schiller, Bardini, Kotlarczyk, Swinarski), or a kaleidoscopic or mosaic method (Korzeniewski, Zegalski, Grzegorzewski). This differentiation also attests to the two fundamental reasons audiences attend a performance of *Dziady*: the pedagogic production that 'teaches' the text, following the nineteenth-century conception of the 'academic theatre,' versus the avant-gardist intervention that rewrites, deconstructs or submits the play in the tradition of *inscenizator* theatre. While this may seem a commonplace, the difference in rationale has raised salient questions in the Polish media about the function of the Romantic canon in contemporary theatre practice.

Morawiec (1984) argues that in the period 1955–87, if one excludes Aleksander Bardini for his relevance outside of artistic criteria, the three landmark productions of the play belonged to Kazimierz Dejmek (1967) at Warsaw's Teatr Narodowy, Konrad Swinarski (1973) at Kraków's Stary Teatr and Grzegorzewski at Warsaw's Teatr Studio (1987). Although some critics refute a single interpretation of the text as the authoritative model, it is clear that even in the mid-1990s every production of *Dziady* was still actively judged against Swinarski's definitive production – an example that throws into relief Marvin Carlson's notion of 'double vision' wherein there exists for the spectator 'a simultaneous awareness of something previously experienced and of something being offered in the present that is both the same and different, which can only be appreciated by a kind of doubleness of perception in the audience' (2001: 51). The title of Grzegorzewski's earlier production, *Dziady – Improwizacje* (*Forefathers' Eve – Improvisations*, 1987), already implies a treatment of the text that is referential and deconstructive rather than complete. Rather than relying on Mickiewicz, these 'improvisations' focused on poetry conveyed spontaneously, an open expression that draws on the director, the actor and the spectator's imagination.

What is crucial to highlight in Grzegorzewski's non-canonical direction is a break with Mickiewicz's worldview, in which God watches over the processes of history, and evil is duly punished. As Małgorzata Sugiera (1988) observes, Mickiewicz provides a clear hierarchy of values wherein no victim is futile and morality is unambiguous. Such certainty is absent in Grzegorzewski, whose vision is profoundly pessimistic, undermining the value placed on personal suffering in the text. Two of the most celebrated scenes focus on men who are isolated in an existential crisis: Konrad in the '*Wielka improwizacja*' ('The Great Improvisation'), who dares to confront God with the suffering of the nation in what is considered the foundational patriotic outburst of heroic despair, and the priest Father Piotr, who has a vision of Poland's redemptive future. Grzegorzewski divided Konrad into two characters, Young and Old, a decision that drew attention to the corporeality of the actors themselves, Boy and Man. In this division, Konrad fails to function as a hero; rather he is reduced to the level of his experience that subverts tragic narratives. This division from traditional narrative was compounded by the delivery of the text with the actors repeating their lines as if the words belonged to someone else. The Young Conrad is too weak to fight God and the Old Konrad has no faith in the efficacy of such a cosmic struggle. Konrad is immersed in pain and despair, but unlike the entire twentieth-century performance canon of *Dziady*, neither emotion is effectively redemptive or cathartic. The most important element of this production is not the struggle or relationship between heaven and earth, rather it is the status of memory and the imaginative work of the director in adaptation that should be kept in mind when discussing the problems of reception. Claims that the performance was jagged, inconsistent or full of uncertainties of theatrical argument often fail to take into account this positioning of history, text and the role of the artist. Małgorzata Dziewulska (2009) has observed that the covenant that traditionally existed between the Polish stage and audiences in the twentieth century was reliant on the ritual of Forefathers' Eve, wherein the ghosts of ancestors are revived in material form through the actor for the spectators. Condemnations that Grzegorzewski broke this sacred covenant by blurring the boundaries between director and playwright and director and actor (the latter he broke quite literally, bringing the devils from Part III into the audience as well as beginning the performance in the foyer of the theatre) should be mitigated through a new lens: the theatrical ritual as an event of history rather than history's evocation.

It is easy to spot the significant change in the role Mickiewicz's text plays in the construction of community and national identity in the seven-year gap between Grzegorzewski's two adaptations (1987 and 1995). In the earlier production, much more appeared to be at stake in the legacy of Romantic tradition, causing such disagreements in the media as that between Elżbieta Morawiec (1988) and Krzysztof Kopka (1988a: 11–12) concerning the heritage of Poland's past in the present day, whether or not the Old Konrad was able to move past the inexorable barriers of history and biology. Sugiera (1988) contended that Grzegorzewski's placing of Pallas Athena, a symbol Wyspiański revitalized as a sign of independence in *Noc listopadowa* (*November Night*, 1904), at the entry to the theatre showed that universally applicable principles had been thrown into question. With a view of the empty square in front of the Palace of Culture – a great irony of Polish history – behind the goddess Athena, Grzegorzewski revealed a collision of incompatible values. Perhaps most striking, however, was the depreciation in the importance of Romantic suffering, previously sublimated through the ordeal of political tyranny. The assembly of five Mrs. Rollinsons attested to a collective trauma that should be challenged rather than nurtured, thus devaluing the mother's anguish, the one who 'suffers for millions,' by turning her singularity of emotion into a parodic chorus that critiqued the Matka Polka trope, a paradigm in Polish Romanticism whose 'fundamental qualities are motherhood, duty and the spirit of sacrifice' (Matynia, 2009: 185). This staging decision equally challenged the status of Father Piotr as the visionary for a martyred country.

If the 1987 production reworked the nation play into the existential crisis of an individual, thereby destabilizing both the myth of the Romantic hero and the substance of the community built upon it, the later production no longer participated in the debate between national literature and individual tragedy. Given the lack of a singular public political or national adversary in the social field in the 1990s, the play struggled to maintain its role as a manifesto for political action. As a result, it could only be read as a deliberate composition of theatrical artifice. Critics, unable to move beyond reception bounded by conceptions of theatre as the locus of community spirit and national autonomy, complained that in Grzegorzewski's vision, meaning was too open, scenes were too sketchily composed, the text was reduced and messily reordered, which meant that the great national drama had been betrayed and the staging was diagnosed as sacrilege. Such censure also kept open the question of the primacy of literature over theatre. Grzegorzewski's aim was not to retain fidelity to the text's production history and, by association, to allow it to retain its privileged position as the guardian of national values. Instead, the director conceived of the presence of the text as a multiplicity, formed by both its historical stagings, the variations of its appearances and associations in the artist's consciousness, which called attention to the radical social change brought about by the political transition after 1989. It is in this pursuit that one may differentiate Swinarski from Grzegorzewski. Swinarski's stagings of *Dziady* and Wyspiański's *Wyzwolenie* (*Liberation*, 1903) succeeded in consummating the symbolic spirit of the community. Community, however, is not at the heart of Grzegorzewski's direction. The free assemblage of scenes, the primacy of the materiality over the symbolism of stage signs, and the auto-reference to previous productions of Wyspiański's texts converge on the audience as the signature of an *auteur* that has no interest in the cohesion of community substance. Swinarski focused on synthesis, cutting off the complexity of the dialectic and the unity of nationhood, while Grzegorzewski focused on the internal opposition and hybridity that undermined a singular vision or experience of nation through his repeated emphasis on antithesis.

In *Dziady – dwanaście improwizacji*, the Romantic hero, Konrad, attempts suicide, although the dagger sticking from his chest is an obvious theatrical prop, which prompted an anxiety in conservative critics that this foretold a reign of spiritual apathy. There were analogies drawn between the end of the Polish hero and the title of Ryszard Przybylski's 1993 study of the play (*Słowo i milczenie bohatera Polaków* [Word and Silence of the Poles' Hero]). Against this trend, other critics tried to discern the legacies of pre-1989 rather than their disappearance. In the early 1980s, Grzegorzewski had already begun to devise a theatre beyond grand narratives. In 1995, the director's work moved to the postmodern precisely because the grand narratives that are embedded in the Romantic text were evoked through references to past productions, then dismantled, braided back together and transformed. The question then is not whether the effects of 1989 are merely a 'dance of phantoms,' derived from worn-out slogans and epithets, but rather how the very 'wearing out' of such reproductions already defines a community.

Grzegorzewski's intercession into the genealogy of productions of Mickiewicz's national drama, and his refusal to conform to the Romantic habit of the audience covenant, has in my mind led to two major shifts. First, critics' recent application of the subtitle *Dziady* to two productions by the director Krzysztof Warlikowski, a student of Grzegorzewski, substantiate a new understanding of the text and its function. Warlikowski's 2001 *Dybuk* was given the subheading 'Polish-Jewish *Dziady*' by Roman Pawłowski (2003), while his 2007 adaptation of *Angels in America* at the TR Warszawa was referred to as 'Today's *Dziady*' (Cieślak, 2007). This is surprising not only because Warlikowski is notorious for his lack of interest in directing *Dziady*, which was still seen in the 1990s as a rite of passage for every major Polish theatre director, but also because his productions depict a country that is secularized, obsessed by consumerism, pluralistic and sexually ambiguous. In other words, the change in meaning of the text in the cultural field, where it now operates as a stand-in for the 'state-of-the-nation' play, extends precisely from Grzegorzewski's disruption to the reception of *Dziady* as a locus of community spirit, fragmenting this monolith of cultural and ethnic identification. And, secondly, returning to Baniewicz's claim that national and religious symbols that sustained Poland through multiple occupations had not been replaced in the mid-1990s, today one does not see an abandonment of the old forms and signs but rather an evacuation of their meaning. While the 1990s may have been an era of larger sociocultural malaise, what emerges after *Dziady – dwanaście improwizacji* is a series of 'ghosts' who to some extent owe their inclusion in contemporary theatre to Grzegorzewski's break with Romanticism. This claim can perhaps best be understood in relation to the identities that had once been excluded from conventional conceptions of Polishness and its connection to the traditional audience covenant.

Given the director's trajectory of deconstructing sacred national mythologies, it is perhaps surprising that Grzegorzewski was selected to head the National Theatre (Teatr Narodowy), which had burned down in 1985 and was reopened after 12 years of refurbishment in 1997. Wyspiański's *Noc listopadowa* (*November Night*) was selected for the premiere. The play, which some critics refer to as effectively the fourth part of *Dziady*, uses the 1830–31 Uprising as a nodal point to frame the tragedy of failed rebellions in the nineteenth century that fundamentally shaped Polish political consciousness in the twentieth century. Pawłowski (2007) noted that for two centuries the Polish intelligentsia shared the fate of their National Theatre, which held the responsibility of defending national identity, guarding cultural traditions and teaching patriotism. In the nineteenth century, the theatre's mission gained more prominence given its power to use the Polish language, a privilege extended only to theatres and churches. Furthermore, at the inauguration of the rebuilt theatre in 1924 Juliusz Osterwa made the solemn pledge to serve the evangelists of the Polish Spirit – in effect, staging the Polish Romantic canon – making the National Theatre a model of common ambition for the rest of the country's theatres. The forced implementation of socialist realism after 1949 eschewed this tradition, but Erwin Axel's directorship was crucial in the reclaiming of nationalist themes and texts in the 'thaw' following Stalin's death in 1953. Kazimierz Dejmek's tenure created a 'Comédie-Polonaise' of sorts, a theatre that maintained the academic literary tradition of the national drama and culture, which in turn shaped the political consciousness of a highly patriotic audience, until his dismissal in the summer of 1968 following his controversial 1967 production of *Dziady*. Dejmek's successor, Adam Hanuszkiewicz, was interested primarily in popular entertainment, and his choice of repertoire largely reflected the values of the Edward Gierek era, defined by intellectual stagnation as well as an increase in consumption and Western influence (Pawłowski, 2007). Reflecting on the mass debate among intellectual elites in the early 1990s on the new role of the National Theatre, Pawłowski acknowledged that the intelligentsia was losing its rarified position as the '*przewodnik*' (leader or guide) of the nation. The anxiety attending the decrease in audience attendance in this period was accompanied by a fear that a strong *auteur* director would not serve the Romantic canon, but create a singular artistic vision.

A large bulk of the reviews of Grzegorzewski's opening production of *Noc listopadowa* simply reiterated this larger anxiety. Breaking with theatrical illusion, shunning pathos, highlighting the fragmentary and melodramatic aspects of the play, each scene exploded the problems of producing Romantic texts in a post-Romantic era. The over-stylization of insurgent activity decoupled historical narratives from their heroic associations, as did the reduction of Konrad's 'call to action' to the level of a theatrical gesture. While *Noc listopadowa* proved to be one of the most technically accomplished productions in the history of Polish theatre, with 55 performers, two orchestras, sophisticated stage machinery, more stage lights than audience members and numerous highly detailed, portable sets, the conservative press universally agreed that the director's deconstruction of Wyspiański ridiculed sacred national symbols, misinterpreted history and attested to an anti-patriotic bias that was wholly inappropriate for the

National Theatre. A stormy debate in a number of the national newspapers followed, in which critics either defended or discouraged the National Theatre as a moral exemplar for the nation. Pawłowski (1997a) endorsed Grzegorzewski against his adversaries, claiming that the production did not revise history but rather its literary image, and that the director's act of debunking national mythologies required the abandonment of pathos and easy sentimentality associated with nostalgic and patriotic-oriented historical rewritings. Ultimately, as the productions that followed the premiere would demonstrate, Grzegorzewski's National Theatre was a mirror for the Polish sociopolitical reality at the turn of the millennium rather than a monument to a sublimated past or messianic future.

Contesting Romanticism

The literary historian Magdalena Chlasta-Dzięciołowska (2007) recently argued that a new generation of theatre artists has appropriated the symbols of Polish Romanticism as a form of understanding the world around them. Although many theatre directors have repeatedly commented on the constraining legacy the national *arcydramat* – i.e., Mickiewicz's *Dziady* – imposes upon them, Chlasta-Dzięciołowska asserts that the play has successfully served to demystify sociopolitical deadlocks and great collective crimes as well as private individual's existential battles. Recent productions of the paradigmatic text have used street slang, graffiti, hip-hop, advertising slogans and examples of shoddy journalism to build a vocabulary of ghostly associations that, she asserts, would not be as potent without the connotations of Romantic aesthetics and philosophical notions. Maria Makaruk, a specialist in Romantic literature, picks up on Maria Janion's eminent and high-profile studies concerning the decline of the status of the Romantic values in postcommunist Poland, maintaining that the function of producing Mickiewicz before 1989 was determined by a stylized interaction with and engagement of Romantic paradigms whereas performances of *Dziady* in the Third Republic, the democratic regime following political transformation, have an entirely different dimension. Makaruk rightly observed that the era of Romanticism was not so much a revolt against existing power structures as a 'laborious restoration of order' that had been destroyed in Europe by the French Revolution, and also grew out of popular forms, such as horror, melodrama and sentimental romances (2012: 9). These forms have resurfaced in a manner that challenges assumptions around Polish Romantic texts. Today the focus on 'community' has been substituted for a deeper preoccupation with the plight of the individual. In this regard, Grzegorzewski's *Dziady – dwanaście improwizacji* stands out as a strong precursor to productions in the first decade of the twenty-first century. The examples I have chosen to analyze have been selected for their critical reception and subsequent influence, as well as for their formal experimentation and aesthetic and conceptual sophistication.

A series of key revisions of *Dziady* commenced in 2007 with Paweł Demirski's *Dziady. Ekshumacja* (Forefathers' Eve. Exhumation), which Monika Strzępka directed at Wrocław's Teatr Polski. While Jan Klata was concerned with the disregarded working classes, Demirski focused on the emerging political elite tied to the religious right. The play was intended as a structural and aesthetic reform of the age-old reverence for Mickiewicz's text and could be read as a series of small skirmishes with Romantic philosophy, canonical readings reliant on metaphysics, and legendary twentieth-century productions that ceded mastery to the playwright. Strzępka maintained that this was not an adaptation of Mickiewicz but an original reinterpretation of the time-honored play. Demirski, treating *Dziady* as raw material for the formation of a political text that has contemporary relevance, asked to what extent Polish cultural life continues to be determined by the philosophical premises espoused by the national bard. Such a treatment requires the opposite of veneration for the text and Demirski's use of stock characters (Konrad, Father Piotr, Mrs. Rollinson) and scraps of dialogue not only fail to conform to the parameters of a 'faithful' performance, they actively resist and argue with the source text. The exhumation referred to in the title gestures towards those topics that continue to be contentious, including Polish Catholicism and disavowed historical transgressions, such as lustration, the communist past, anti-Semitism and unacknowledged war crimes. Digging up the corpse of Polish Romanticism, insincere or trivial patriotism is presented in contrast to the interrogation of the assumptions that found cultural identity. Strzępka insisted that 'authentic' patriotism requires an interrogation of the self, even if it is painful, not a covering up of uncomfortable crimes or prejudices (Wysocki, 2007a). Theatre critic Joanna Derkaczew (2007a) agreed, maintaining that this exhumation of Polish forefathers was not from the ground but rather from under the carpet where taboo subjects had been swept for decades. Although some critics found this examination anti-patriotic, Strzępka's main goal was not to undermine national pride but to reshape the conventions associated with traditional forms of patriotism that require a blurring of former wrongdoing. The

Romantic hero and his promise of salvation on a national scale is opened for ridicule, which directly engages Swinarski's 1973 production that highlighted the hero's ability to overcome material and human limitations. The first two rows of the audience were seated in church pews, a gentle mocking of the pious connotations associated with past productions that position the audience as a church congregation. Despite the attempt to deconstruct the original, Chlasta-Dzięciołowska argued that Mickiewicz's text was, paradoxically perhaps, granted access to the stage precisely in its subversive, rebellious condition. The 'provocative nature' of the original is preserved by Demirski, Chlasta-Dzięciołowska (2007) claimed, reminding us that Mickiewicz, who wrote the play in self-imposed exile in Dresden and then later in Vilnius, also wrestled with his own guilt complex as a deserter who did not directly involve himself in the fight for independence. She concludes that this performance remains faithful not to Mickiewicz's text as much as to his thinking. Both *Dziady* and its exhumation were therefore produced out of corresponding creative energies set up by powerful passions, intellectual discourses and contradictory arguments.

Robert Rumas' stripped-down set was inspired by the constructivist aesthetics of Andrzej Pronaszko, a prominent member of the 'Młoda Polska' (Young Poland) movement and later the avant-garde theatre in the 1920s–30s, who helped develop the modernist visual simplicity associated with Polish monumental theatre. This design indicated that the farcical overtones would dominate any sacred ritual. *Dziady. Ekshumacja* opens with three veterans plastered with medals discussing their past exploits, failed uprisings and events that trouble national narratives such as the Jedwabne pogrom and the Prague Spring. One of the veterans is semi-catatonic and falls asleep as his fingers make the memorable victory sign from the Solidarity movement. The dead and the living are referenced alongside one another, intermingling allusions to the old PRL and the new Fourth Republic, a plan for a moral revolution first articulated in 1997 by the Polish conservative philosopher Rafał Matyja in the magazine *Nowe Państwo*, which was being actively implemented by the Kaczyńskis' Law and Justice Party in the mid-2000s. United by lingering grievances and strong xenophobia, the veterans' conversation ends in an argumentative babble as each man attempts to tell his story without any wish to hear the stories of his compatriots. The tales of the military achievements are related on All Soul's Day, which unintentionally evoke the unwanted spirits who foreground and undermine the philosophy of the Fourth Republic, the victims of pogroms, the Volhynia massacre, Soviet aggression and former communist governments.

Whereas in conventional productions of *Dziady* good and evil are neatly separated between stage right and left in a composition that literally frames the dramatic rhetoric as opposing sides of a moral binary, Strzępka put the Angel and the Devil in the center of the stage picture. The two actresses are dressed in sexy Halloween-like outfits that barely are decipherable from one another and the connotations of the naughty devil and the kinky angel have similar pornographic dimensions. Neither of these opposing moral agents interferes in the action of the play, thus excluding the possibility of divine intervention in the political field. In an atmosphere of constant struggle and self-preservation, amid personal betrayals and political denunciations, Strzępka forces the spectator to play an active role in decoding the slippery moral terrain introduced by Demirski. One critic argued that the performance did not occur against general slogans such as 'politics' or 'Church,' but rather highlighted the contradictions that are born out of these fields, thus creating a coherent warning against the unique variety of nationalist radicalism incited by Romantic philosophy (Bryś, 2007). In keeping with the overall intent, transcendental stage signs, such as the legendary hardboiled eggs Konrad broke in Swinarksi's production that acted as a condemnation of the bourgeois privilege of Warsaw salons, are reduced to comedic devices. The tabernacle in the center of the stage is transformed into a dripping kebab spit and the supernatural numerology of 44 is reduced to the country code for phone calls to the UK. Writing in *Teatr*, Jolanta Kowalska contended that the most painful part of the performance resulted forcefully from 'the mutual alienation between the elites and the public, and the lack of any communication with the exception of the occasional quarrel concerning the settlement of the past' (2007a: 29).

While the audience never see the melancholic, lyrical Gustaw make his miraculous transformation into Konrad, in 'The Great Improvisation' the hero confronts the audience in the absence of God, transforming the scene from a patriotic awakening to a critical examination of the premises undergirding patriotic duty. Making eye contact with spectators, Konrad asks: 'How significant is our collective traumatic past? Are we in a position to judge our former oppressors? Is there more to patriotism than faith? Who will give their blood for the country?' If Mickiewicz's text is a call to arms that demands individuals relinquish their rights and self-interests for the sake of the community, Demirski asks who among the audience is actually willing to step forward. By 'exposing weaknesses in the Romantic philosophy of action,' Kowalska argued that the production indicated that it is much easier 'to throw stones from the rampart than to build a responsible state' (2007a: 31). Demirski insinuates the construction of the state is not a problem to be thought through with theoretical or idealistic distance. Konrad demands names from the audience, indicating that what is needed most today is not military action but participation in democratic processes. In such a confrontation, the sublation of campaigns that require great bloodshed, such as the much-celebrated Battle of Grunwald often cited by the religious right that founded the Polish-Lithuanian union in the fifteenth century, which scholars have only recently attempted to re-examine without nationalist bias, are acrimoniously delegitimized.[1]

Demirski hatched a more ambitious project in Wałbrzych with greater results in his next co-production later in 2007, again with Monika Strzępka. *Był sobie POLAK POLAK POLAK i diabeł* (There was a Pole, Pole, Pole and the Devil) can be seen as a continuation of the exhumation project, the all-out confrontation with Polish Romanticism propelled by long-simmering frustrations with public hypocrisy and political turpitude that marked the construction of the Kaczyńskis' Fourth Republic, that chime with Klata's critique of neoliberalism. Rather than working with biography or adaptation to directly assail a venerated leader or source text, Demirski wrote an original play using the critical conventions of positivist philosophy and Romantic poetry to comment on 'Polish provincialism, vulgarity, greed, historical hypocrisy, empty martyrdom and stale holiness' (Wysocki, 2007c). Set on half a football pitch with the audience seated on bleachers, Demirski maintained that the sublime status of the sport in Poland made it the pitch-perfect location for any discussion of national values (cited in Kyzioł, 2007). At the beginning of the performance, body bags are dug up that contain the carcasses of deceased characters caught in a temporary purgatory. Unlike the metaphorical practice of disinterring of the *arcydramat*[2] in the previous performance, these exhumations were materially exhibited in a gesture towards slapstick humor, visual gags and cabaret. Neither completely dead nor entirely stripped of life, these zombie-esque bodies inhabit an undefined space where national themes are argued in juvenile fits of rage, depression and hyperactivity. The macabre setting led Derkaczew (Derkaczew 2007b) to conclude that this was the first Polish post-mortem whose grotesqueness audiences had only ever encountered in the graveyard scene in *Hamlet*. Derkaczew, however, failed to note the obvious link with Kantor's 'undead' in *Dead Class* who also occupy benches while collapsing traditional barriers between satire, tragedy and black comedy. Unlike in Mickiewicz, death does not free these heroes from their worldly sorrows. The humor here, however, could be more easily aligned with *Scary Movie* (2000), the famous parody of classic Hollywood horror movies, or lampoons such as *South Park* in which sanctified subjects are treated with the total irreverence. This style, familiar to young Polish audiences who obsessively watch American television, not only makes the content maximally accessible to a new generation of theatregoers, it also responds to the director Michał Zadara's petition to Polish theatre-makers to 'find new, lightweight communicative forms for important topics' (cited in Kyzioł, 2007).

Demirski targets the entire political spectrum from the liberal TVN24 watcher to the conservative Radio Maryja listener, blithely merging quotations from political cartoons, newspaper headlines, nationalist songs and speeches by John Paul II. Such citations create a multiplicity of ready-made languages, each of which, Kowalska argued, contains a different worldview and hierarchy of national memories that are irreconcilable (2007b: 32). The disparate array of characters makes for a 'slice of life' depiction of current trends, associations or prejudices in the mass media. These included a bishop who rubs baby oil on his chest while fantasizing excitedly about gay sex; a German tourist dressed in colorful Bermuda shorts and a Nazi military uniform, who accuses Poles of being an inferior race; a Polish general in black sunglasses, who waxes nostalgic about the PRL, an obvious reference to the last Communist leader of Poland and imposer of Martial Law, General Jaruzelski; a teenager depressed because his parents have immigrated to the West without him; and a survivor of Auschwitz. In a ghoulish series of dance routines, gags and soliloquies, Demirski and Strzępka sustain a powerful satire on contemporary themes ranging from German resentment over lost territory, anti-social behavior and hooliganism, pedophilia in the Catholic Church, Poland's participation in globalization and Holocaust memorials. These civic concerns are contrasted with teenage ennui, devotion to football and depression. The personal remains steadfastly political, as can be seen in the pairing of the abandoned teenager, who longs for a successful business career in Warsaw, with the woman who is searching for a husband with a large bank account and, preferably, a foreign passport, in order to escape her unhappy life in rural Poland. Their ideals of unlimited consumption are shaped by brutal competitiveness, relentless self-promotion and, ultimately, 'unrealizable dreams of a high standard of living' (*ibid.*). The focus on monologues and frenzied, one-sided verbalizations – none of which succeed in gaining footing as the dominant discourse, much like the fighting between the three veterans in *Ekshumacja* – serve to reinforce Demirski's conclusion that a breakdown in social communication has accompanied the abandonment of Romantic values for a neoliberal paradigm. Interestingly, the reign of the free market also combats the figure of the 'universal Pole' advocated by many theatre practitioners in the twentieth century.

The final production I will consider in the recuperation of the Romantic canon for social critique was Paweł Wodziński's adaptation of *Dziady* at the Teatr Polski in Bydgoszcz in 2011. Wodziński graduated from the Academy of Dramatic Arts in Warsaw in 1993 and went on to work as both an actor and director at the Teatr Dramatyczny before founding the Towarzystwo Teatralne (Theatrical Society) at the Teatr Rozmaitości – later rebranded the more international 'TR Warszawa' by Grzegorz Jarzyna – with, among others, the left-wing intellectual Paweł Łysak. Their main aim was to create a theatre that played a social role and functioned as a crucial component of public discourse. Shortly after, Wodziński was invited to become artistic director of the Teatr Polski in Poznań, bringing Łysak along as assistant director, where he inaugurated the Centre for Contemporary Dramaturgy, which hosted workshops for young playwrights and readings from new plays. Throughout his career, Wodziński has been a proponent of contemporary writers such as Sarah Kane and Ingmar Villquist, and he is also well-known for his productions of Polish Romantic texts. Joining the ranks of Jan Klata and Monika Strzępka in their biting interrogations of Romanticism's ideals, Wodziński's recent *Dziady* was the third in a triptych of Polish Romantic plays in which he separated out the play's conventional title from the playwright and the theatre space from the performative act. These included *Krasiński. Nie-Boska komedia. Instalacja teatralna* (Krasiński. Un-divine Comedy. Theatrical Installation, 2008), followed by the epic *Słowacki. 5 dramatów. Rekonstrukcja historyczna* (Słowacki. 5 Plays. Historical Re-enactments, 2010), and culminating with *Mickiewicz. Dziady. Performance.* (2011), which was invited to the 2012 Warsaw Theatre Meetings. *Dziady* is a compulsory text for middle-school students in Poland, who are required to read the second part of the play in which Mickiewicz lays out his folk-inspired philosophy on love and death. The remaining parts, more rubato in style, politically engaged and wildly melodramatic, are saved for higher-level students. While Wodziński was aware, as is any Polish director, that a production of the *arcydramat* will inevitably bring in hordes of school groups, his intention was not pedagogically oriented.

Perhaps the most memorable convention of this adaptation was a series of scathing and unsympathetic quotations about Polish culture from eighteenth- and nineteenth-century Western intellectual and artistic elites such as Johann Wolfgang von Goethe, Heinrich Heine, Voltaire and John Frederick Smith. Non-Polish actors read out the quotations in English, which were simultaneously screened on a side projection in their mother tongue. Accusing Poles of being primitive, backward, servile and stupid, Wodziński gave a salutary blow to an audience anticipating a reaffirmation of national identity, martyrdom and the significance of Polish culture, implying that the country is still peripheral to the West and suffers from parochialism, which was formally at odds with the use of English, French and German that required a cosmopolitan sophistication of the audience. Criticizing in equal measure Polish megalomania and martyrdom and, simultaneously, the West's blatant xenophobia and ignorance of its Eastern neighbors, it is important to point out that such inflammatory language is also often deployed by politicians on both sides of the Polish political divide, from staunch proponents of Westernization to those wishing to negatively influence debates around EU membership. The final section of the performance referenced the so-called '*bitwa o krzyż*' ('battle for the cross'), a debate over a large crucifix erected spontaneously by Polish Scouts in front of the presidential palace in Warsaw five days after the Smolensk air disaster that I discussed at the opening of this chapter. Bronisław Komorowski, the newly elected Polish president from the central-left party Platforma Obywatelska, requested the cross be moved to St. Anne's Church, which sparked a nationwide debate over Polish patriotism. The security and police force required to watch over the public feuds created by the cross reportedly cost the Polish government more than three million zloty. Using a metal barrier to cut across the center of the stage, Wodziński envisaged the senator's palace as the site of this conflict, producing two distinct areas occupied by the political elite and the marginalized protesters. At the Senator's Ball, the elites participate in a grotesque mockery of a formal nineteenth-century dance illuminated by colorful neon lighting while the grimy protesters watch from a distance. The ball presents the sham of an egalitarian society that covers over mutually exclusive worlds that fail to have any contact with one another. The angry mob watches passively as the political and intellectual elite inside the palace dance like puppets connected to the strings of an unseen master. Crawling on the floor of the grotesque dance is a young maid in white, the embodiment of Romantic martyrdom, who squirms around at the feet of the 'enlightened' in a state of semi-paralysis, lacking the necessary strength to stand up. The sublime and the base are intermingled in Wodziński's sketches of prankish frivolities, successfully destabilizing religious and nationalist associations with the text while giving voice to a desire for community-building that is then undermined in the final scene when the camp-dwellers return, this time in faceless masks. These indistinct figures, who could either be interpreted as religious protesters positioned within Polish patriotism or as refugees excluded from it, are symbols of a social rage that has not been tamed by the *dziady* rites, which have been rendered culturally moribund across the political spectrum.

What we find in Strzępka, Demirski and Wodziński's productions of the Romantic canon is the absence of Christian iconography that dominated virtually every performance of *Dziady* in the twentieth century. What they also have in common is a fascination with the instability of identity and the loss of fixed meaning that has accompanied the abandonment of metaphysical thought. The worlds they present advertise a degree of spiritual numbness or vacuity and moral disorientation characterized by violent eruptions of anger and resentment linked to religion, class and cultural dis-belonging. Easy differentiations between stage left and right cease to be metaphors for good and evil, and angels and demons invade the playing area formally reserved for Romantic heroes, offering materialist readings of transcendental texts. These directors are preoccupied with the negative space left by the abandonment of Christian philosophy and symbols in the wake of Grzegorzewski's deconstructive productions of the 1990s, and look instead toward the growth and cultivation of non-essentialist publics that are not reliant on former notions of national exclusivity and community and that act as pockets of resistance against the moral ambiguities conditioned by the free market that elaborate dissensus. While solutions to forms of cultural and economic alienation are not offered by these directors, new class distinctions actively generated by economic processes, impacting those exploited by capitalism without having regulatory power over it, and forms of cultural association that displace social formation and activist collection are made visible.

Solidarity in dispute

Alongside the ethics and philosophy behind Polish Romanticism, Solidarność (Solidarity), the most significant movement in modern Polish history, has been at the forefront of debates around cultural values and the implementation of new political structures. Inaugurated on August 31, 1980 in the Gdańsk Shipyard, the first independent Polish trade union federation was a movement that used civil resistance in an effort to support workers' rights and prompt political social change. Not only did the Round Table Talks in 1989 between leaders of the Solidarity movement and the government lead to the dissolution of communism in Central and Eastern Europe, it produced a new political rhetoric that dominated the shift towards democracy and neoliberalism in the 1990s. In the heated debates between post- and anti-Communists that raged from 1989 to 1997, Solidarity hero Lech Wałęsa created controversy in his attempt to give more power to the office of the presidency, echoing the reliance on authoritarian power and strong leadership in the Polish Second Republic during the interwar years. However, his defeat in the 1995 election enfeebled this position, adding strength to a parliamentary system. Jacek Kurczewski identifies the 1997 constitution – the result of parliamentary disputes, power struggles and negotiations – as an essentially normative and republican project (1999: 192). The apparent nationalist slant to the preamble was an attempt to cover over the rifts between left- and right-wing politicians, focusing on a shared cultural history rather than the rifts in ideology that divided the country. What developed in the 1990s was an antagonistic split between two opposing and opposed ideologies, the sublimation of pre-communist Poland, perceived as a 'natural order' organized around native values, and a push towards modernization. Kozłowski (2008) observes with great nuance the implicit identification with the United States, a country that successfully yoked these ostensibly conflicting beliefs, an affirmation of natural values intertwined with the imperative of constant capitalist modernization, as opposed to the more welfare-oriented EU.

Given the centrality of Solidarity in Polish discourse, it is surprising how little attention it has been given in the theatre. Sławomir Mrożek's *Alfa* (*Alpha*, 1984), which portrayed Lech Wałęsa's internment, is one of the few plays that dealt with the movement. Andrzej Wajda's classic film *Człowiek z żelaza* (*Man of Iron*, 1981) remains the paradigmatic cinematic response. Mixing fiction with documentary footage, Wajda brilliantly expressed the hope inspired by the early stages of Solidarity, thereby creating a material manifestation of cultural memory, before controversy indelibly marked the mythic legacy of Solidarity in the 1990s. This vision was largely dismantled in the exhibition *Dockwatchers*, curated by Aneta Szylak at the Wyspa Institute of Art in the Gdańsk Shipyard on the twenty-fifth anniversary of the movement in 2005. Using Wajda's film as a point of reference, Szylak's aim was to look beyond officially represented history in order to consider how the collective memory is triggered or inscribed by personal experience. Just one year prior to the exhibition, Jan Klata was given access to the abandoned shipyard for an adaptation of *Hamlet*, entitled *H.* (2004), programmed by Maciej Nowak. Reviewers, for the most part, were keen to support the performance, although they found the focus on the historical site led to a disruption to the logical structure of the play's familiar plot. Nonetheless, *H.* was filmed and disseminated by the Polskie Wydawnictwo Audiowizualne (Polish Audiovisual Publishers), who specialize in recording the most significant cultural events in the country. The disparity between the critical reception of the adaptation and the interest in its documentation indicates the larger effect of the performance in the cultural sphere.

The pamphlet that accompanies the DVD provides two dramaturgical readings of the performance that appear to be in ideological conflict with one another. While Małgorzata Dziewulska argues in her short essay *Dlaczego Szekspir?* (Why Shakespeare?), that Mickiewicz's hero, Konrad, is a direct descendant of Hamlet in an effort to align the ideals of Polish Romanticism with Shakespeare – she even goes so far as to suggest that Konrad and Hamlet speak with 'the same voice' (Dziewulska, 2006a) – Piotr Gruszczyński's review insists that the purpose of Klata's production is to criticize the theatre itself for its 'numbness and detachment from real life' (Gruszczyński, 2006: 21). Exemplifying this point, Gruszczyński singles out Klata's acting troupe in *The Mousetrap*, whose feeble and unskilled performances represent old conventions that no longer address contemporary problems. The elitism of Dziewulska's argument is transparent in her observation that 'Shakespeare is so mature that infantile minds cannot accept him' (2006a: 7), unflinchingly attributing the moral duty to think for the masses and prompt social change to the intelligentsia precisely in the mode developed by Mickiewicz and, later, Wyspiański. Although Dziewulska's position is heavily influenced by an outmoded Romantic perspective, it is true that Hamlet has been as important for thinking through national problems as Mickieiwcz's *Dziady* in the last century. It is possible to trace three separate and distinguishable approaches to *Hamlet* in Poland: first, as a 'commentary upon current political and social experiences and dilemmas'; second, literary reworkings that position Hamlet as the archetypal Pole fighting for the national cause; and, third, as a meditation on Polish national character (Kujawińska Courtney and Kwapisz Williams, 2005). In his 1904 study of *Hamlet*, Wyspiański argued that the puzzle of Hamlet encapsulates the locus of the Polish revolutionary and melancholic spirit, engendering a crucial visible confrontation between the actor and the assumption of a dramatic character. Klata's performance was heavily ghosted by Andrzej Wajda's 1989 production that can again be seen in a wider production history of the play from Wojciech Bogusławski's introduction of *Hamlet* on the Polish stage in 1789 to Swinarski's much anticipated but unfinished 1975 production, aborted prematurely due to the director's untimely death in an airplane crash, which correspond in multiple ways to the approaches I distinguish above. Wajda attempted to describe and summarize the condition of the actor as a mode of both maintaining and critiquing patriotic sentiment in the private and civic spheres, which was as crucial a question in 1989 as it had been under Martial Law seven years previously when the acting elite risked persecution and pecuniary to boycott state-controlled theatre, film and television as a public means of social solidarity.

In his 1904 essay, Wyspiański suggests Wawel Castle as the appropriate location for a Polish staging of *Hamlet*. Given the castle's historical significance as the burial site for Polish kings, Wawel is universally recognized as the most sacred space in the country, standing as the locus for the 'spiritual' nation. Wyspiański was equally interested in the aesthetic of Wawel, which he felt fittingly matched the monumental scenery of Elsinore Castle. Klata's substitution of the Gdańsk Shipyard, socialist workplace turned post-industrialist ruin, for Wawel is emblematic both of the sacred status Solidarity now holds in Polish culture and of the wreckage of the movement's initial promise. Furthering this comparison between locations, the Ghost of Hamlet's father rides into the main hall mounted on a white horse dressed in the armor of the Polish Hussars, the elite cavalry of the Polish-Lithuanian Commonwealth who were undefeated for more than a century. The use of this figure is not only a direct reference to earlier theatre traditions founded on national symbols but also forms a contrast between the passivity of Claudius' court and the forsaken values of the Hussars. Rather than situating Claudius as an obvious villain, however, the new king appears to be well-spoken and considerate, a man whose tastes have developed beyond the customary vodka and cabbage that the former king would have greedily consumed. The world Claudius promises is more refined and progressive than the outdated values embodied by the Ghost. Whereas Demirski juxtaposed Konrad's traditional call to arms with a democratically inflected critique of patriotic fervor, this contrast required the audience to consider whether they would be enticed to answer the nostalgic and outdated call to arms of the Hussar, whose presence signaled the famous image of Józef Piłsudski seated on his mare Kasztanka, or if they would be persuaded by Claudius' troubling nouveau-riche, EU-oriented gentility and sophistication. Privileging neither side of this binary, Klata provoked thinking about a mode of mobilization and collectivity that did not simply adhere to the available models articulated by politicians across the political spectrum.

Klata made the memorable comment, 'Myślę, że Hamlet jest Polakiem' ('I think that Hamlet is a Pole') (cited in Wąsiewicz, 2004), implying that, like Poland, his only route to protesting the rotten court is an inane rebellion. Making use of contemporary promenade theatre practices, the audience began the performance on the outside of the shipyard, watching Hamlet play 'turbogolf,' a sport practiced in Germany where traditional golf has become too expensive and disused factories outnumber available courses. This version of the sport deliberately destroys abandoned buildings, choosing unbroken windows in place of holes, and appeals to those who cannot afford to pay course fees as well as privileged youth who are attracted by turbogolf's destructive energies. Defined by fury rather than melancholy, and focusing on the conflict without careful consideration for psychological motivation, the opening scene frames the actual protagonist of Klata's production not as the eponymous hero but rather as Hamlet's problem itself, which is, for Gruszczyński, 'the problem of all the [Polish] spectators' (2006: 19); that is, how to reconcile the forsaken ideals of the past with the floating or destabilized ethics of the present. A fusion of point-scoring and game-playing through the metaphor of fencing dominates the action, and sets up a striking contrast with the real threat proffered by Fortinbras' army and the Ghost's cavalry uniform. In the new world of the free market, actual violence is largely disavowed, which makes the vast scale of death in the play all the more traumatic.

Klata considered the crucial Polish question in 1989 to be: 'take revenge or let go of guilt?' (cited in Wąsiewicz, 2004), which links to his decision to make Hamlet read the 'Our Father' to Polonius, including the line: 'forgive us our trespasses as we forgive those who trespass against us.' The question of culpability and retribution replaces the 'To be or not to be?' speech, which is given to some amateur actors who audition for the role of Hamlet. By reading out Hamlet's confused thoughts in this soliloquy, Gruszczyński maintained that the amateurs relieved Hamlet of the responsibility of his hopeless task (1996: 21). One might add to this conclusion that their flawed performances reconfirmed the impossibility of performing this speech with perfect eloquence. Referencing Wajda's 1989 production, Klata implies that, ultimately, no one is capable of bearing the burden of this role. The question of revenge re-emerges with striking force when Hamlet confronts his mother in the now badly damaged rooms of legendary Hall 42 where Anna Walentynowicz, whose dismissal in August 1980 provoked trade unions to form the Solidarity movement, had worked. The deterioration of this space helped to express Klata's fascination with the corrosion of Solidarity's legacy. One is tempted to interpret the confrontation between Hamlet, emblematic of Klata's generation, and Gertrude, whose naïve optimism could be associated with the early days of the Solidarity movement, as the overriding subtext of the performance. Today, the walls are still covered in signs from the workers' protests and Ophelia's corpse is found floating among the once mighty ships now slowly rusting in the post-industrial hush of the port.

Klata observed that Hamlet's rebellion has less to do with August 1980 and is more easily aligned with the workers' struggle of the early 1990s, a fight was doomed to failure in the onset of capitalism, which rendered the shipyard laborers, paradoxically, the first victims of their own hard-won battle. At the conclusion of the performance, Fortinbras stares at the row of dead bodies that once made up Elsinore's court and asks 'Gdzie jest wszystko?' ('Where is everything?') as the Ghost of Hamlet's father ominously rides by on his white horse in the background. The contrapuntal strategy here lucidly depicts the conundrum of Klata's contemporaries, often referred to as Generation NIC (Generation Nothing), the first generation to mature to adulthood in a 'free' postcommunist Poland. If Claudius represents the consumerist, ego-driven ethics of the free market, then the Ghost that haunts the scene acts as a reminder of lost Romantic morals. Rather than reinforcing the right-wing Law and Justice Party's call for a return to such values – indeed, Fortinbras is easily recognizable as the then Polish President Lech Kaczyński – Klata presents us with open-ended allegory that requires the spectator's participation through interpretation. Not only is this adaptation an examination of an older generation betraying their formal ideals, it also presents a younger cohort – Hamlet, Ophelia, Horatio, Rosencrantz, Guildenstern – who are shaped by their choices. Theatre critic Jacek Cieślak observed that this performance would have been considered sacrilegious if it had been produced just a few years earlier, but was met with laughter at its 2004 premiere. Cieślak (2004) focused particularly on the reinterpretation of exalted signs: the 'V' signal for Solidarity's victory is reduced to Uma Thurman's memorable gesture in her dance with John Travolta in Quentin Tarantino's *Pulp Fiction* (1994); patriotic symbols are replaced by technical gadgets; Hamlet and Ophelia communicate through greeting cards and mobile phone melodies; Claudius cannot remember the words for his forgiveness prayer; and Gertrude plays an infantile game of hopscotch to an erotically charged Grace Jones anthem. This makes for a banal picture of post-Solidarity Poland, and Fortinbras' climactic triumph proves to be of little of value in the wreckage of the shipyard.

A little more than a year after the premiere of *H.*, Paweł Demirski wrote *Wałęsa. Historia wesoła, a ogromnie przez to smutna* (Wałęsa. A Cheerful Story, and Because of This Enormously Sad, 2005), which presented a more direct and less metaphorical exploration of the former Polish president during the twenty-fifth celebration of Solidarity. Set between 1980, when Wałęsa famously laid a wreath of flowers at the graves of the victims of the 1970 workers' protest, and the 1989 Round Table Talks, these dates might indicate a heroic narrative, as Wałęsa's popularity was not challenged until he faced the economic problems that plagued the 1990s, allegations of collaboration with the SB, the secret police in the PRL, and general dissatisfaction with his presidency. However, casting a very young actor, Arkadiusz Brykalski, who looked nothing like the Polish leader, allowed audiences to consider social discourses framed around Wałęsa without resorting to biography or, worse, the sort of hagiography one expected from the failed Hollywood biopic that was meant to star Robert De Niro, and was later, unfortunately, brought to life by Andrzej Wajda in his 2013 film *Wałęsa. Człowiek z nadziei* (*Wałęsa. Man of Hope*) that only succeeded in offering a highly gendered picture of a working-class hero and his supportive, if beleaguered wife, who perfectly matches the Matka Polka trope that I detail in Chapter 4.

Demirski recalled identifying with election posters prior to the 1989 elections that included silhouettes of sleeping children with the subtitle, 'Żeby mogły z nas być dumne' ('So that they may be proud of us'). What intrigued the playwright about the legacy of Solidarity was the extent to which his generation could be proud of their parent's struggle (cited in Wojciechowska, 2005). Maciaj Nowak resolved to give the Wałęsa project to artists in their twenties, who were free to interpret Solidarity without the emotional input of those who had directly experienced it, thus drawing on the distinction Ewa M. Thompson (2011: 222–3) makes between *communal* memory, a group's shared memory of a particular experience they have witnessed, and *collective* memory, memory acquired not through direct participation but through reading and hearing about historical events. Resisting the nationalist-oriented nostalgia engendered by forms of communal remembering, the performance positions Wałęsa's generation as an object of interrogation. Anti-naturalist stage techniques such as the use of banners as overt political rhetoric, the reduction of character to caricature and the rotation of cast members from protesting workers to policemen and from dissident intellectuals to state bureaucrats overlapped provocatively with the play's dialogue, largely based on Wałęsa's 1987 autobiography *Droga nadziei* (*A Way of Hope*), as well as documentary materials, fragments of speeches and interviews. Demirski was interested in press coverage from foreign sources that might expand the context of the story away from the 'Polish thinking' about these events (cited in Baran, 2005).

Wałęsa was attacked by the Communists in the 1980s for his bad manners and mulish obstinacy, and, following this cue, the very same tactics were revived by the anti-Communists to defame him in the 1990s.

Using the historical record to create a performance text allowed Demirski to negotiate propaganda on both sides of the argument. This purposeful shift away from biography also substantiated an interest in changing the language of national independence associated with Wałęsa to a 'language of rebellion' and revealing how deeply ingrained the false propaganda of the communist security services had become in the Polish mentality (Kuźmiński and Olszewski, 2008). Rather than mimicking Wałęsa's familiar mannerisms or gestures, Brykalski remained a largely featureless 'everyman,' carefully avoiding established perceptions of the leader as charismatic, obstinate or combative. In one dynamic scene, the workers stare silently at their leader, waiting to hear if Solidarity will continue or evaporate. Wałęsa squirms under the pressure of their gaze, quoting U2's 'New Year's Day,' which was dedicated to the Polish opposition leader in 1983. Counterpoising his lack of resolve with the lyrics of a Western band, director Michał Zadara emphasized the effect the Western gaze had on the Polish workers' struggle. Having been educated in Germany, Austria and the US, some commentators suggested that Zadara was even more distanced from this subject than Demirski and other members of his generation raised in Poland. Zadara rejected these claims, maintaining that rather than limiting his cultural perspective on these events, his studies abroad gave him privileged access to the West's absorption of the story of Solidarity. Differently contextualized, Zadara (2010) claimed that Western historians tend to focus on the economic and political aspects of the movement and disregard the religious and eschatological. Both director and playwright expressed disappointment that the Round Table Talks turned out to ultimately function as a victory for late capitalism and not left-wing socialist-oriented politics.

While some, such as Zadara, regard Solidarity as a story of emancipation, a paradise lost in contemporary national mythologies, others believe that for the generation born during the 1970s, the movement is oblique and devoid of cultural meaning. According to Demirski, this myth 'does not motivate [young people] to change the world' (cited in Kuźmiński and Olszewski, 2008). No longer inferring a sacrifice on behalf of others, Solidarity is now interpreted as a fight for personal gain. Zadara finds this recalibration both dangerous and misleading, suggesting it implicitly supports xenophobia and self-interest.[3] Just as Solidarity is a contested and politically charged referent that remains open-ended and thus easily instrumentalized in cultural debates, the legacy of the Polish Romantic hero is a figure that must be extremely sensitive to changes in the historical situation and resulting social metamorphoses. In diverse modes, Tadeusz Kantor and Jerzy Grzegorzewski unsettled the paradigm for theatre production as set out by Polish Romanticism that dominated twentieth-century political theatre in Poland. What is crucial in Grzegorzewski's directorial intervention into the text is a profound break with the inherited covenant between stage and audience that formally unties the theatre from the locus of community spirit predicated on the exclusionary logic of a singular national identity, which explains why his work is inhabited by a defamiliarizing effect. Understood not in its limited sense, Kantor's resistance to essentialist nationalism, rejection of the singularity of memory, evacuation of meaning from the degraded object and disruptions of the theatre space as a location for the 'collective deciphering' of a 'historicopolitical identity' (Kobialka, 2009b: 198) were crucial progressions both for the inclusion of new Polish identities and modes of theatrical reception in the twenty-first century that were taken up by the new generation of directors from Klata and Demirski to Strzępka and Wodziński. This then is the challenge for stagings of the Romantic hero today, to remain responsive and dynamic, not caged in nostalgia or nationalistic rhetoric. This hero is no longer tied to the inevitability of an eternal return, a 'rotation theory' that is linked to cycles of oppression and deliverance. If freedom is the true beginning of the Romantic hero it follows that this figure must be extremely sensitive to the changes in the Polish historical situation and the resulting social metamorphoses (Gruszczyński, 1996: 8–9). Anna R. Burzyńska observed that with Grzegorzewski's death in 2005 it appeared that the Romantic tradition had been broken once and for all. What should be kept in mind is that it was primarily through interventions and tussles with Romantic thought and conventions, rather than through their canonization or exaltation, that directors forged their reputations over the last century. Burzyńska has also noted that although it is impossible to return to an experience of a cohesive or singular community reading and experience of a production that is based on the Romantic covenant between performer and audience engendered by the subversive controversy of Dejmek's 1967 *Dziady* or the clandestine, conspiratorial solidarity of Jarocki's *Murder in the Cathedral*, the 'potential of community' remains a vital reference point in Polish theatre today (2012: 46–7). While I acknowledge the referent community continues to have cultural significance, I aim to trouble the articulations or mobilizations of this term that seek to turn difference against itself, facilitate historical disavowals, mistake appearance for essence, or purport to resolve social contradictions. Having considered the historical political potential of Polish Romanticism, its subsequent disfigurement and dismantling, and its later revitalization as a site of social critique rather than national formation, what I will develop in the following chapters are political theatre's attempts to make visible identities that have been traditionally excluded from the restrictive notion of 'community' that was performed in the rituals of public mourning in the wake of the Smolensk disaster. As I will demonstrate in the remainder of the book, the desublimation of the Romantic hero and the abolition of the individual as the symbol of a singular national will have formed a crucial part of a wider process of deepening and broadening democratic pluralism through dissensus, the production of counterhegemonic discourses and counterpublics, and the unmasking of enduring and continually redrawn exclusionary limitations of society's shared values and common ideals.

Notes

1. When Konrad calls for recruits one could not help but think of the war in Iraq that Poland had been manipulated into joining in 2003 by the US in an effort to preserve healthy international relations with the West. War and national service in 2007 had in many ways lost their age-old connotations of nation and brotherhood and were connected with a transnational, global form of warfare guided by economic concerns rather than current cultural values.
2. *Dziady* is referred to as the '*arcydramat*' in Polish, which indicates, in effect, that the text is *the* exemplary work of Polish Romanticism.
3. Highlighting with irony the nostalgia for former social solidarity, Zadara used Halina Kunicka's deeply sentimental song from the era 'To były piękne dni' ('Those Were Beautiful Days') in the performance and ghosted Agnieszka, the young revolutionary famously played by Krystyna Janda in Andrzej Wajda's *Człowiek z żelaza* (*Man of Iron*, 1981). The change in signification of the term 'solidarity' is then enacted in the final scene of the play, which juxtaposes two trials in Warsaw. The first is set in the late 1970s: a heaving courthouse clearly supports workers from the Niezależny Samorządny Związek Zawodowy 'Solidarność' (Independent Self-Governing Trade Unions 'Solidarity'), who are fighting the communist authorities. In contrast, the contemporary court of law is practically empty. No voices of solidarity are raised for the staff of a private company litigating against their employer, thus stressing the isolation created by the advent of the free market. Struggles for 'freedom' are no longer collective emancipatory acts, but singular attempts to create a dignified life. What is analogous between 1980 and 2005 is the political rhetoric used to impede or prohibit workers' action. In the PRL, the government warned that strikes led to a perilous decline in productivity that directly impacted the proletariat, while politicians in the early twenty-first century warn that it is the taxpayers who foot the bill for strike action.

3

Beyond a *teatr kobiecy*

Premiering at Kraków's Stary Teatr on June 6, 1989, Andrzej Wajda cast the actress Teresa Budzisz-Krzyżanowska to play Hamlet in a production that coincided with the first partially free elections in the country, an outcome of the agreement produced at the Round Table Talks in April of the same year. Wajda famously declared, 'Hamlet is the image of life itself' (cited in Baniewicz, 1990), and as such he was unable to 'direct' the text, only to face up to its monumental challenges, effectively paraphrasing earlier observations from directors such as Roman Zawistowski (1902–87) and Konrad Swinarski (1929–75). In his 1904 study of *Hamlet*, the neo-Romantic Stanisław Wyspiański argued that the puzzle of Hamlet encapsulates the locus of the Polish revolutionary and melancholic spirit, engendering a crucial visible confrontation between the actor and the assumption of a dramatic character. *Hamlet* in 1989 was Wajda's attempt to describe and summarize the condition of the actor as a mode of both maintaining and critiquing patriotic sentiment in private and civic spheres, which was as crucial a question in 1989 as it had been under Martial Law seven years previously.

Reviewers of the day were especially fascinated by the decision to cast a woman, Budzisz-Krzyżanowska, who Wajda proclaimed to be the most talented contemporary actor in Poland. Hamlet, Wajda contended, was 'gender neutral,' a floating signifier through which many actors have passed and will continue to pass. While this is a clear allusion to Wyspiański's canonical essay on the play, the gender of the actor is implicitly understood as male in Wyspiański's formulation. Entering the actual dressing room of the Stary Teatr, where the audience was squeezed in on wooden benches, Budzisz-Krzyżanowska changed into period costume, a black velvet doublet and hose. Spectators observed the actress' transformation into Hamlet, a copy of the play and the production program on her dressing table. Only visible through the dressing-room door, Wajda inverted the social function of the main stage of the Stary – *the* paradigmatic space for sustaining national cultural identity and maintaining active resistance to foreign domination in the twentieth century. What had been the realm of 'Aesopian' language that frustrated state censorship and spoke symbolically about oppression and national identity was transformed into a realm of lies, fiction, hypocrisy and politicking. The dramatis personae around Hamlet, with the exception of Horatio and Fortinbras, were portrayed as frivolous and superficial stereotypes only visible in fleeting glimpses. In the intimate space of the backstage, the inner sanctity of the theatre, Hamlet was able to work through processes of demystification of the political system, relieved of the burden of having to 'play' at madness, a clear allusion to the 'double speak' engendered by Soviet-style communism. Rather than offering the typical blood-soaked conclusion to the tragedy that precipitates Fortinbras' arrival in Elsinore, Wajda focused again on the transmutability of Hamlet as a role, allowing Fortinbras – played by Jerzy Radziwiłowicz, an actor whose artistic standing was politicized by his participation in radical films and theatre productions that championed national independence – to assume the same ritual of transformation from contemporary clothing into period costume. This purposeful recycling of the Hamlet role and narrative moved beyond political literalism to indicate a collective struggle, an innate social antagonism between the individual and the world that was not confined to oppressive communist regimes but that provocatively anticipated the ambiguous promise of late capitalism, culturalism and national autonomy. Furthermore, separating the labor of the actor from the embodiment of the character not only highlighted the meta-theatrical dimensions of the play, it also foregrounded the intellectual and ethical *work* that playing Hamlet prompted in response to the volatile social and moral order of the Polish reality in 1989. Historically, the role of Hamlet in Poland is a mantel that must be donned at moments of political uncertainty, and Wajda indicated that this work was as relevant for women as it was for men.

While Wajda managed to reverse the discursive binary that situates women in the private sphere (background), while men play out the public, political stage (foreground), conservative gender norms were quickly reinscribed in Polish culture after 1989. One of the main aims of feminists in Poland over the past three decades has been to eschew the mainstream tendency to view the political transformation as lacking gender components. Feminist theorist Magdalena Grabowska argued that in scrutinizing the legacies of Polish feminism, one needs to deal with at least three revolutions, the nexus of which offers plural or competing notions that challenge singular or authoritative understandings of feminist activism and experience. The first of these, and often the most neglected, is the unfinished revolution for gender equality under communism that emerged from Second World War, which climaxed in the self-limiting revolution of Solidarity in the 1980s that eventuated the reassertion of patriarchal gender constructions in the dominant social order after the collapse of communism. Grabowska identifies with the Foucauldian tendency to critique any scholarly establishment of 'pure' origins that implies linear or causal continuity. Therefore, Grabowska does not identify these historical legacies as unified or leading on from each other but rather sees them in a negative dialectical relationship that is uneven and imbalanced, full of breakages and discontinuities. At the beginning of the new political era, the most visible problems for feminism included the lack of political consciousness for women after state-imposed gender equality, which was undermined by patriarchal family structures that did not dissolve under communism; the cancellation of social security provisions, including the right to abortion; subsidies for childcare and the availability of contraception; the growth of patriarchal nationalism and Catholicism; and the exclusion of women in leadership roles in the opposition movements that led the political transformations (Grabowska, 2012: 388–90).

Agnieszka Graff, a US-educated Polish scholar who has emerged as one of the most significant voices of Polish feminism in the past two decades, argues that the political alienation imposed by communism led to the destabilization of gender hierarchies, largely resulting from the criminalization of political organizing in public that brought men into the private sphere, the home in particular, in order to organize subversive or nationalist political activities. The domestication of male leadership resulted in the increased participation of women in underground structures. However, constitutionally authorized equality for women resulted in the 'double burden' of new forms of employment without relief from the standard expectations of domestic work. Rather than seeing the 1990s as a space for increased freedom and representation for women, the return of men to the public sphere in politics, a space from which women were powerfully excluded, and the concomitant reinforcement of a sharp division between the public and the domestic, conversely led to the restructuring of gender hierarchies (Graff, 1999). As the pre-eminent Polish feminist literary historian Maria Janion famously noted: 'To my surprise, it transpired that a woman was to be a "family creature" in liberated Poland, a creature who – instead of engaging in politics – should take care of the home. It took some time before I realized that democracy in Poland has a masculine gender' (cited in Chowaniec and Phillips, 2012: 5). Cultural theorist Teresa Kulawik has also criticized the exclusion of women from the political sphere, which was seen by many liberals and conservatives as a 'purification' of the Polish nation that restored men and women to their 'natural' roles (cited in Grabowska, 2012: 387). The most obvious signifier in the erosion of women's rights was the devastating change in 1991 to the laws governing abortion, which had been both legal and freely available, along with contraceptives, to Polish women since 1956.

The legacy of communism remains contentious and highly disputed in regards to the development and negotiation of gender equality. On the one hand, the state-enforced deployment of gender difference was used an ideological tool that often had the adverse effect of dividing women, which, the writer Joanna Bator argues, aided the rise of the Catholic Church and the failure of pro-choice activism in the 1990s (1999: 20–2). Such organizations as the League of Polish Women were seen as a state tool that functioned without social legitimization or grassroots support, and therefore contributed to the depoliticization of feminism under communism rather than its espousal, defense or encouragement (Walczewska, 2006: 127). Grabowska warns against codifying women as homogenous and sharing universal conditions of life under state socialism (2012: 386), while historian and gender theorists Basia Nowak (2010) and Małgorzata Fidelis (2014) support the idea that communism was a time for women's self-education and involvement in the workforce that allowed them to be directly involved in the construction of greater economic and sexual autonomy. The UN's Fourth World Conference on Women in Beijing in 1995 was the first opportunity for postcommunist feminists to enter the global feminist forum, although many felt marginalized or unappreciated, and there was a pervasive feeling of having joined the conversation two decades too late. Impulses for the mobilization of feminist actions that took their cue from second-wave feminism arose as a reaction against masculinist public policy and a need to marshal liberalist doctrine from the West against the exclusion of women from politics. One of the primary points of contention was the Western focus on secularism, which in Poland produced tension between the urban intelligentsia and working-class women, who tended to identify as committed Catholics. Although there was resistance to the colonization of Polish feminist movements through the borrowing or transplantation of Western theory, or through the reliance on Western activists and funding bodies, feminist theorist Ewa Krakowska has celebrated the tools Western feminism provided for women in Poland after 1989 to re-examine their past and present lives. Far from being divorced from the struggles of Polish women, Krakowska asserts that Western feminism was adaptable to the conditions of local needs (2012: 74).

Feminism in the 1990s was marginalized and even seen as a derogatory term, given its pejorative associations with communist rule, and feminists were treated with condescension as inconsequential remnants of counterculture or, worse, as pro-communist sympathizers. In the negotiations of the political transformation, the Solidarity movement quickly sided with the Catholic Church to the detriment of women's liberation and from its inception the new regime was patriarchal and religiously fundamentalist. Women's coalitions, groups and NGOs struggled to find strength, support and a unifying platform based upon an agreed principle of collective action, while conservative politicians and the Church successfully worked at limiting women's rights. Equally, the 1990s offered very little in the way of what might be deemed feminist theatre practice. Even companies that were working on the fringes of the mainstream, many of which attracted attention in the West, reinforced stereotypes of women as victims, hysterics, whores or mothers, and in relation to scenography, women were often contained within the domestic space. Images of the male body as the stand-in for metaphysical representations of Polish cultural life dominated Krystian Lupa's productions of the 1990s, much-lauded by Polish critics and scholars. For instance, Piotr Skiba in Lupa's *Bracia Karamazow* (*Brothers Karamazov*, 1990), naked and exposed under a tattered blanket, symbolized spiritual alienation, and Andrzej Hudziak in *Kalkwerk* (1992) paced nervously back and forth across the stage of the Stary Teatr as a sign of dynamic male anxiety in contrast to his wife, played by Małgorzata Hajewska-Krzysztofik, whose body is confined passively to a wheelchair, a metaphor for stasis rather than an alternative narrative on disability. However, the director's 1999 staging of *Prezydentki* (variously translated as *First Ladies* or *Holy Mothers*, 1990) by the Austrian writer Werner Schwab dealt directly with the moral incoherence and political relativism that directly impacted on women's lives. Opening with a series of television images of Pope John

Paul II discussing abortion, drugs and pornography, the entirety of the action centered around three women gossiping, arguing and reminiscing in a semi-decrepit dining room decorated with mirrors, teacups, plates and religious iconography. Impoverished, isolated and marginalized, the tone of the women's conversation shifted unexpectedly between vulgarity and religious devotion, with topics ranging from excrement and sex to piety and Catholic faith. This mixture of religiosity and bodily excess was highlighted by Mariedl, played by Ewa Skibińska, who believes that ritual humiliation will bring her closer to salvation and so uses her bare hands to clear clogged toilets in the houses of the rich that she cleans. The women's collective degradation represented a broader social malaise at the end of twentieth century wherein the establishment of democracy and the liberalization of the market had not lived up to its promises but had instead created a disenfranchised class of working and unemployed women.

Anna Augustynowicz was the most notable director of her generation to address feminist concerns in the 1990s. Before completing her studies at the Department of Directing at the PWST in Kraków, Augustynowicz premiered as a director in 1989 at the Teatr im. Wojciecha Bogusławskiego in Kalisz with Marek Koterski's *Życie wewnętrzne* (Inner Life, 1986), an unflinching depiction of modern-day sexual relationships and unfulfilled ambitions on the eve of Poland's major political transformation. From the outset, Augustynowicz's direction was celebrated for its cool analytical distance between form and subject matter, a style that was equally steeped in metaphor and focused on the minutiae of everyday life. Also in evidence from this early production was a playful deconstruction of language that broke up grammatical coherence and included so-called 'low' theatrical language such as gibberish and slang, breaking with a long-established link between the theatre, verse poetry and elevated oratory. By rejecting conventional verbal forms, Augustynowicz and Koterski sought to interrupt gender clichés and cultural stereotypes embedded in traditional theatrical language bounded by an inherently patriarchal delimitation in their abstract, philosophical and rhetorical devices.

In 1991, Augustynowicz was invited to direct Stanisław Wyspiański's *Klątwa* (*The Curse*, 1899) at the Teatr Współczesny in Szczecin, where she became artistic director a year later. One of her greatest accomplishments in Szczecin has been the establishment of the Malarnia (Paint Shop), a small laboratory theatre in which she premiered a number of young, mostly foreign playwrights from across Europe, including Stig Larsson, Clare McIntyre and Werner Schwab. This introduced themes prevalent across Western Europe, such as McIntryre's *Low Level Panic*

(*Bez czułości*), first produced at London's Royal Court in 1988, which deals with women's social and personal anxieties stemming from the ubiquitous public presence of pornography and the threat of sexual violence. The plays produced at the Malarnia went a long way to undermine a pervasive feeling that the contemporary theatre lacked new (women's) voices. When Augustynowicz staged Austrian playwright Werner Schwab's *Moja wątroba jest bez sensu albo zagłada ludu* (*My Liver is Pointless, or People's Annihilation*, 1997), theatre critic Roman Pawłowski (1997b) argued in the mid-1990s that there were not many pieces as uncompromising as Schwab's play and that it was one of the best dramas translated into Polish in recent years. By placing the families in a row of three framed boxes, reminiscent of a medieval triptych, the director added a religious dimension that was further confounded at the climax of the play – a birthday party where the hostess attempts to poison her fellow tenants – which was suggestive of the Last Supper. However, as the critic Joanna Chojka (1998) noted, this religious dimension did not allow the production to operate as a morality play but rather as an example of socially engaged theatre, probing rather than sermonizing. This exploration called to mind Augustynowicz's previous venture into the absurd in Witold Gombrowicz's *Iwona, księżniczka Burgunda* (*Ivona, Princess of Burgundy*, 1935) in 1996. In this production the infamous court that eventually destroys the mute Iwona was rendered as a ceremonial empire of high fashion, where costume and appearance reign supreme. The prologue opened with a flamboyant catwalk fashion show set to heavy, pulsating techno music. Augustynowicz rendered the superficial world of selfishness, vanity and polite manners that Gombrowicz critiques in his play as a modern society obsessed with appearance, celebrity and glamour. This differed from Ingmar Bergman's production, which had been shown the previous season in Kraków, in one particularly significant mode. While Polish productions of the play are frequently associated with ritual, religious themes and tragedy, it was Bergman's production from the Royal National Theatre in Stockholm that deployed the use of Catholic imagery – Iwona dies on a crucifix – while Augustynowicz's playful and more light-hearted staging focused on gender, sexuality and style. Editor of *Dialog*, Jacek Sieradzki (1997) has argued that while there was an increasing tendency to produce incorporeal theatre in Poland in this period, in which the focus was placed on abstract ideas and rhetoric, Augustynowicz always drew the spectator's attention back to the presence of the actor's body through her play with gender, use of nudity, bold video close-ups and exposure of non-normative bodies that signified one of the key symptoms of the corporeal turn in Polish theatre.

The body again became the site of spectoral fascination in *Iwona*. Outside the theatre, Augustynowicz planted an actor, who most reviewers believed to be a real beggar, kneeling with a sign reading, 'Jestem chory na AIDS' ('I'm sick with AIDS'), which prompted anxiety among audience members who reportedly discussed whether he appeared to be ill. This coincided with the decision to cast two men in drag, Wiesław Orłowski and Jacek Piątkowski, in the traditionally female role of Iwona's Aunt and to turn the Chamberlain into a homoerotic stripper. The actress Beata Zygarlicka commented that costume in Augustynowicz's productions is always applied to highlight the painful concealment of nudity through one's enslavement to conventional forms (cited in Liskowacki, 2011: 65). After seeing Zygarlicka in Marcin Liber's *ID* (Szczecin Teatr Współczesny, 2009) perform as Andreas Krieger, the German shot-putter who underwent sexual reassignment surgery, Augustynowicz observed that the performance confirmed her theory that the actor's body transcends age and sex, and that gender is merely another semiotic stage sign, no different in its formal function than costume (*ibid.*: 66). Although I will trouble this assertion later in this chapter, I am sensitive to significance of Augustynowicz's argument, which offered a challenge to essentialized understandings of gender that pervaded both the mainstream and avant-garde theatre of the 1990s.

Augustynowicz's daring and divisive productions had an enormous impact on the status of the Teatr Współczesny in Szczecin, and in 1998 the director was awarded the prestigious Paszport prize by the magazine *Polityka*. Once viewed as a parochial backwater, the theatre under Augustynowicz's tenure had a profound impact nationally, leading Jacek Wakar (1997) to observe that directors in Kraków and Warsaw often waited to mount new plays based on their success or failure at the Szczecin Współczesny. After receiving the prize, Augustynowicz subjected the Polish Romantic text *Balladyna* by Juliusz Słowacki to digital technology. The industrial setting of polished steel scaffolding at first suggested Adam Hanuszkiewicz's seminal 1974 production of the play at National Theatre in Warsaw that shocked audiences with the use of real motorcycles spinning around the stage. However, it soon became clear the extent to which the director had divorced herself from the play's production history. The costume design evoked popular images from contemporary science fiction and the proliferation of media devices evidenced the inability of the characters to communicate even with a technological intermediary. This was also the first production in Poland to deal directly with virtual reality (VR). The nymph Goplana, who jealously covets Balladyna's beloved Grabiec, puts on a VR helmet in order to experience a virtual relationship with her would-be lover, thus privileging agency in female erotic desire. The real *coup de théâtre*, however, was the director's intervention in the final scene. Traditionally Balladyna is struck down by lightning, a sign of divine retribution for her unmerited claim to power through bloody and unjust means. In Augustynowicz's staging, it is the paparazzi that are ultimately responsible for the heroine's demise. In a world ruled by the media and spin, the flash of a camera ultimately strikes Balladyna dead. Without entirely affiliating herself with the category of feminism, Augustynowicz's interventions into suspect and disavowed discourses on gender in *Iwona* and *Balladyna* reconfigured predominant cultural categories of 'woman' that placed prominence on social constructivism over biological essentialism. At the end of the 1990s, literary and theatre scholar Elżbieta Baniewicz (1999) commended Augustynowicz for her frank portrayals of sexuality, a highly taboo topic about which Polish society was often hypocritical. Baniewicz further wondered why no male directors had approached themes concerning sexual violence against women with the same courage as Augustynowicz, warning that it is easy to believe such social concerns do not exist if they are not frankly depicted in the theatre.

Difficult optimism

The beginning of the new decade did not initially herald a positive change for women's equality. In 2002, a letter written by Maria Janion to the EU Parliament that was signed by Polish women from across the professional and artistic spectrum claimed that their freedom had been sold to the Catholic Church as part of the negotiations for Poland's acceptance into the European Union, a political body that was ultimately more concerned with economic liberalization in the country than the unevenly enforced EU policy of gender mainstreaming. The letter was ignored and never received a response. Graff (2014) has claimed that the price of abandoning gender equality and justice was the growth of populism and ultra-conservative nationalist sentiments. In exchange for women's rights there was religious education in schools and, as a result of this deal, the Church, who backed the extreme right in an effort to work against modernization, supported democratization and the development of the free market in Poland. The right-wing continued to attack appeals for gender and sexual equality as anti-nationalist and anti-Catholic. Third-wave feminism has been a key movement – although many scholars feel it is too splintered and pluralistic to be condensed into the term 'movement' – in enriching not only Polish feminisms with queer and postcolonial theory but also discourses on otherness that include race, ethnicity, religion and sexual orientation. Transnationalist scholarship has challenged essentialist notions of women's identities, seeking coalition in difference and diversity espoused by third-wave feminists that engage with complex genealogies, multiple sites of oppression and multiple sites of loyalty in relation to nation and Catholicism. In 2006, theatre scholars Krystyna Duniec and Joanna Krakowska wrote an influential article in the journal *Res Publica Nowa*, with the subtitle 'W stronę teatru lewicowo-feministycznego?' ('Towards a leftist-feminist theatre?'), in which they argued that feminism had been appropriated as the critical lens of the New Left movement, a liberal, socialist-oriented political platform that emerged in the early twenty-first century that broke the longstanding fear of communism that hindered left-wing politics in the 1990s. Duniec and Krakowska maintain that although theatre in the 1990s received significant attention for its ability to provoke and scandalize or 'offer psychotherapy for depressed adolescents,' it failed to function in its past role as a center for the diagnosis and analysis of social problems. Younger directors' reliance on brutalism was not productive, as this form of drama – which was overly interiorized and profoundly nihilistic – did not pose an appropriately external perspective on politics or society. It was not until the following decade that the theatre began to discover gravity, situate hopelessness in a social context, and to negotiate a 'difficult optimism' by portraying characters that traverse boundaries of diversity, limit rather than elaborate violence, demonstrate independence rather than mourn cultural disintegration and highlight social alienation. Regrettably, these scholars neglect to reflect on the fact that brutalism was already politicized and sought to dismantle a number of the master narratives on which essentialized Polish identity was being devised and reproduced for mass culture. The violence depicted in the Polish productions of playwrights such as Sarah Kane, Mark Ravenhill and Marius von Mayenburg was reflective of an experience that was made political through the exteriorization of psychic pain, social malaise, alienation and disenfranchisement.

Although, Polish second-wave feminism had a short, even abrupt, genealogy in the 1990s, it received a similarly striking backlash to that in the US and Western Europe. Graff has argued that the standard Western chronology of feminist waves is complicated in Poland and local forms of activism frequently merge standard second-wave identity politics with third-wave accents, such as the strong presence of camp aesthetics and queer theory. Graff further contends that the backlash rhetoric against feminist activism takes a contradictory turn. While one the one hand it is assumed in conservative public discourse that feminism is a luxury Poland can ill afford, it is also commonly believed that as a matriarchal country there is no need to assert women's rights. Graff concludes that this presents an 'ideology which both obscures and justifies the fact of inequality, while asserting a vague sense of national pride in the face of an equally vague external threat' (2013a: 104). In *Matki-Polki, Chłopcy i Cyborgi... Sztuka i feminizm w Polsce* (*Mother Poles, Boys and Cyborgs... Art and Feminism in Poland*), art historian Izabela Kowalczyk makes a case for the positioning of postfeminism, in which women presumably have some control over their objectification, in the work of contemporary women artists as a pivotal intervention. Kowalczyk (2013) traces a genealogy in visual arts commencing from the early 1970s when feminism as a contemporary movement and a critical attitude was still largely absent in Poland. Artists such as Natalia LL, Maria Pinińska-Bereś and Ewa Partum drew attention to the problems of portraying women as objects of consumption and the male gaze, while openly acknowledging their anti-feminist positions or at least disappointment with available forms of feminism that purported to comprehensively speak for and on behalf of women as a single or authoritative movement. As part of the second wave, Teresa Murak and Izabella Gustowska attempted to map an essentialist femininity or womanhood, producing works that highlighted the specificity and particularity of the female body and experience, which Gustowska identified as 'sztuka kobiet' ('women's art') rather than 'sztuka feministyczna' ('feminist art'). Katarzyna Kozyra and Alicja Żebrowska denied such commonplace gender binaries, offering a transition to the third-wave feminist or postfeminist positions that embrace gender crossings, fluid mappings of identity, the 'girl' as the central figure, and stylistically favors irony, kitsch and playfulness. What is missing from Kowalczyk's analysis is a discursive engagement with the complicity neoliberalism plays in the aesthetic and thematic choices of these latter artists and the larger tendency in postfeminism to conceive of feminist movements as generational waves that provoke conflict rather than sustain relational dialogues, even if they do so unintentionally. As cultural theorist and feminist Angela McRobbie points out, the second wave is often seen to have been more or less appropriated by society at large, inclusive of its more conservative elements, while postfeminism argues that the outdated politics of pre-1990s feminism is no longer required and should thus be relegated to history (2004: 254–63). Although Kowalczyk traces a discernable move in the visual arts from 1970s feminist concerns to those of the seemingly post-feminist second decade of the twenty-first century, it is much more difficult to trace such a coherent line in the theatre, and many of the productions highlighted by critics as representing 'women's issues' realign their central protagonist with patriarchal expectations around female beauty and enforced heterosexuality.

Two plays that received enormous critical attention in 2005 were Joanna Owsianko's *Tiramisu*, which outlines the devastating effect of the rat race on young female workers in an advertising agency, and Dana Łukasińska's *Agata szuka pracy* (Agata in Search of a Job), which draws attention to the discrimination against women in the Polish labor market. Pawłowski (2005a) argued that the common feature of these plays is their attention to a civic responsibility, which denotes a more widespread return in Polish theatre to its intellectual roots. Pawłowski observes in light of these texts that younger playwrights have taken over the duty of the intelligentsia from the older generations standing up for values in dialogue with tradition and defending the socially marginalized. However, while feminism has unquestionably offered a crucial critical lens for the recognition of excluded and marginalized subjects, the fact that these plays were written by and about women did not unconditionally signify an explicitly feminist commitment. As feminist theatre scholar Geraldine Harris has cogently argued, one of the key challenges for theatre and performance critics is the need to 'acknowledge and respect not just different feminisms but the distinction between a play "about" feminism, one written as a feminist play, and one simply written by a feminist' in order to eschew prescriptive formulas in critical scholarship (Harris, 2014: 291). Both of these plays offered a critique of feminism that tended to rely on stereotypes and supported representations of gender that are transparent and easily decodable, which failed to offer alternative directives that either moved away from dominant social norms around gender or built on existing feminist frameworks.

Gendered subjects

In *Performative Democracy*, Elżbieta Matynia argues that processes of denationalization have been accompanied by dematriotization, which includes a shifting from the feminine to a focus on and critique of male images and subjects. The desublimation of 'woman' has provided space for women's self-authorship and a confrontation with the romantic-symbolic culturalist strategies that rely on women as objects of exhibit (2009: 158). As opposed to productions that tend to cite rather than contest an established set of gender conventions, Duniec and Krakowska (2006) reflect favorably on a number of stagings in the early 2000s that portrayed previously unseen representations of domestic violence, sexual abuse, prostitution and pedophilia that defy an enduring reiteration of social norms.[1] Krzysztof Warlikowski is singled out as the most significant director to champion the rejection of gender privilege and patriarchal hierarchies in their multiple forms, which began with particular force in his early feminist reworking of *The Taming of the Shrew* in Warsaw's Teatr Dramatyczny in 1998. The use of graphic profanity, pornographic images and homosexuality caused outrage that thrust him into the public eye, but the most profoundly feminist gesture was his earnest exposure of the brutal acts of male violence perpetrated on the female body in the play that are as a rule rendered as comedic and normative both in Polish theatre and beyond.

At the end of the decade, Warlikowski's *Hamlet*, his inaugural production at the Teatr Rozmaitości in 1999, is now considered iconic and highly emblematic of a new mode of theatre directing after the political transition of 1989 that deconstructed social taboos and again confounded patriarchal orders that valorize masculinity and devalue femininity. A number of his directorial signatures can be detected in this production including androgyny, sexual ambivalence, haunting soundscapes, polychronicity, an overlaying of multiple narratives and the replacement of (standard) female with (taboo) male nudity. The privileging of the personal family narrative over the state affairs of the court emphasized the private spaces normally associated with femininity that are excluded from the masculinized political realm, which overlaps with the aims of Andrzej Wajda's 1989 production. Elsinore became a highly theatricalized open-ended space in which characters performed on the sidelines, commenting on rather than enacting the scenes, often in almost total darkness. Małgorzata Szczęśniak's designs combined with Paweł Mykietyn's evocative acoustic scenography encapsulated the director's staging of social spaces that have been described by Grzegorz Niziołek as 'a place of scars, of painful and repressed experiences' (2015: 55). Reviewers consistently returned to descriptions of Hamlet's body, played by Jacek Poniedziałek, highlighting not only his suppleness and flexibility as a performer, but also the beauty of his musculature. The conservative critic Janusz Kowalczyk (1999) observed that the male striptease, a favorite signifier in the catalogue of familiar Teatr Rozmaitości aesthetics, signals a lack of inventiveness that is nothing but a 'conglomerate of perversion.' While this claim problematically diagnoses the desire to see naked male bodies as perverse, what Kowalczyk further neglects is that the concentration on the corporeal is not secondary to Warlikowski's directorial intention. This is not merely a stage effect or shock tactic but is rather at the center of Warlikowski's compositional methods wherein the body itself establishes formal unity through its simultaneous exposure, sublimation and denigration that does not prudishly exclude the possibility of the spectator's arousal. The pleasure of viewing the exposed male body at moments of emotional vulnerability and philosophical contemplation that foreground subjectivity also contrasted with the standard misogynistic habit of staging female nudity only to emphasize women's helplessness and objectivity. Emptied entirely of pathos and sentimentality, the meekness of Hamlet's voice was shown in stark contrast to the raw sexuality of his physical strength, forcing audiences to lean forward to catch his colorless, throwaway utterances. Just as Augustynowicz played with language as a mode of gender exploration, this notion of an intimate voice can be seen as an important extension of the Teatr Rozmaitości as a performance laboratory rather than a national theatre in which the actor's voice is powerfully associated with screams, shouts and fervent proclamations of the national spirit, particularly from strong male heroes in Polish Romantic texts. In this opposition between theatres as laboratories or as political manifestations, one can better understand the accusations that Warlikowski's Hamlet was bloodless, speculative or shadowy in contrast to 'louder' or more impassioned Hamlets in Poland in the twentieth century. Although this Hamlet was overtly sexualized, his emotional and psychic pain, naked body and fragile voice did not promote normative ideals of male potency, but portrayed masculinity as strenuous, contingent and culturally constructed. Ultimately, Warlikowski was interested in exploring male vulnerability in opposition to portrayals of 'weak' men in much Polish theatre in the 1990s that carried an implicit and highly gendered criticism, which was often paired with portrayals of female strength as immoral, selfish or malevolent.

Warlikowski's next production for the Teatr Rozmaitości was Euripides' *Bacchae*, the first significant production of the play in Poland since 1945. With the exception of Jerzy Grotowski and Włodzimierz Staniewski, very few memorable performances of Greek tragedy were produced after the Second World War,[2] the most famous being Andrzej Wajda's *Antygona* (*Antigone*, 1984) that placed the play's central themes in the context of communist despotism. Although there is a preoccupation with the trivialities and pettiness of family life, Warlikowski rarely stages the domestic space, and if he does it is mutilated, ruined or corrupted. Crucially, such spaces are inclusive of men, and are not displayed as inherently and organically female. Indeed, if a woman's freedom is limited to the boundaries of her household, it is portrayed as stifling rather than natural. While Włodzimierz Staniewski veers towards Jungian universalizing narratives that evoke the constant or eternal in humankind through music that are reliant on normative gender roles in his productions of Greek tragedy in Gardzienice, Warlikowski used Euripides as a means of diagnosing changing material circumstances and psychic states in contemporary society, highlighting instability and the obstacles presented by political rapprochement. The expression of female sexuality was not restricted to traditionally beautiful or youthful bodies, and female empowerment was not simply dissipated by Agave's acknowledgment that she has killed her own son and must be exiled from the state. The Bacchants were middle-aged women participating freely in their own brand of faith, a pointed mix of Catholicism and paganism, which juxtaposed the low-key spirituality of Kadmos and Tiresias, who resembled aging hippies as they twisted their bodies into painful yoga positions.

Suffering in this performance failed to transubstantiate male victims into martyrs and women into strong or repentant mothers, known as the Matka Polka trope, a paradigm in Polish Romanticism whose 'fundamental qualities are motherhood, duty and the spirit of sacrifice' (Matynia, 2009: 185). Matka Polka is a standard trope of nationalistic Catholicism that emerged in the nineteenth century that frequently appears in Polish literature, visual arts and theatre. Although she is distinguishable from the Virgin Mary and the Polish motherland, there are strong resonances among these figures. Matka Polka was required to be strong and selfless, known for her fortitude and adherence to duty, which was primarily based around the nationalistic education of her children in the home. Romantic sacrifice forcefully adheres to a circular trajectory. While Matka Polka sacrifices herself for her son, her son in turn must struggle and ultimately sacrifice himself on behalf of the motherland. Despite being seen as a symbol of courage and strength, Anna Reading observed that the idealization of Matka Polka renders this figure an empty signifier 'with no meaning of her own' (1992: 20–1) and Elżbieta Matynia has observed how she further reveals that the adoration of the feminine in Poland often masks gender discrimination (2009: 130).

While *Burza* (The Tempest, 2003) exerted a deconstructive force on discourses of power and *Krum* (2005) presented forms of self-determination beyond gender norms that engaged a strong feminist futurity, it is undoubtedly Warlikowski's production of Sarah Kane's *Cleansed* (*Oczyszczeni*, 2001) that offered one of the most biting critiques of systemic patriarchal power in Polish theatre history. In the early 2000s, the popularity of what Aleks Sierz coined 'in-yer-face theatre' in the UK was just making its imprint on the German and Polish stages. Critic Łukasz Drewniak (2002) recognized an overlap between Warlikowski's aesthetics and avant-garde directors working in Berlin such as Christoph Marthaler, Thomas Ostermeier and Johann Kresnik, although Hans-Thies Lehmann was quick to commend Warlikowski's sophisticated treatment of Kane in opposition to many German directors' eager capitulation to depictions of violence (2002: 41). *Cleansed* imagines a world without God, where sexuality and desire are posited as the ultimate horizon of human experience, and where love is the single salvationary hope of humankind. Iterations of sexuality in the play are complex, manifold and divorced from gender, which is rendered an unstable category through sex change and non-camp forms of cross-dressing. The production opened up a debate on a national scale not seen before. In some respects, its primary political force was the generation of dissensus. Fierce criticisms tell us perhaps more about shifting experiences of theatregoing in the country, no longer reliant on community-building (consensus) and concurrence among members of the press than about conceptions of 'good taste,' political correctness or appropriate conduct in the theatre. Warlikowski did not address 'a group of like-minded people,' but rather activated the audience's continued attentiveness through obvious displays of discomfort.[3] Foreclosing graphic depictions of violence in Kane through the transposition of the actual to the figurative effectively undermined conservative politicians and critics' protests that the British playwright was promulgating violence as pure shock tactic and also reconceptualizing the tendency on Polish stages to uncritically perpetrate violence on female bodies. Nevertheless, censure poured in from major theatre reviewers, including Elżbieta Baniewicz (2002), Janusz R. Kowalczyk (2002), Jerzy Pilch (2002) and Jacek Kopciński (2002), who variously accused Warlikowski of being devoid of artistic vision, rendering an obsessive, one-dimensional portrait of reality, failing to engage his actors in convincing characterization, falling short of a diagnosis of the contemporary historical moment and resorting to kitsch, sadistic, vulgar or shocking images.

Cleansed produces bodies through dynamic processes. Theatre scholar Cristina Delgado-García is cautious about the mode in which the presence of physical bodies on stage will undo the open-ended gender-fluid bodies produced through Kane's text, cautioning, that 'the physical and psychic hybridity of subjectivity in the playtext can be effectively neutralized by the performers, whose already signified, distinct physical contours can act as a centripetal force' (2012: 243). One might invoke here performance theorist Erika Fischer-Lichte's argument in her seminal article 'Reality and Fiction in Contemporary Theatre,' translated into Polish in 2005, regarding what she terms 'perceptional multistability,' the shifting of perception between figure and ground, between the actor's phenomenal body and that of the dramatic character. Fischer-Lichte argues that there is a divergence between the order of representation, the understanding of the semiotics of the actor's body purely in reference to the construction and articulation of the dramatic character, versus the order of presence, the 'unpredictable and even chaotic' associations, memories and imaginations conjured by the actor's particularity, their being-in-the-world (2008: 88). Teetering back and forth between these two modes of viewing the actor's body, which compete against one another for dominance and the stabilization of meaning-making, the spectator experiences frustration and even confusion. In other words, this divergence affects a particular phenomenon experienced as the very crisis theorized by Victor Turner as a liminal state, a state 'betwixt and between' wherein the standard dichotomy between fiction and reality is first collapsed and ultimately undermined (1995: 95). Because the actor's body refuses to disappear completely behind the veil of dramatic fiction – a process that one might argue *disciplines* the actor's body – the resulting tension is more conducive to performances of gender variance than the disembodied, genderless, discursive bodies produced through readings of Kane's text that Delgado-García advocates.

The responses to Warlikowski's *Cleansed* then produced something in the vein of what feminist performance theorist Rebecca Schneider has termed 'binary terror,' the terror that accompanies the dissolution of the binary habit of sense-making, which is proportionate to the social safety insured in the maintenance of such apparatuses of sense (1997: 13), which in this case are linked to gender rigidity and sexual 'normalcy.' While Delgado-García privileges the textual body as a 'fluid loci of hybrid non-identity' (2012: 234), Warlikowski deals directly with physical bodies that are determined through and by the presence of genitalia that can nevertheless be exchanged, as the phallus moves for example from Graham (Redbad Klynstra) to Grace (Małgorzata Hajewska-Krzysztofik), or is removed entirely from the body (Jacek Poniedziałek). In this shift away from the stability of phallic power, Warlikowski's insight is to confront the audience with proof of the actors' anatomical sex while divorcing their bodies from attendant understandings of gender that are toxic to queer and feminist subjects. It is precisely the force of the actors' 'physical contours' that is inverted and rerouted through new forms of social relationships and self-identification in a mode similar to the critical feminist art of Katarzyna Kozyra and Alicja Żebrowska, who direct attention to the problem of visibility and invisibility of certain types of bodies, linking strategies of visual culture to structures of power that are constructed through corporeal representation.

Any such exchange was foreclosed in Grzegorz Jarzyna's lauded 2002 production of Kane's *4.48 Psychosis* at the TR Warszawa. Jarzyna placed the focus of the text on a central individual, played by Magdalena Cielecka, on the brink of total psychic collapse. Cielecka returned to the dark and destructive impulses that she had first explored in Jarzyna's production of *Iwona, księżniczka Burgunda* (Iwona, Princess of Burgundy) at Kraków's Stary Teatr in 1997. Although gender is not fixed in Kane's text, Jarzyna's casting of Cielecka and her central figuring of character – and the later doubling of her exposed nude and obviously female body by an elderly actress – went far to impose categorical fixity with regards to more essentialist dynamics of gender. Kane's textual reference to hermaphroditism was erased while Jarzyna highlights the display of female genitalia. Whereas the doubling of bodies in Warlikowski suggests the multiple physical embodiments open to subjecthood, thus breaking with the hierarchical paradigm that positions bodies as normative *or* abject, Jarzyna reaffirms binaries and implicitly reveals his proximity to heterosexuality as the standard model.

Feminist and queer performance theorist Sue-Ellen Case has focused on Kane's repetitive use of 'I,' the personal pronoun, in her examination of *4.48*, framing this both as 'the personal "I" of early feminism, with its desire and its social positioning marked,' and as the 'I' of the subject of the state 'speaking of self through the past of its violent oppressions and of its future in reincarnations of violence' (2007: 110). Case thus positions Kane's 'anticipatory' gesture in the play as the activation of the future in a present determined by its past. Jarzyna, however, offers an ambivalent approach that moves back from 'subject' (Kane's lines are not specified for particular characters) to a characterological position (Cielecka) that coalesces national anxieties with a female body. Pawłowski (2002) praised Cielecka in his review for *Gazeta Wyborcza*, pointing out the overlap of creative audacity between Kane, who stripped away 'the illusion of fake emotions, alleged wisdom and false ideologies' about madness, and the actress, who did not attempt to convey psychological reasons for her condition. While Warlikowski's *Cleansed* stirred up feelings of 'rebellion, anger, joy and compassion,' Jarzyna's *4.48 Psychosis* primarily evoked a mood of grief and anguish (Gruszczyński, 2002a), which is rendered as exclusively female. The potential for erotic communions, romantic attachments or expressions of love present in *Cleansed* was entirely absent in Jarzyna's bleak vision. For Gruszczyński (2002b), the main difference lay in the confrontation with the actors' bodies: 'Warlikowski's performance led to the boundaries of intimacy, forcing everyone to overcome embarrassment, thus opening up new gates of perception. In Jarzyna, physicality gave way to the poetry of the text,' making the theatrical effect weaker and less shocking. One might add that Jarzyna's production lacked 'shock' value precisely because it reinscribed familiar tropes: the 'madness' experienced by Cielecka is easily legible, mapped as it is onto to standard misogynic expectations of female hysteria.[4]

Beyond the nuclear

Graduating in 2002 from the Kraków PWST directing program at a time when women were discouraged from the profession, Maja Kleczewska has become one of the most significant directors in Poland since 2000 to intervene into normative conceptions of gender and forms of kinship. Although Kleczewska claimed to resist being part of the Polish feminist movement (cited in Targoń, 2007), her productions have chimed with a number of key feminist perspectives. Placing women in tragic situations from which they can rarely find an exit in her first few early productions highlighted social conditions of oppression. Beginning with Moira Buffini and Anna Reynolds' *Jordan* at the Teatr im Juliusza Słowackiego in Kraków (2000), an intimate and intense monodrama about a working-class woman's confession of infanticide, Kleczewska quickly followed this success with Hugo von Hoffmannstahl's *Elektra* in Jelenia Góra (2001). In both plays, female characters are working through the cramped confinement of the nuclear family, which results in violent murder. Later, the cult of the Polish family particularly favored in right-wing rhetoric emerged as a dominant trope in Kleczewska's radical adaptations of classics, which have become associated with her idiosyncratic use of kitsch and ubiquitous citations of pop culture. The disintegration and abjection of the family is largely understood through searing critiques of heterosexual marriage. In the opening scene of *Fedra* (*Phaedra*, 2006), staged at the National Theatre in Warsaw, Danuta Stenka in the eponymous role stands defiantly with two large greyhounds, her eyes disguised behind black sunglasses, possibly in defense against the intrusive lens of the paparazzi and the gaze of the audience. This image is opposed to the corpse-like Theseus in a coma, the inert master of the house who has lost power while Fedra rejects the role of mother and queen by fully inhabiting her desire and teasing out her erotic fantasies despite the psychic pain they cause her. Fedra's desire for the king's son is self-conscious and cannot be divorced from the pleasure such an obvious act of rebellion against the father produces. Connected to tubes in a hospital bed, the king's disembodied mythical status is foreclosed, he is more or less a torpid phallic object, and further articulations of masculinity throughout are equally impotent or ineffectual. Hippolytus stabs himself in the hand to determine whether he is capable of any human feeling and the Minotaur sits transfixed in front of a television screen, fully content to be lost in the disembodied, virtual maze of video games. In contrast, the study of a mature woman's isolation, discontent and sexual agency is foregrounded, while the emergence of parasitical or debased masculinities is registered physically by the king, emotionally by the son and intellectually by the Minotaur.

Critiques of marriage emerged with equal force in Kleczewska's *Woyzeck* (2005) and *Sen nocy letniej* (*Midsummer Night's Dream*, 2006), in which cultural understandings of normality and perversity were reversed. Woyzeck is depicted as an impecunious barber who has sex with the Captain, an effeminate homosexual, in order to support his child, while Maria, who works in a bridal shop that ironically produces the fantasy of marriage through pristine white gowns, indulges in a sexual affair with the Drum Major, a local mafia boss who leads a group of skinheads, an obvious reference to the growing problem of neo-Nazis, particularly in rural Poland. The production thus exposes commonplaces around idealized heterosexual relationships, which in reality compel infidelity through economic need, claustrophobia and emotional inadequacy. In mainstream Polish theatre, women are often seen to cheat on their husbands while men are more entitled to indulge their sexual caprices, inclusive of prostitution. Kleczewska offers a counternarrative to this cliché that inhabits the unsettled space between critique and parodic humor. It is the man who works as a prostitute to earn money for his child while the woman enjoys sexual adventures without being submitted to the narrative of 'town whore.'

In *Midsummer's Night Dream*, Kleczewska did away with the typical focus on the naivety of the lovers, choosing instead to depict a world in which young people understand their sexual desire, an awareness many critics found upsetting or overly cynical. Conversely, I would suggest that while sexuality is intensely celebrated, the compromises of marriage are condemned in favor of multiple intimacies. Puck, a gender-variant drug dealer, walks around the stage in a wedding dress in a promenade of exhibitionism, placing the horror of this symbol on the clothing rather than, as is typical, on the woman wearing it. This is not a form of drag in which a queer male reimagines himself; it is rather the ritual undermining of the wedding dress as a symbol of feminine success, a female phallus. In the concluding scene, it is not the lovers who are married as a sign of the return to the standard moral and rational order of Athens from the eroticized phantasmatic forest. Instead, Puck officiates a marriage between the corpses of Pyramus and Thisbe, collapsing the boundaries between funeral and wedding ceremonies. While critics found this a depressing and cynical take on contemporary notions of love and fidelity, I contend Kleczewska opened up new ideas of intimacy that refuse to simply reproduce the mechanisms underpinning marriage that maintain gender inequality. When Puck pronounces 'Till death do we part' to the corpses of the mythical Greek lovers, there is an overlap of conventional heterosexual marriage with its own conclusion, thus ultimately repurposing the strategies of the marriage plot in modern romantic comedies. It is not simply that, as critic Małgorzata Ruda (2006) argues, the characters 'suffer from incurable loneliness in a world where magic has vanished,' but rather that what was experienced as 'magic' is composed of structural conditions that promote troubling and ritually perpetuated inequalities. In Kleczewska's production, 'magic' is criticized rather than sentimentally evoked, reminding spectators that nostalgia for the magic of romance favors narratives of femininity that can only be resolved in the conventional spectacle of the wedding, in which the free reign of adolescent sexuality is finally contained and restricted by the bounds of the nuclear family. Nuanced readings of Shakespeare's play offer a number of objections to marriage but these are typically overturned by Puck's concluding blessing in which he 'restores amends.' Rather than seeing marriage as unquestioned good, this production uses the double casting of Oberon/Theseus and Titania/Hippolytus as an ominous and depressing foreshadowing of failed marriages that the young lovers ultimately reject. While alternative endings are normally eschewed in the privileging of the wedding plot, marriage is here shown as a coercive means of submitting women to relations with men that find their apex in a circulatory and interminable series of betrayals and humiliations. This comes with particular force when Oberon hires a male stripper to entice Titania. Falling for his seduction, Titania is humiliated when the stripper pulls away from her at the very moment she responds to his advances, while

Oberon observes the scene with casual amusement. The typically playful and comic pull-and-shove between Titania and Oberon is thus treated with earnestness, a site of contest rather than fun. It is not simply that this 'degradation is the inherent price of love,' as Olga Katafiasz (2006: 4) suggests, but rather that Kleczewska highlights how alternative understandings of kinship, desire and relationships need to be incorporated into the tired language of romantic comedies that ultimately favors male dominance while reinforcing women's subjugation.

This is mirrored by Kleczewska's scenographic choice to break down the normative boundaries that keep Athens, the seat of masculinist power, set firmly apart from the realm of the faeries, the feminized world of sexual freedom. The action takes place in a nightclub, a marketplace for desire, whose mirrored floor, dark lighting and red leather sofas offer multiple opportunities for queer-time orgies. Fleeing the harsh moral world of their parents, the lovers engage in a counterpublic space that allows – as I will discuss in the following chapter with Krzysztof Warlikowski's *Kabaret Warszawski* (*Warsaw Cabaret*, 2013) – for the transgression of prohibitions without the opportunity to return to the 'real world.' By breaking the familiar juxtaposition between the forest and the city, the counterpublic Kleczewska presents does not rely on the existence of an outdated or oppositional moral order. This troubled and troubling 'in-between' is precisely the world the characters and, by extension, the audience inhabit. What critics appear to be mourning in their resistance to the production is the fragmentation of social groups and families into desiring individuals. Moving away from the traditional happy ending that eschews the midsummer dream, which permits the transgression of prohibitions only to be resolved by the return to the heterosexual marriage, Kleczewska offers a new model for desiring, cohabiting and relationships by refusing to stage the moment of reunion between the 'correct' lovers through the benign rationalization of the night's intrigues. The end of the dream is not happily and easily reconciled through the return to the prescriptive heterosexual structure. Rather, the conclusion of that very structure is staged through the marriage of corpses; the world of sexual fluidity refuses to be co-opted into such an institution. Without offering recourse to the orthodox and prevailing binaries of chaste/deviant, rhetorical/corporeal or rational/sensual, Kleczewska simultaneously exposes the nostalgia for traditional gender values that many critics lament while advancing an example of resistant understandings of sexuality beyond conservative and state-enforced models of the nuclear family.

In the 2004 staging of *Macbeth*, her most lauded production by Polish critics, Kleczewska again rejected the nuclear family by omitting all references to Banquo's children and claims to the legitimacy of the transference of authority and wealth through familial inheritance. Characters pursue power for its own sake, not as a means to legacy. What caused the most outrage from critics was not the prolific and often sexually explicit forms of violence in the production, but the choice to depict the Witches as drag queens. Before visiting Macbeth and Banquo, two male transvestite-witches teach a female prostitute how to attract a man through a display of suggestive 'feminine' gestures. Replacing the explicit mystery and supernatural quality of the witches, which is commonly determined by their gender, with the citational practice of drag, Kleczewska stages 'woman' as a category that is exposed to contest rather than shrouded in obscurantism. When the three witches arrive at Macbeth's house, where they flirt and sexually provoke the men, their predictions are treated lightly as something of a titillating joke or simply as pre-coital banter. In his article for *Didaskalia*, theatre scholar Tadeusz Kornaś seems to miss the point when he suggests that the drag queens do not care about their role as oracle, but rather relay a vague whisper of 'unreality,' which he sees as the modern equivalent of prophesying in a world where there is no God (2004: 3). The problem with this formulation is that femininity is framed as both performative and veiled, a secret that refuses to be uncovered as the last vestige of mystery in a secular world. Kleczewska's investment in femininity and seduction as well as femininity and destruction (the witches' prediction as the harbinger of Macbeth's ultimate demise) are here not 'merely' fantastical. The feminist turn in this production is to reveal how that which is treated as an ineffectual female game, and potentially a male sexual fantasy, is in practice the very *effect* that constructs Macbeth's reality and leads to his downfall. The witches are habitually represented as mad, disfigured or evil women. Against the seeming inevitability of this paradigm, Kleczewska's transsexual witches do not pathologize or delight in making obscure women's sexuality, knowledge, agency and power. Rather than depictions of excessive gore or explicit violence, it was perhaps *this* intervention into gender politics that led local newspapers to report warnings that 'hypersensitive' audiences and schoolchildren should steer clear of Kleczewska's production (see, for example, Kłopocka, 2004).

Kornaś sees the transsexuals in *Macbeth* as possessing a 'frontier status'; that is, living on the borderlines of social life, caught between genders, outside of the purview of the family as well as mafia hierarchies of influence and control. As such, Kornaś argues, transsexuals are excluded from the race for power in the play (2004: 4). This theorization is not surprising given that drag queens and transsexuals are often described as vulgar by critics, and their 'otherness' is reinforced through persistent references to non-Polish culture, such as the early films of the Spanish director Pedro Almodóvar that incorporate drag and the Australian cult movie, *The Adventures of Priscilla, Queen of the Desert* (1994). Drag queens are queer in the sense that they remain staunchly unreadable, mysterious, perverse and genre-defying. Agnieszka Olczyk wrote in *Didaskalia* that the transsexual witches in *Macbeth* are 'strange beings,' and 'indefinite – not just sexually' (2004: 6). Sexuality and gender variance, therefore, function as ciphers for ambiguity, abnormality and the uncanny, a perspective that requires a stable category of 'woman' that is not decentered through postmodern performance. Tomasz Plata (2007) maintains that the use of drag in Warlikowski is often a citation from pop culture that indicates a large-scale spiritual crisis in the social field, while in Kleczewska drag queens are a dangerous figure on par with mass cultural representations of the mafia, simultaneously threatening and ominous. In both of these formulations, drag remains a form of pastiche, but not one that produces subversive laughter or parody. The drag queen is a dissident figure only insofar as s/he remains excluded from natural discourses that constitutes 'our' culture (*nasza kultura*). Joanna Derkaczew compared the use of drag and transvestism between Kleczewska and Warlikowski, arguing that for the latter there is always first the question of drag queens, gender, sexuality and then, consequently, a diagnosis of culture (cited in Plata, 2007). Kleczewska, Derkaczew reasons, inverts this order. The drag queens that appear in *Macbeth*, for example, are not an interrogation of sexuality that will shed light on cultural values, rather they are framed as figures of foreignness or strangeness, that which is culturally excluded. Sex, in relation to biologically determined anatomies and culturally constructed genders, is not the most crucial concern for Kleczewska. The semiotic stage function of drag is therefore metonymic. As figures that stand in for those identity positions that are undervalued, marginalized or attributed as the embodiment of social 'evil,' Derkaczew contends that the witches might just have easily been figured as the elderly, the unemployed or Muslims if Kleczewska was interested in a different reading of the play. Not only does this fail to attend to the multiple and nuanced distinctions between these identities, registering sexuality and gender as metonymic is an attempt to universalize these categories so as to downplay their relevance and neutralize their discursive power. As a result, such attempts ultimately belie a return to normative readings of sexuality and gender.

Similar to Kopciński, who suggested that the drag queens were a perversion and the embodiment of the 'degeneration of the modern world'

(2005: 25), Plata puts forward a model of heterosexuality that invests in the idea that crossing the normative and highly policed boundaries between genders is always framed as a crisis and a symptom of moral and social degradation. The hierarchical mode in which masculinity asserts cultural dominance, as the indistinct ground from which male drag is rendered legible, remains unquestioned. Although Judith Butler's work is well-known in Polish academic circles, the normative social constructions of gender that appear naturalized through their constant repetition or 'citation' are never evoked by these critics. What's more, upholding masculinity as the norm, men performing hyperbolical displays of 'femininity' are permitted and tolerated only insomuch as femininity is already assumed to be a 'poor copy' of an originating masculinity. It is not coincidental that these critics fail to comment on Kleczewska's interventions into the extreme objectification of the female body, such as the brutal gang rape and murder of Lady Macduff, which equally situate gender as a social role; that is to say, the normative social constructions of gender that appear naturalized through their constant repetition or citation, such as in this instance the well-known formula for horror films that finds its climax in the sexual attack and subsequent killing of a peripheral female character.

It is revealing to consider how Kleczewska has been evaluated by male critics. In a critical forum on Kleczewska's work, Plata (2007) asked, 'Co to znaczy teatr kobiecy?' ('What does a feminine theatre mean?'). Plata's question prompted another critic, Joanna Derkaczew, to defend Kleczewska against the supposed confines of a 'feminine' theatre that is reduced to a preoccupation with feelings or emotions or other constricted notions of what preoccupies women. Derkaczew opposed the assumption that the objectification of the female form is being interrogated by Kleczewska precisely because she is a woman who, by association, must be working through 'female' themes. Opposing such marginalizing connotations, Derkaczew suggested that Kleczewska's theatre contests and negotiates problematic patterns set out by popular culture. One might add, Kleczewska does indeed stage normative gender models, but only as a means of rendering gender readable through the citation of dominant norms that exposes them to dispute.[5] Does this, however, make her oeuvre a so-called *teatr kobiecy*? Opposing descriptions of Kleczewska by male critics reveal the extent to which work by women directors continues to be perceived in relation to gender. Plata observed that the power of sexuality in Kleczewska's work is new and intriguing because it is consciously and definitely articulated by a woman, and he further emphasizes this point in his observation that Polish theatre has perhaps never been so clearly marked by a woman's perspective. Drewniak, on the other hand, claimed that Kleczewska directs with an 'almost masculine hand,' by which he means her work stands out for the precision of her scenic composition, actors' emotions and stage images (cited in Baniewicz, 2007). And while Kleczewska is often compared with Warlikowski, not only because of her aesthetics but, perhaps mostly, as a response to the ambiguity of gender and sexual identities and relationships in her productions, critics do not submit Warlikowski, whose masculinity and rumored homosexuality is eclipsed, to the same criteria of gender analysis. While avant-garde directors continue to challenge, destabilize or undermine received and damaging understandings of gender, the next radical step must be taken by those producing the dominant discourses of Polish theatre's critical reception.

After 1989, it has been imperative to amend the habit of interpreting the political transformation as lacking gender components and to stop codifying women's experiences as uniform or homogenous. Indeed, one of the global challenges for feminism has been the need to eschew the logic of equivalence that forecloses diverse identifications. Teresa Kuwalik has argued that the upholding of 'pure' Catholic-national identities in Poland has entailed the elimination of women from public space and the restraint of their sexuality as a purification of the nation after communism. As both the civic and the social have become increasingly sexualized, the nationalist right continues to reinforce conceptions of nationhood through gender binaries. Despite Andrzej Wajda's foregrounding of the primacy of women's participation in the political arena in his canonical *Hamlet*, the exclusion of women from the public sphere in the first decade of the formation of liberal democracy was pernicious, wide-ranging and destructive. Wajda implied in his use of drag in *Hamlet* that normative categories of gender have been crucial not only in modes of resistance to political subjugation, but also in their inscription into the dominant articulations of a national voice.

The performances I have outlined in this chapter have disrupted the ongoing solidification of binary tropes that position women as either eroticized victims and sexualized objects or asexual martyrs that safeguard conservative national narratives and restore traditional hierarchies in a return to a Polish 'normality' that is antithetical to communism. The primary objectives of staging gender for these directors over the past two decades has been to repudiate a perceived 'proper' femininity, to advocate and contest legacies of feminism, to represent innovative and lateral forms of kinship and intimacy, and to disrupt the reinforcement of heterosexuality as originary and natural. If theatre counterpublics do not take account of feminism in its *many* articulations, they are doomed to reproduce the very exclusionary community they purport to indict.

Notes

1 These productions included Grzegorz Jarzyna's *Uroczystość* (TR Warszawa, 2001); Marek Modzelewski's *Koronacja* (Teatr Narodowy Warszawa, 2004); Tomasz Gawron's *Gry i zabawy* (Teatr Dramatyczny, 2004); Anna Bednarska's *Z twarzą przy ścianie* (Teatr Polski im. Hieronima Konieczki Bydgoszcz, 2004); and Przemysław Wojcieszek's *Cokolwiek się zdarzy, kocham cię* (TR Warszawa, 2005).
2 For a discussion of postwar Polish productions of Greek tragedy see Niziołek (2001: 13).
3 Various reports document audience members looking ostentatiously at their mobile phones, sighing with frustration or disgust and yelling out for the production to be shut down.
4 This positioning of female subjectivity in relation to hysteria, mania or depression in many ways corresponds with similar problematic tropes in productions directed by Włodzimierz Staniewski for Ośrodek Praktyk Teatralnych 'Gardzienice'. Disturbingly, this tendency has not disappeared, as this genre of theatre continues to develop and evolve in the work of Teatr ZAR and Teatr Pieśń Kozła.
5 Derkaczew further accused Plata of bestowing a dubious validity on Polish cultural identity as pure and unadulterated, and ultimately opposable to pop culture, when in fact, she argues, Polish identity is constructed, not innate, and therefore permeable. Kleczewska's cultural critiques drive precisely at this assumption of a 'core' and demonstrate how any understanding of contemporary Polish culture is already embedded in negotiations with, through and against pop culture (cited in Plata, 2007).

4

Gay emancipation and queer counterpublics

In 2013, two figures in Polish public life made homophobic claims that caused a scandal on a national level. The fact that both of these figures, one from politics and the other from the professional repertory theatre, are directly and intimately connected to 1989 as a transformative political moment in Polish history should not be divorced from the significance of their statements nor from the outrage that followed their publication. The events began when Lech Wałęsa (2013), leader of the Solidarity movement and a key player in the Round Table Talks that led to the establishment of liberal democracy in Poland, stated that homosexuals as minorities have no right to a prominent role in politics and should not be entitled to a front bench position in the Sejm, the lower house of the Polish parliament. Wałęsa further claimed that this injunction should be carried out in spatialized terms wherein non-heterosexual politicians should be placed on the backbenches or even outside the Sejm chamber. In short, the former president of Poland suggested no less than the implementation of a gay ghetto in the seat of the country's main legislative body. This was soon followed by the actress Joanna Szczepkowska's (2013) assertion that, not unlike in the Vatican, a powerful homosexual lobby ('*homoprawda*' or 'homolobby') dominates the Polish theatre, an elite group who privilege fellow gay artists in casting and force heterosexual actors to publicly undress in order to attract gay audiences.[1]

In both cases, the visibility of gay or queer bodies, or straight bodies being read as queer, in the highly politicized arena of the parliament or publicly subsidized theatres is directly connected to the perceived over-impact of homosexuals on Polish culture. Wałęsa's statement exposes a lack of grounding allotted to gay people in the national imaginary and further condenses a bedrock of state-sponsored homophobia in public discourse that had not been as apparent throughout most of the 1990s, at a time when sexuality was not recognized as a political category that underpinned civil liberties and homosexuality in particular was all but excluded from the civic sphere. Queer theorist Błażej Warkocki claimed that homosexuals functioned like extraterrestrials in the Polish collective consciousness, their existence rumored although never directly verified (2004: 151). The emergence of a public dialogue on alternative sexuality around 1998 was first and foremost framed by conservative anti-homosexual attitudes that found their legitimation in Catholic doctrine, and terminology such as 'closet', 'coming out' and 'homophobia' only arrived belatedly. Although Solidarity's pervasive social resonance has been destabilized in the past two decades and the myth of Wałęsa as the embodiment of the movement's initial values almost entirely debunked, this blunder has, unintentionally, revealed the opportunity of homophobic rhetoric at this level of politics and suggests that homosexuality, like communism, is aligned as an alien, antagonistic force that threatens the health of Polish cultural identity and democracy.

Szczepkowska's accusation of a 'homolobby' in the theatre is worth looking at in more detail, as it exposes a number of phobias that may not be reduced to the term 'homophobia' but nevertheless demonstrate the mode in which criticisms of contemporary Polish theatre are projected onto the open presence of homosexuals in that professional sphere. Szczepkowska has vehemently argued in a number of articles and interviews that her views are being censored and distorted by the media, who have unfairly labeled her 'homophobic', a term that she claims homosexuals hide behind in order to shut down public debate. Szczepkowska's defense is that she has simply provided a substantive criticism of a real and verifiable social phenomena that is not a revelation of an underlying homophobic attitude. Critics of Szczepkowska have focused on a conflation in Poland of anti-Semitism with homophobia, referring to an ideological positioning of prejudice rather than an overlapping of discriminatory content.[2] Anti-Semitism stands as a model of intolerance in Poland, with the Holocaust and the March 1968 purges as paradigmatic events. Political theorist Rafał Pankowski notes that the structure of the radical right party League for Polish Family's anti-gay rhetoric 'employed clichés strikingly resembling those used historically against perceived enemy ethnic groups such as Jews and Germans' (Pankowski, 2010: 123), which evidences a significant process of displacement with regards to scapegoating. As I will discuss in the next chapter, since the publication of Jan T. Gross' *Neighbors* in 2001, the seminal study of Polish collusion in Hitler's 'Final Solution' and the resulting public re-examination of Polish involvement in the Holocaust and subsequent pogroms and purges, the articulation of explicit anti-Semitic attitudes have become strictly taboo in the public domain, although such viewpoints may remain strong in private quarters. Szczepkowska frames the 'homolobby' as a conspiracy aimed against the heterosexual majority, a phobia that mirrors popular anti-Semitic beliefs that see Jews as a threatening force to a Christian majority. The underlying paranoid logic is nearly the same and creates an equivalent paradox: Jews/gays both have to remain in hiding so as not to offend wholesome Polish sensibilities and at the same time Jews/gays must reveal themselves so that 'normal people' can be on guard against their influence or duplicity (Graff, 2006: 444). While Szczepkowska and Wałęsa do not oppose homosexuality per se – that is, individual homosexuals have a right to practice their chosen lifestyle in private – a homosexual collective is framed as a menacing social threat.

I would suggest that this anxiety is further advanced by the lack of clarity surrounding relevant terminology around alternative sexualities. The political distinction in the West between queer, the opposition to socially constructed and restrictive categorizations of sexual identities, and gay (*gej*), which stems from inter- and transnational emancipatory movements based in identity politics, remains vague and unfixed in Poland, which creates destructive results in public discourse and calls attention to a temporal disorientation in queer studies in the country. Terminology remains a site of battle and contestation in Poland. Warkocki has written extensively about the appropriation of and subsequent disempowerment of queer terminology in the Polish mainstream. 'Coming out,' for example, has been decontextualized in literary studies from its homosexual context and employed as a useful term to determine the unveiling and immediate transformation of identity. As in a number of global examples, 'camp' has been similarly assimilated in popular culture and recontextualized as a sophisticated aesthetic. Warkocki claims, however, that camp is homosexual and political, a subversive response to an oppressive reality, and that 'gay' is still an antonym to 'universal' (2014: 7–17). This position has been supported by lesbian activist Anna Laszuk (2009), who has asserted that the word 'queer' has never been adequately translated into Polish, which has led to a drastic de-politicization of the term.

Queer theorist Robert Kulpa and sociologist Joanna Mizielińska observe that while the development of civil rights, women's liberation and gay activism in the West unfolded over a linear timeline, the abrupt cultural shift in 1989 in Central and Eastern Europe (CEE) meant that these movements were adopted all at once without an identical foundational historical narrative. It has been difficult to make a straightforward reconciliation between the arrival of queer studies being too late and simultaneously brand new. What became/is/will be had in CEE appears to have already been in the West (Kulpa and Mizielińska, 2011: 20). It is obvious that one could not speak about a 'Jewish lobby' without its pejorative connotations being immediately evident. However, 'gay' and 'queer' remain what Claude Lévi-Strauss termed 'floating signifiers,' signifiers without referents that fail to produce any particular meaning or association (1987: 63). This was evident when the former prime minister Jarosław Kaczyński argued that punishing gays does not undermine the moral limitations of a democratic system, and the Polish government rejected a European Parliament resolution on homophobic violence in Europe, maintaining that use of the term 'homophobia' functioned as an imposition of the language of the homosexual political movement in Europe and was in conflict with 'the whole of Europe's Judeo-Christian moral heritage' (cited in Pankowski, 2010: 173, 189). Without a strong historical narrative of resistance and visibility, Polish LGBTQI individuals and communities remain vulnerable. What should be empowering terminology instead provides space for a homophobic imaginary to reign unimpeded and, what's more, these 'floating signifiers' are marshaled for the benefit of the extreme right, justifying the banning of literature in public schools, abolishing the commissioner for the equal status of women and men, promoting homophobic violence and linking homosexuality to pedophilia.

Certainly the case for the recognition of homosexual rights as a collective body is essential to notions of democracy, a system that is not, despite Wałęsa's claim, reliant on the will of the majority, but rather on the extension of equal rights to those excluded from that majority. The media expert Karina Stasiuk-Krajewska argued that there is a defining gap between homophobia, the codified vision of a world threatened by homosexuality, and a cultural prejudice. She warns that if the heavy charge of 'homophobia' is too loosely applied in the Polish public sphere then the term will lose its necessary impact (cited in Kalukin, 2013). However, what Stasiuk-Krajewska neglects in this argument is precisely the mode in which a cultural prejudice functions at the level of public discourse, a point that the recent debates around anti-Semitism have brought to the foreground. Equally problematic is Szczepkowska's easy recourse to anti-communist rhetoric – she claimed, 'This is exactly how the media manipulated innocent citizens in the days of Communism!' (cited in Michalski, 2013) – as a mode of defense against the apparent manipulation of her words. Anti-Communists often mobilize this type of hysteria around Soviet-style censorship and oppression or else resort to the anti-gay dictates of a Church that is itself grappling to cope with dissenting viewpoints in post-Solidarity Poland. The feminist academic Agnieszka Graff used the Szczepkowska scandal and the ongoing debate between Catholic conservatives and liberals over the provision of IVF treatment to consider the limits of freedom of speech in Poland. In 2006, Graff claimed that the issue of homosexuality had trumped reproductive rights as the symbol of ideological tension in Polish politics and society (2006: 445). Deploying the American expert on rhetoric Stanley Fish, Graff more recently argued that in Western democracies, freedom of speech is a functional myth, and its limitation depends on speech that turns into violence or encourages violence. Given that homophobic rhetoric can turn into homophobic violence, Graff (2013b) asks whether the freedom of the 'Episcopal word' should also have its limitations.

A shift of perspectives and approaches to understanding alternative sexualities can be traced in recent theatre history. Rather than queering the national dramatic canon, the performance examples that I will look at largely come out of new writing and intertextual collage in sympathetic dialogue with queer subjects, or the production of Western texts that first met with critical resistance by opening a window onto queer studies and/or gay activism in Poland. In 1999, a production of Mark Ravenhill's *Shopping and Fucking* depicted a brutal vision of contemporary sexuality, drug addiction, urban violence and homelessness with considerable amplification, provoking a Warsaw city councilor, Joanna Fabisiak, to write a public statement condemning the lamentable 'experimental' art, funded by an outraged taxpaying public. The play was certainly othered by its overt Britishness, which, given the difference in attitudes towards consumerism between the UK and Poland at the time, audiences found more intriguing than enlightening. This alterity was sustained by the decision not to translate the title from English. Nevertheless, alongside Grzegorz Jarzyna's equally scandalous *Unidentified Remains* at the Teatr Dramatyczny, *Shopping and Fucking* paved the way for a new decade of taboo-breaking. In 2001, a playwright working under the pseudonym Ingmar Villqist produced an anthology of one-act plays entitled *Anaerobes* that brought questions around sexuality directly into the Polish context. The eponymous text from the collection portrays two men raising a child together, one of whom longs to abandon their modern family for a less conventional, although more identifiably gay, lifestyle. The representation of a serious relationship between men, which did not follow the default recourse to effeminate stereotypes that abounded in the theatre in the 1990s, led critic Roman Pawłowski to defend the piece as groundbreaking. The only issue I take with this defense is that Villqist's characters typically discuss their feelings more than their sexual relationships and there are no erotic or even intimate acts openly depicted. While some critics argued that this allowed the play to reach a broader audience, it also follows the paradigm set by such American television sitcoms as *Will & Grace*, seemingly pioneering in their approach to social taboos, but highly restricted in their honest representation of gay men and women, a process of desexualization that is easily instrumentalized for a liberal agenda of 'tolerance.'

Unflinching portrayals of homosexuality are vital precisely because they do not require social tolerance that is reliant on the invisibility of same-sex desire and sexual acts, ostensibly banned on the grounds of common decency. A more frank account of gay men's lives occurred with force four years later in Bartosz Żurawiecki's one-act play *Sekstet* (2005), which portrays the interweaving sexual relationships among six men at the higher end of Warsaw's socioeconomic ladder. In this play, however, the subject matter was more revolutionary than the writing, affirming Żurawiecki as a stronger novelist and film critic than dramatist. While the text presented a keen interest in cross-generational perspectives on sexuality and the performance generated some perspicacious comic relief, it was ultimately outstripped by Marek Modzelewski's *Dotyk* (*Touch*, 2005) in its limited focus on 'privileged' gay culture and its pedestrian critique of systemic prejudice. Conversely, Modzelewski's play at the Teatr Powszechny in Warsaw produced a more effective recalibration of Polish gay identity, focusing on two simultaneous coming-out conversations between a husband and wife and a father and son. These 'outings' brought to the fore ingrained bigotry in Polish families. The play ultimately asks whether it is ethical to pursue individual desires or instincts – *Instinct* was the original title – over the values of one's community.

Two novels published in 2005 offered more frank depictions of gay and queer sexuality. The novelist Michał Witkowski explored the forbidden passion and secret lives of homosexuals over a 50-year period in *Lubiewo* (*Lovetown*, 2005), in which two aging queens lament the passing of communism and the birth of a 'liberated,' Western-oriented younger generation, obsessed with drugs, monogamy and identity politics, that uses 1989 as a marker of generational difference in homosexual lives.

Witkowski frequently performs his novels at the TR Warszawa, where the playful renegotiations of his fiction as performance gesture towards queer literary theorist Nick Salvato's definition of camp, an 'affectively ambivalent queer parody' (2010: 180) that simultaneously identifies with and parodies its object of fascination, which, in this case, is sexual obsession, gay promiscuity and the decline of local same-sex erotic practices. These performances are a critical antidote to the literary reception of the novel that has transformed queer characters into exotic but ultimately non-threatening others. Bartosz Żurawiecki's *Trzech panów w łóżku, nie licząc kota* (Three Men in Bed, Not Counting the Cat) is a whimsical novel that portrays a burnt-out yuppie who becomes obsessed with a gay couple in his search for existential meaning. The explicit and even compulsive handlings of gay sex in both novels, which rather astonishingly have sold tens of thousands of copies in Poland, broke a longstanding evasion of outright homosexual content in Polish fiction, although many reviewers shied away from any mention of the virtually ubiquitous eroticism present in the novels.

Typically relegated to opaque significations, such as a sublimated fascination with the male body or a 'tender friendship' between men, homoeroticism in Polish literature started to become more visible in the 1990s from such writers as Izabela Filipiak, Marcin Krzeszowiec and Grzegorz Musiał. An immoral and essentially carefree lifestyle accompanied by the unrelenting struggle against the futility of a childless existence are concepts that figure with equal weight in Żurawiecki and Witkowski, thus opening the writers up to criticism from both the conservative right, whose prejudices were confirmed by the narratives, and from gay groups who struggle to 'prove to the heterosexual majority that they are "people just like everybody else"' (Łukasz Smuga cited in Fordonski, 2007). The latter position was exemplified by the NGO Kampania Przeciw Homofobii (KPH, Campaign Against Homophobia) poster advertisements 'Let them see us' in cities throughout the country – nearly all of which were destroyed, marked over or torn down on account of their attempt to make homosexuality too conspicuous – that showed butch gay and ultra-feminine lesbian couples, reinforcing rather than contesting gender stereotypes. Krzysztof Tomasik's monograph *Homobiografie* (Homobiography, 2009) attempted to establish a rapprochement between homosexuality and national identity, determining the degree to which the production of a national subject has been historically reliant on homosexuals through his outing of Polish national icons. Warkocki situates Tomasik's journalistic study within a more generalized shift in cultural perception and visibility that evidences a unique epistemological breakthrough, arguing that the book positions homosexuality as a crucial element in Polish culture, a sociocultural fact and not simply a twenty-first century fad (Warkocki, 2013: 127). While the book no doubt undermines the exclusionary rhetoric of the extreme right and redresses the problem of homosexuality as 'inexpressible and hence not subject to discoursivization' (*ibid.*), such a study also concedes to the primacy of nation and nationality in conceiving of subjectivity and is therefore in danger of enfeebling protean queer identities.

Przemysław Wojcieszek's *Cokolwiek się zdarzy, kocham cię* (*Whatever Happens, I Love You*), which premiered at the TR Warszawa in 2005, follows the development of a sexual relationship between two teenage girls, Magda and Sugar, and was the first serious representation of lesbian identities in the theatre. Warsaw is represented in the play as the focal point for young Poles wishing to create a new identity for themselves, although the urban space simultaneously dislocates as it liberates. This storyline reflects a larger queer renegotiation of traditional Polish identity that has relied on a move from the rural to the urban space. Magda's journey to Warsaw from an unnamed village is provoked by her father's refusal to tolerate her sexuality. While the salary Magda earns at a fast-food chicken restaurant might be nominal, it should be diametrically opposed to the bankruptcy suffered by the company Magda's homophobic father works for in the impoverished countryside. The combined forces of employability and anonymity in the cosmopolitan center free up room for Magda's self-regulated identity, although her love for Sugar is indelibly intertwined with a hatred of her country, symptomized by her longing to move to Prague or Berlin. These cities are not attractive on account of their superior working conditions, rather they promise the tolerance for alternative sexual identities she sees as lacking in Poland.

Easily the most controversial element of *Whatever Happens* was the introduction of Sugar's brother, Piotrek, a soldier who returns from the war in Iraq. The liberal and uninhibited nature of the girls' relationship is foiled by the sudden re-emergence of the modern-day combatant, representing conservative Catholic populism symbolized by the St. Christopher medal Piotrek wears proudly around his neck. Deeply nationalistic, the brother inadvertently denigrates his country when he passes out in a drunken stupor while wearing a Polish flag he had earlier exhibited proudly on his shoulders; an act that offers a compelling reappraisal of Polish heroism that the critic Zdzisław Pietrasik (2005) deemed one of the most iconoclastic scenes in the theatre since 1989. Piotrek longs for the arrival of his father, whom the mother threw out of the house because of his drunkenness and violent behavior, foolishly believing that he can

Figure 1 *Cokolwiek się zdarzy, kocham cię* (Whatever Happens, I Love You), directed by Przemysław Wojcieszek. Roma Gąsiorowska as Sugar and Agnieszka Podsiadlik as Magda. Photo by Stefan Okolowicz, © TR Warszawa.

restore moral balance to a home gone awry through the rule of women. Repeating the pattern set by the father, Piotrek first uses violence against the girls and, when this fails, resorts to alcohol. Piotrek's only cultural reference to lesbianism is the German pornography he watched in Iraq, which reduces sexual relations between women to a supplement of male desire. The hypocrisy between his revulsion at the girl's mutual love for one another and his enjoyment of pornographic imagery associated with female-female sex is at the heart of Wojcieszek's critique. Pietrasik (2005) rightly observes that Sugar's sexuality defies not only Piotrek's Catholic values but also undercuts the narrative that makes him conceive of himself as a brave soldier, connecting Iraq to battles such as Monte Cassino in the age-old fight for Polish freedom. Critic Jacek Cieślak (2005c) convincingly argued in the left-leaning newspaper *Rzeczpospolita* that although Magda's final monologue specifically addresses the difficulties of homosexual love, she effectively expresses the more universal longing of many of her contemporaries, for whom individual relationships are more important than national identity or patriotism.

The conservative backlash in the media to the performance is highly indicative of the debates happening at the inauguration in 2005 of the Kaczyński brothers' so-called 'Fourth Republic,' whose stated aim was to introduce a 'moral renewal' of Polish culture through a return to Christian values. Roman Pawłowski, who included one of Wojcieszek's screenplays, *Zabij ich wszystkich* (Kill Them All) in his anthology *Pokolenie porno i inne niesmaczne utwory teatralne* (*The Porn Generation and Other Disgusting Theatrical Works*, 2003) – a collection that has been as influential in Poland both for its texts and its positioning of a generation as 'in-yer-face theatre' was in the UK – came under attack for his defense of Wojcieszek's play. In one review, the conservative Catholic newspaper *Nasz Dziennik* accused the progressive newspaper *Gazeta Wyborcza* of manufacturing a liberalist reality that had no basis in modern-day Poland, which the historian Stanisław Krajski (2005) even went so far as to compare to Stalin's communism, where only singular views of freedom were legitimized. While this claim is, of course, already reliant on a highly manufactured conception of domestic values, the hostile response can be best understood through a centralization of the conflict between Sugar and her brother. The performance was condemned as a mishmash of biased and journalistic social observations, an accumulation of verbal gags, and a grotesque representation that tickled the 'Porn Generation' but did not draw discerning audiences.

This followed from Pawłowski's allegation that Lech Kaczyński's ban on the Warsaw gay pride parades in 2004 and 2005 was unconstitutional. Reviewer Kalina Zalewska (2005) accused Pawłowski of 'demagoguery,' asserting that pride parades promote sexual promiscuity as much as diversity. Unsurprisingly, Zalewska couches her argument in reference to privacy, insisting that the Warsaw council's decision was not a violation of the constitution but rather an absence of consent for the promotion of sexual licentiousness, thus conflating homosexuality with decadence and immorality. The critic reveals what she sees as Pawłowski's hypocrisy: while he openly criticizes Żurawiecki's *Sekstet*, which stresses a 'prevailing tendency' in homosexual circles to regularly exchange partners, Pawłowski praises Wojcieszek for his portrayal of a loving and monogamous lesbian relationship. Zalewska's observations were then reiterated by the critic Temida Stankiewicz-Podhorecka (2005), who insisted the play was 'flat, vulgar and dirty' in *Nasz Dziennik*. What is most striking in this piece of journalism is the author's utter dismay that the director not only does not condemn the pathology and sexual deviance of the characters, by which she means their homosexuality, but that Polish Catholicism is itself presented as a topic available for critique. Her primary concern is that contemporary liberal or progressive theatre is epitomized by a disdain for Catholics, who are represented without fail as scoundrels, oafs and criminals. In his response, Pawłowski shows no surprise that Zalewska and Stankiewicz-Podhorecka are more outraged by the denigration of a religious symbol, the St. Christopher medal, than by the gendered violence suffered by Sugar at the hands of her brother. Furthermore, both critics align Piotrek's idealization or 'moral renewal' of the family unit with the program promised by the Law and Justice Party. Repeated emphasis on Catholicism and morality expressly neglects the positioning of the rebel in the play. The girls' insistence on the integrity of their relationship and a resistance to tropes of victimhood provide a re-engagement with and departure from traditionally perceived images of rebellion as a characteristically national practice that in much Polish drama results in catharsis or uprising. Such a departure has led performance theorist Wojciech Baluch to observe that, unlike in ancient tragedy, there is no guarantee in Wojcieszek's plays that rebellion will lead finally to the restoration of order and, consequently, to a feeling of happiness or safety (2008: 171). The very quantity of conservative press coverage signals, although unwillingly, the complexity of the play, which, beyond making Polish lesbian identities more visible, ultimately acts as a condemnation of the national value system promised by the conservative coalition.

The concurrence of the stagings of *Dotyk*, *Sekstet* and *Whatever Happens* with Kaczyński's banning of the gay pride parades created a gap between the public and private performance of non-normative sexuality. The directors and writers expressed an anxiety about the encroaching Fourth Republic and the liquidation of the promise of the Third Republic, which exceeds a standard critique of capitalism, choosing to tackle the problems of visibility and the process of coming out at a moment of profound public homophobia from the Warsaw city council as well as local hooligans who destroyed or vandalized the poster campaign 'Let them see us.'

On the one hand, this provoked Pawłowski (2005b) to defend the theatre as a space for moral freedom, a bracketing of social differences and inequalities, while on the other it highlights theatre as an exclusionary practice, confirming public space as synonymous with compulsory heterosexuality and validating the act of parading as an exclusively nationalistic practice. To protest, march or parade becomes an activity that cannot be divorced from conservative conceptions of sexuality. Contrasting public marches such as the Equality March and indoor theatre events that contain sexuality also touches upon theatre and film theorist Anne Fleche's anxiety that the theatre space itself, insofar as it requires an enclosure or frame in its self-designation, can be tantamount to the closet (1995: 253–67). This follows precisely the structural logic of Zalewska's objection to public gay demonstrations, and her firm belief that the theatre is a more appropriate place to discuss sexuality than the street, where, as Stankiewicz-Podhorecka (2005) pointed out, 'there might be children.' Indeed when Krajski opines that overly effusive displays of emotion in a public space unnecessarily stress a person's sexual identity, as does 'unnatural attire,' one is also reminded of sociologist Roman Kuhar's discussion of the transparent closet, in which publicly displayed images of heterosexual desire are so ubiquitous that they are effectively rendered invisible (2011: 146–66). As a result, any open performances of homosexuality, through clothing or gesture, disturb the heterosexual space and are read as exhibitionist or in poor taste, which affirms gay rights activist Krzysztof Zabłocki's claim that signs of homosexuality in the Polish public sphere are still largely masked or invisible (cited in Fordonski, 2007).

Wojcieszek's next play, *Darkroom* (2006), returned to the congruence of homophobia and Polish Catholicism. The performance confronted the prevalent binary that divides heteronormative monogamous relationships from perceived homosexual promiscuity in its depiction of an elderly former communist playboy, now a devoted listener to the ultra-conservative Radio Maryja, and Łukasz, a young gay man who is looking for a partner on a permanent basis. Originally intended as an adaptation of a the novel by Croatian writer Rujana Jeger, Wojcieszek quickly rewrote the story from scratch, reimagining the characters in a Warsaw context, which included symbolically charged references to the then recent election of the Law and Justice Party as well as the banned pride parades. Setting the play against the background of the Kaczyńskis' 'moral renewal' boldly reinvents what might have otherwise been a conventional comedy. The title is meant to indicate a 'labyrinth of human emotions' (Wyżyńska, 2006), but also serves as an obvious allusion to the dark room used for anonymous sexual encounters in gay nightclubs. Breaking down barriers between conflicting attitudes, Wojcieszek explores most provocatively the formation of a friendship between Łukasz and Stanislaus, the elderly conservative, who at the beginning of the play wipes his palm on his trousers after shaking hands with a homosexual. Wojcieszek was conscious of the reception of older audiences to the play, for whom homosexuality remains a new and provocative topic in the theatre. There are several overlaps with *Whatever Happens*, such as the confrontation of radically different attitudes and the move from the rural to the urban space. In *Darkroom*, however, the city fails to live up to its promises. The three male characters are all unemployed, which causes them to feel guilty, anxious or apathetic. The play resists any pedagogic tendencies, and offers instead a humorous meditation on the conventional gap between generations and an appraisal of homophobia that does not rely on gay stereotyping. Nostalgic references to communism are not limited to the old man, once the head of the Office of Foreign Trade, but are also evident in Łukasz's karaoke selections, such as Ewa Demarczyk and Violetta Villas, both of whom were famous in the PRL. The fact that Wojcieszek was frequently asked in interviews if he feared a counterattack from Radio Maryja's creator Tadeusz Rydzyk attested to the priest's huge influence and acknowledged authority.[3] The director was quick to distance himself from the 'John Paul II generation,' instead choosing to denounce the Kaczyńskis' planned Fourth Republic as a civilization incompatible with the European Union.

What was of vital importance was the emergence of a counterdiscourse to the conservative desire for queer identities to remain in the closet. Critic Piotr Schmidt (2007) cites performances that premiered in 2007 that openly portrayed men kissing or copulating, such as *Lincz* (Lynch), *Terrordrom.Breslau* and *Zaśnij teraz w ogniu* (Now Fall Asleep in the Fire), which did not court shock or public outrage. These frank depictions indicated either that homoeroticism had become an acceptable – or at least recognizable – element in Polish society or that such relationships were simply a director's artistic vision not based in any reality. Schmidt, who places emphasis on the theatre's duty to teach diversity, settles on the former conclusion, resuscitating the notion that what happens on stage always already reflects that which can be identified or traced back to experienced cultural identity. It is important to remember that although these productions were intended to be accessible through a queer dimension, they simultaneously reinscribed basic stereotypes. This was particularly identifiable in *Terrordrom.Breslau*, produced by Wrocław's Teatr Polski. Snubbed by his male lover, the protagonist Hakan urges fellow citizens through political manifestoes into acts of terror, creating uncontrollable flows of violence redoubled by live media coverage. Perhaps what the critics struggled most with in this much-anticipated production by Wiktor Rubin, then a young director known for his theatrical risk-taking and experimentation with new forms, was the use of homosexuality as a cipher for social problems at large, thus simultaneously reinforcing the idea that gay men are emotionally unpredictable and mentally unstable. Another disturbing feature was the use of gay sex as a metaphor for capitalism, a system that purportedly 'fucks' men. While this attempted to be deliberately non-normative, it only emphasized traditional gender roles uncomfortable with male passivity, which unintentionally chimes with Pawłowski's observation that one of the attractions of the radical right in

2005 was their reassertion of a strong Polish masculinity. Reformulating the equation of happiness with hyper-masculinity – a belief that positions the failure of capitalism as the point of intersection between politics and gender – the production did not espouse a real alternative to the conservative right, who promote conventional masculinity as a symbol of powerful democracy and the will to self-governance. What is most revealing in these performances is the insight that unflinching portrayals of homosexuality can be just as normative and regulating as a reliance on the closet.

Producing counterpublics

Three productions by Krzysztof Warlikowski, Paweł Demirski and Monika Strzępka in recent years demonstrate a radical change in public understandings of queer subjectivities and gay rights in Poland that go beyond the epistemology of the closet, engaging in what feminist theatre scholar Jill Dolan has termed 'utopian performatives' (2005: 5). The first of these, Warlikowski's revolutionary staging of Tony Kushner's *Angels in America*, produced by TR Warszawa in 2007, directly attempted to rectify the lack of a concrete gay emancipatory movement in Poland cited by Kulpa and Mizielińska as a cause of disequilibrium in political struggle and the dynamics of oppression. Warkocki argued that this was the most significant production of the first decade of the twenty-first century (2013: 308–9). Warlikowski's determining staging provoked a new public discourse around homosexuality that allowed for a crucial representational counterdiscourse to the Kaczyńskis' neoconservative Fourth Republic, and that established a broadly identifiable historical shift in the treatment and perception of homosexuality and HIV/AIDS that was in sympathetic dialogue with, and later considered a significant component of, the 'rainbow revolution,' a manifestation of Polish gays and lesbians who protested against conservative Catholic groups and the loss of privileges granted to citizens across virtually the rest of Europe. Tomasz Miłkowski (2007) writes disparagingly about the homophobia and hatred generated by the builders of the Polish Fourth Republic and the 'yoke of socially and historically embedded resentment' in Polish society that cannot simply be reduced to a fear of AIDS. Superimposing the New York of the 1980s over Warsaw at the turn of the millennium, Kushner's attack on Ronald Reagan functioned as a stand-in for Warlikowski's caustic critique of the

Kaczyńskis' blatant opposition to liberal pluralism and their own particular brand of neoconservatism that combined notions of cultural exclusivity and superiority with Christian values and a championing of the free market that make them no less responsible for defining a social movement that responds to economic globalization and the decline of national culture. Theatre scholar David Savran (1995: 208) has famously drawn attention to the 'decisive historical shift in American theatre' produced by the play in the early 1990s, and Warlikowski's production can be seen as producing a comparable social and artistic impact. Just as the appearance of the translation of Edward White's 1982 novel *A Boy's Own Story* (translated as *Zuch* in Polish) in 1998 made the possibility of a gay literature possible for the first time in Poland (Warkocki, 2013: 214–15), *Angels in America* gave explicit form to a possibility of a theatre that did not attempt to universalize specifically gay identities but focused on their visibility as an expression of their particularity. Warlikowski expertly collided black humor with irony, fantasy and absurdism in his critique of modern sexual relationships. The argument at play in this adaptation, to embrace a 'tolerant indifference to differences,' is constructed to incite reflection on audiences' ability to willingly ignore or readily reject those elements of cultural phenomena or individual identity that do not seamlessly map onto social norms.

Figure 2 *Anioły w Ameryce* (Angels in America), directed by Krzysztof Warlikowski. Jacek Poniedziałek as Louis Ironson and Tomasz Tyndyk as Prior Walter. Photo by Stefan Okolowicz, © TR Warszawa.

This production was in many ways a culmination of Warlikowski's oeuvre, which has consistently disrupted accepted historiography, broken down traditional gender roles, frustrated dominant cultural discourses and commentaries, reconsidered synchronic notions of time, favored the individual over the collective and interrogated sexuality in place of nationality. Many agree that Warlikowski was groundbreaking in his portrayal of the reality of homosexual relationships in Poland in his earlier production of Sarah Kane's *Cleansed* (*Oczyszczeni*, 2001) at the TR Warszawa. It is generally acknowledged that the production included the first male homosexual kiss ever to be performed on a public Polish stage, which was complicated by the fact that finding professional actors willing to portray a gay man openly in love with his partner still proved difficult in 2001 (cited in Dolińska, 2002). Not only did the homosexual couple portrayed by Jacek Poniedziałek and Thomas Schweiberer offer alternative physical appearances to stereotyped gays that are commonly seen as effeminate, passive, flamboyant or camp, the sacrifice Carl makes for his love of Rod (he literally loses his arms, legs, tongue and penis) and Rod for Carl (his throat is slit) went a long way to combat associations between homosexuality, superficial sexual exchanges and rampant promiscuity.

Angels in America also confronted the highly circumscribed and stringently homophobic public discourse on HIV and AIDS in Poland. The first recorded performance to deal with the subject, as late as 2005, was Maciej Kowalewski's *Miss HIV*, based on a real-life beauty contest held annually in Gaborone, Botswana.[4] The contest, in which all participants are infected with the disease, is supported by the country's government in an effort to promote tolerance and reduce the stigma attached to HIV. Significantly, the five contenders of various ages and social classes were heterosexual women, thus challenging the received perception of HIV as a disease exclusively contracted by homosexuals and drug addicts, as well as the accepted premise that the disease simultaneously ennobles and stigmatizes a patient. Kowalewski used HIV as a conceptual tool to comment on the media's hypocritical treatment of illness in general, concurrently exploiting subjects it purports to bring to light, sponsor or protect. For Warlikowski, HIV and AIDS was an important lens through which to critique nationalism. Despite many reviewers' focus on themes such as forgiveness, tolerance and compassion in *Angels in America*, the director was adamant that the crucial problem in the play was the depiction of a healthy lover living with an AIDS patient (cited in Kijowska, 2007). When Prior Walter appears in a stupor at the end of *Millennium Approaches* wearing a crown of thorns and a purple robe, this directly engaged the image of Christ's Passion for Polish audiences. Cultural commentator Rafał Węgrzyniak (2009) has argued that the Passion is virtually absent in the work of the younger generation of Polish directors, likely the result of widespread progressive secularization and the ongoing culture war between conservative Catholics and progressive liberals. Disarticulating this familiar stage picture, which has appeared in the work of other major Polish directors in the twentieth century such as Leon Schiller, Jerzy Grotowski and Konrad Swinarski, from its traditional associations by associating Christ with a homosexual AIDS patient, Warlikowski troubled the legacy of artists as transmuters of Polish Romanticism and threatened the conjunction of national identity with heterosexually bounded Catholicism. By making the disease the enemy around which Poles could rally, Warlikowski complicated a tendency that implicitly participates in the idealization of heteronormative and nationalist exclusionary identity formation.

Warlikowski's next major production to deal with queer identities and the cultivation of an oppositional consciousness was *Kabaret Warszawski* (*Warsaw Cabaret*, 2013), produced by his own theatre company Nowy Teatr. If *Angels in America* foregrounded the visibility of gay men within a clearly defined 'coming-out' narrative, *Kabaret Warszawski* offered a critique of identity politics that rejects minoritizing concepts of the subject by eschewing singular sexual identities (gay) in favor of anti-identitarian energies (queer). *Angels* was also Warlikowski's last attempt to stage a single text. Moving instead towards a form of intertextual collage that allows the theatre to speak in a multiplicity of voices that the director does not feel is available in the ready-made play, two moments of artistic force spawning from heightened political tension are contrasted: the dissolution of the Weimar Republic in Berlin and the aftermath of 9/11 in New York City. The juxtaposition between these cities and historical moments revealed existing phobias in contemporary Warsaw. The first half of the performance was a revision of John van Druten's 1951 play *I Am Camera* based on Christopher Isherwood's collection *Berlin Stories* (1939), germane in its associations with the recent resurgence of neofascism in Central and East Europe, while the second part adapted John Cameron Mitchell's 2006 *Shortbus*, a film that depicts a group of New Yorkers who meet weekly in a utopic salon where sexually diverse practices and normally controlled libidinous desires can be freely enacted. While diversity in *Angels in America* is rendered as the fight for the acknowledgment of recognition of a specific minoritarian subject, *Kabaret Warszawski* can be seen as an attempt to produce a counterpublic that eschews homonormative claims to difference and assimilation by highlighting the inclusive tendencies of diversity as a *queer* politics. The impetus for this production resulted from a growing wave of aggression Warlikowski and his ensemble recognized in the extreme right in Poland. Influenced by Polish artist Artur Żmijewski's video installation 'Democracies' (2007–12) – a series of 30 short films that document various manifestations of political activity in public space such as protests, rallies and parades in which anti-Semitic and homophobic feelings erupt on a mass scale – Warlikowski's project mirrors Żmijewski's belief that culture is a field for political thought and action rather than a stable set of moral values and traditions. Both artists further demonstrate the extent to which the instrumentalization of nationalistic, traditional values tends to energize the very problems they claim to purge.

Using conventions of cabaret allowed Warlikowski and his ensemble to break the fourth wall, engage the carnivalesque as a means of providing a space for self-determination that promoted personal contact with the audience. Appropriating the specific form of cabaret from Weimar Berlin was a productive tool to embody scathing anti-normative critiques of ultra-right-wing movements that merged art with power, magnifying new forms of extremism and their means of justification. Warlikowski merged the Nazi dictatorship with the American Dream and the mass commodification of culture through projected images of the opening ceremony of the 1936 Berlin Olympics, which revealed participation and implicit collusion on an international level as many teams performed the Hitlergruß, the infamous Nazi salute. The critic Nikołaj Bierman (2013) observed that this footage reveals how the evil of the swastika becomes a striking contrast to the apparent modern, global 'good' as the Americans enter the arena. Fascism and globalized consumerism were again paired in the emblem of the swastika, which was inscribed on costumes of the cabaret dancers in the bright red and blue colors that form the Pepsi-Cola logo.

In Sally Bowles' raucous song and dance routines, Christopher, van Duten's protagonist based on Christopher Isherwood, succumbs to an authoritarian father figure, symbolized by a buffoonish Hitler, who is himself an elated spectator at the cabaret. This depiction of Hitler reflects Agnieszka Graff's warning that economic stagnation in Poland has produced a crisis of masculinity, a generation of young men frustrated with the democratic system who are targets for non-democratic slogans. The reinforcement of masculine heroism in Poland in the twentieth century was understood as the only mode in which to build horizontal trust among young men in the ongoing struggles against occupying forces. Graff (2014) argues that this process of engagement today

Figure 3 *Kabaret Warszawksi* (*Warsaw Cabaret*), directed by Krzysztof Warlikowski. Magdalena Cielecka in an ecstatic dance routine as Sally Bowles. Photo by Magda Hueckel, © Nowy Teatr.

is radicalizing young men to the radical right, which is resulting in the increase of a fascistic climate. Subverting the typical portrayal of Hitler as a menacing or forbidding personage in exchange for a lighthearted and friendly father figure with strong, but down-to-earth views made his current appeal plausible. Moreover, the performance style of cabaret places primary significance on sexuality, presenting bodies on stage that undermine gender cohesion and amplify popular homophobic and misogynistic beliefs through humor and parody. The repetition of Hitler's clownish gestures provided a critical distance that revealed the perverse underlying temptation for an embattled straight white masculinity. The fact that Hitler takes pleasure from watching the cabaret that mocks him only further illustrates the elasticity of contemporary liberal democracy in accommodating such neofascistic positions.

Warlikowski has commented that there are no longer homosexual themes and 'gay' characters in his work, but rather performative attempts to subvert hegemonic culture (cited in Urbaniak, 2013). For most Polish critics the most memorable moment in *Angels in America* was Maciej Stuhr's exclamatory disclosure as Joe Pitt, 'Mom, I'm gay!' The act of coming out here was a confession and not a statement of autonomy or independence. In the intersectional economies of queer sexualities in *Kabaret* that resists the homonormative eroding effects on identity, the possibility of such a coming-out narrative is foreclosed. Jacek Poniedziałek's performance as Justin Vivian Bond, the New-York based transgendered performance artist, strategically enacted a trans-identity that continues to be more taboo than homosexuality in Poland. Bond is a member of the Radical Faerie movement, a countercultural network that embraces new-age spirituality and promotes queer paradigms beyond 'hetero-imitation.' In *Kabaret*, Bond's appearance is reminiscent of Ariel in Warlikowski's 2003 *Tempest*, an impish and erotically charged presence that breaks strong cultural norms. The multivalent erotic energies in the adaptation of *Shortbus* signal the absence of a sexual revolution in Poland, which has made it difficult to establish alternatives in public discourse outside of the nuclear family fetishized by the Church. Savran suggests that the conclusion of *Perestroika*, the second part of *Angels in America*, breaks down the multiple romantic dyads produced through the combination and interchange of the four principle characters (three gay men and one straight woman) and thus provides 'a utopian concept of (erotic) affiliation' that undermines known understandings of the family unit (1995: 209). Warlikowski continued this deconstruction of the standard heterosexual nuclear family in *Kabaret Warszawski*. Placing the dialogues from *Shortbus* in a Polish context allowed discussions of sex through an unrestricted exchange of partners without prudery, vulgarity or reference to pornography to offer a framework that thinks beyond the integrationist liberal pluralism of *Angels in America* towards more radical forms of social transformation. The queer, idiomatic world Warlikowski and his ensemble produce in *Kabaret Warszawski* is a potent and ongoing act of what queer theorist José Esteban Muñoz terms 'disidentification,' a process that is descriptive of 'the strategies a minority subject practices in order to negotiate a phobic majoritarian public sphere that continuously elides or punishes the existence of subjects who do not conform to the phantasm of normative citizenship' (1999: 4). The physical relationship established with the audience through eye-contact and physical touch, the sharing at one point of a marijuana joint and a concurrent use of the audience seating area as performance space created a mutual co-presence between performer and spectator that was affecting, temporal and inclusive, in line with Victor Turner's notion of '*communitas*' which Jill Dolan has defined as 'the moments in a theatre event or a ritual in which audiences or participants feel themselves become part of the whole,' inciting a sense of belonging within the group (2005: 11).

The physical space of the theatre itself functions like the utopic salon in *Shortbus*, where the enactment of social optimism through open-ended expressions of sexuality constitute audiences as counterpublics. It is fair to argue that Warlikowski's explorations of cultural alterity have established a new category of audience. As queer theorist Michael Warner has suggested, the creation of such a public is a 'cultural form' that is necessary to the circulation of discourse through the larger social imaginary (2002: 12). While the first section of *Kabaret Warszawski* critiques radical right-wing ideologies through *I Am Camera*, the second half disidentifies with normative articulations of sexuality in Polish society and simultaneously enacts a 'utopian performative,' which Dolan defines as the 'small but profound moments in which performance calls the attention of the audience in a way that lifts everyone slightly above the present, into a hopeful feeling of what the world might be like if every moment of our lives were as emotionally voluminous, generous, aesthetically striking, and intersubjectively intense' (2005: 6). This utopian performative thus draws together the audience in a collective act of political praxis that embodies hope, validates personal experience beyond the strongholds of the normative social body and produces an alternative to uniformity and oppression. The queer public that is produced not only among the performers but also the audience exceeds the more exclusionary limits of identity politics carefully outlined by the sociologist Steven Epstein (1998).

Challenging politics

Many critics have placed Warlikowski's stagings of gay and queer identities in opposition to Monika Strzępka and Paweł Demirksi's 2011 production *Tęczowa trybuna 2012* (*Rainbow Stand 2012*) at the Teatr Polski in Wrocław. In the same year this production premiered, a media frenzy grew around the Euro 2012 football tournament set to take place across Poland. As in most countries, football and nationalism are strongly linked and often gender-bound, and hooliganism and binge drinking among young men is a growing problem in the country. As a result of the aggressive male bonding enacted at most matches, it was reported that a coalition of football supporters decided to start a campaign for stadiums to establish separate stands for gay fans who might otherwise be verbally abused or physically threatened by homophobic supporters.

Strzępka, who was fascinated by the seeming paradox presented by macho hyper-heterosexual football heroes appearing in blatantly homoerotic advertising geared towards gay consumers, such as the famous pictures of Cristiano Ronaldo in slinky Armani underpants, claimed that she and playwright Paweł Demirksi had been in contact with the gay men who had created the coalition while developing their new play, which quickly became the most hotly anticipated production for the Warsaw Theatre Meetings in spring 2012. Demirski observed that such schemes as the 'Rainbow stand' are ideally suited to Western Europe, where a number of gay-friendly zones have been established at Barcelona, AC Milan and Borussia Dortmund football clubs (cited in Piekarska, 2011). However, Demirski and Strzępka eventually revealed that they had fabricated the gay-rights project and the group's host website. Their ostensible goal in creating the 'Rainbow stand' was an attempt to test the ability of a grassroots organization to find a platform from which it could actively intervene in Polish politics and public space initiatives, such as the building of the new national stadium in Warsaw. It should of course be noted that the ethics of the 'Rainbow court' are themselves questionable practices. Creating a separate stand for gay supporters not only establishes a ghetto within the stadium, it also poses a potential threat to their safety in its obvious demarcation of their sexuality. Both Demirski and Strzępka confirmed that despite the myth of modernization and feigned respect for minorities that have accompanied the rhetoric around the Euro 2012 tournament, it was almost impossible to make any headway with the initiative. Unless one has a contact at the Ministry of Sport or the National Football Association, any bottom-up activism around the championship proved to be wholly ineffective.

There have been two major defenses of *Tęczowa trybuna 2012* that propose the production had the potential to galvanize audiences into political consciousness and activism. The first I will consider is Warkocki's use of feminist theorist Nancy Fraser as a means to analyze the political dimensions of Strzępka and Demirski's project. Fraser is part of a tripartite of recognition theorists, including Axel Honneth and Charles Taylor, who believe that 'contemporary politics has seen a shift away from ideas of class, equality, economy and nation towards those of identity, difference, culture and ethnicity' (Thompson, 2006: 3), which positions social justice in relation to subversion of hegemonic culture through the equal recognition of disparate and distinct identities. Fraser has argued that 'recognition designates an ideal reciprocal relation between subjects in which each sees the other as equal' (2003: 10). What distinguishes her thinking from that of Honneth and Taylor is a particular concern that the rise of the politics of recognition is concurrently motivating a decline in the politics of redistribution, wherein the identity politics of marginalized minority groups eclipses the old-fashioned tenets of class politics. Warkocki is concerned primarily with this equivocal relationship between recognition and redistribution, and champions Strzępka and Demirski for highlighting economic hierarchies and inequalities that Warlikowski's productions eschew. While this line of argumentation is tempting, it is important to recall that identity is produced through a plurality of cultural means, not all of which can be reduced to economics. Queer theorist J. Jack Halberstam (formerly Judith Halberstam) has similarly criticized David Harvey for his narrow focus on capitalism in his analysis of postmodernism that exclude processes of heteronormativity, racism and sexism (2005: 8). Fraser herself forecloses the binary between multiculturalism and social democracy, suggesting that this politically limiting either/or can be reworked into a 'broader overarching framework' that accounts for the underlying and often obscured links between recognition and distribution (2003: 35). The danger of her careful argumentation is that while the two are certainly imbricated, the precarious balance between economism and culturalism can threaten to sway violently in either direction. 'Perspectival dualism' is the task Fraser outlines for critics to ascertain how they are related to one another in any given social formation. Certainly it is true that the subordination of the working classes in Warlikowski's productions is not foregrounded. However, could this criticism not be reconceptualized as a different formulation: how can experiences of oppression that are not reducible to social class (homophobia is not directed at a certain class of gays and lesbians, but is ubiquitously bestowed) be characterized? Queer theorist Eve Kosofsky Sedgwick has demonstrated an approach more analogous to Warlikowski's, which demonstrates how 'questions of normative sexual definition are central to both the smooth running of patriarchal capitalism and to fascist and imperialist ideologies' (Edwards, 2008: 45), which, in turn, suggests that challenging sexual hierarchies and norms and modes of discrimination directly impacts on forms of economic oppression related to class. While *class* hierarchies might be challenged by Strzępka and Demirski, the simultaneous reinforcement of a hetero/homo binary in the establishment of the 'Rainbow stand' actually works within a normative discourse of *sexual* hierarchies rather than providing an alternative that empowers rather than segregates a marginal positionality.

Dramaturge Igor Stokfiszewski (2011) staunchly defended *Tęczowa trybuna 2012*, arguing that the production was an attempt to initiate a social movement by artists that is part of a broader trend to transform the political imagination in both the social field and in legislative processes. Questioning the homogenous nature of Polish collective identity, manifested in such mass spectacles as the European football championships, and breaking with the standard social passivity of audiences, Stokfiszewski suggested that the production tested the ability of cultural institutions to adequately operate at the level of civil society. Stokfiszewski also argued that the production and its concomitant activist platform exposed a fundamental weakness in Polish theatre criticism – most reviews carefully omitted analysis of the relationship between civil actions and performance – concluding that reviewers were insufficiently able to deal with real political acts. Even if Strzępka and Demirski's movement did not achieve the desired social effects, Stokfiszewski reasoned, it developed specific knowledge about the mechanisms of the functioning of democracy and paved the road for future initiatives.

Tęczowa trybuna 2012's focus on Euro 2012 did indeed demonstrate that the structural dynamics of power in Polish democracy are flawed, and further established how these inadequate structures interpenetrate cultural and sexual identity, economic status, citizenship and nationality. Taking the construction of the football stadium in Warsaw for Euro 2012 – the total investment in infrastructural change was €20 billion – as an example testifies to the indelible link between capitalist accumulation and expressions of national fervor. However, what we do see in Warlikowski is the way state actors are key in the designation and naming of minority groups, and are therefore one of the primary generators of misrecognition. The homophobic rhetoric of the nationalist Catholic right worked across economic stratifications, indeed this rhetoric was primarily concerned with cultural identification that imparts what Pierre Bourdieu calls 'common symbolic forms of thought' and 'social frames of perception' (2003: 175) that cast homosexuality as antithetical to Polishness. What's more, whereas Strzępka and Demirski have conceived of radical forms of social transformation in left-wing politics in general, Warlikowski's theatre has been crucial in the development and encouragement of a *queer* audience who have developed a taste for queer bodies, queer readings and queer encounters that occur in what Halberstam has termed 'queer space,' 'place-making practices within postmodernism in which queer people engage' thus enabling the production of queer counterpublics (2005: 6). Working outside and within the public sphere simultaneously – this is a fitting description of the Nowy Teatr, which was only recently offered a permanent space from the Warsaw city council – the creation of a counterpublic sphere allows us to 'imagine models of social relations' (Muñoz, 1999: 33) that are not confined to more limited understandings, even if misconstrued, of US-inherited identity politics. Warlikowski envisages his theatre as an unpretentious venue for those who have no place to socialize and do not feel safe at home (cited in Urbaniak, 2013), a refuge safely distanced from what is perceived as an increasingly dangerous public space.

Noisily touted as a seminal production on gay themes, Demirski claimed he was not only concerned with the connections between football, nationalism and homophobia on a mass scale, but also wished to protest against the ill health of democracy in Poland in general in devising *Tęczowa trybuna* (cited in Grzebałkowska and Karaś, 2011). Indeed, the play touches on a number of other themes, such as the dubious attempts to make poorer neighborhoods in Warsaw adjacent to the stadium, such as Praga, more cosmopolitan for the sporting events. Demirski also asserted that he could just have easily chosen a different topic from gay rights, such as the floods in 2010 that displaced Warsaw residents and cost the government more than US$3.6 billion in damages. Although one might attribute the significance of *Tęczowa trybuna* to its ability to test the boundaries of healthy democratic systems, if one fails to see sexuality as a key interpretive focal point for this performance then gay rights simply stands a metonym for a whole range of identity politics that is founded on opposition to discrimination on the basis of race, gender or creed. Such easy shifts between disparate categories of revolt, opposition and activism undermine the individual historical and political trajectories that frame activists' platforms. Given this open-ended focus on democracy and its faults, it is possible to invert Warkocki's criticism and suggest that Demirksi is more concerned with a universalizing tendency that privileges class over particular and local understandings of sexual identity.

Theatre historian Joanna Krakowska defined Alain Badiou's theory of the universal, 'breaking the grip of a community of truth,' in painstaking detail in her scholarly article for *Dialog*, intending to affix meaning to the curious coincidence of the Polish translation of Badiou with the premiere of *Angels in America* (2007: 88). Krakowska perhaps goes a step too far in her otherwise perspicacious defense of Badiou when she claims that Warlikowski's theatre is not and never has been a gay theatre. The theoretical turn necessary here is a substitution of terms. While I admit that Warlikowski has not founded an intentional 'gay theatre,' one that conforms to the Western model of a chronological progress-to-rights narrative, his work is queerly constitutive in that it produces effects in the world most intensely associated with non-normative identity and sexuality. The simple deployment of Badiouian universalism somehow falls short of the mark, and reminds one of Demirski's argument that one's duty is to assert a radically tolerant left-wing position wherein gay rights is reduced to the level of a metonym for a variety of political movements or social concerns. If *Angels in America* attempted to provide a concrete referent for the floating signifier 'gay,' *Kabaret Warszawski* provided what Michel Foucault called a 'reverse discourse,' a reaction against the homonormative identity politics underlying this form of signification, while simultaneously pointing to the importance of the production as a direct reaction to the lack of a historical legacy of gay liberational politics in Poland. Rather than pit Warlikowski against Strzępka and Demirski, as Warkocki attempts to do, it is imperative to show how each of these theatre-makers is contriving radically different political aims. While Warlikowski subverts nationalist hegemonic culture specifically through the enactment of divergent sexualities, Strzępka and Demirski rehearse democratic public practices that use sexuality as only one of a host of transferable political factors.

Future potentials

Although officially tolerated under communist rule, homosexuality was tacitly suppressed and often used as a means of blackmail. The situation did not change significantly in the years directly following 1989 as the majority of the population took guidance from the Church in the social and economic chaos and confusion that followed the collapse of communism. As I have argued, the Church continues to be used as an instrument of propaganda by the political right and as a voice for heteronationalism. Homosexuals are still framed in conservative rhetoric as a threat to the family, a concomitant symbol of the collapse of society, a demonized figure produced through sin and perversion and a pathologized body in need of medical treatment and prayer. Homophobia continues to mark the boundaries of normative masculinity in public discourse. The theatre has been a crucial space in which to stage alternative paradigms, embody counterdiscourses and enact queer worlds. In this respect, Polish cinema has staggered critically behind the theatre. Although a handful of recent films with gay characters and themes has broken a longstanding taboo,[5] even a detailed overview of cinema since 1989 exposes an almost exclusive heteronormative bias and in most cases cinema directors have endorsed prevailing stereotypes around strong masculinity and victimized female bodies, while desexualizing homosexuality. The belatedness of gay characters in cinema, and their reliance on predictable coming-out narratives as the focal point for their plot structures, demonstrate how theatre has been far more avant-garde in its depiction and interrogation of alternative sexual identities. In opposition to film, theatre has been a crucial territory to challenge social norms around sexuality, providing legitimate sites for the embodiment of (private) pleasure and the cultivation of self-esteem, identity and counterpublics. Although many of the productions I have discussed remain in the realm of political theatre, the aesthetic register has significantly changed. Moving from Warlikowski's 1999 *Hamlet* to *Kabaret Warszawski* in 2013, there is the clear establishment of gay and queer identities, but this is a trajectory that does not map clearly onto Western models that begin with gay emancipatory movements and end up at queer studies; rather, the movement between these remains overlapping and interpenetrating. This trajectory does, however, reflect how understandings of homosexuality remain bound by the struggle to be visible within the body politic while attempting to protect a queer position of difference.

Notes

1 Szczepkowska is perhaps most notably associated with her appearance on national television in October 1989 when she declared, 'Ladies and gentlemen, on 4 June 1989 communism ended in Poland,' a statement that has been mobilized as a symbol of the sociopolitical changes in the country after the first partially free parliamentary elections since the conclusion of the Second World War.
2 See, for example, Dmitruczuk (2013) and Kalukin (2013).
3 Tadeusz Rydzyk, a Roman Catholic priest and Redemptorist, is creator and head of the conservative Radio Maryja radio station. He has been involved in a number of controversies, including support of the death penalty and claims of anti-Semitism.
4 Significantly, the production was staged in Warsaw at Le Madame, a gay nightclub and performance art venue that was a stronghold of left-wing thought. The building, which also housed the offices of the Polish Green Party, was purchased by the Law and Justice Party, who used the opportunity of closing down the venue as an excuse to openly express their deep-seated aversion to EU environmental politics and homosexuality. Warsaw was polarized by the event, and a large public demonstration was organized in retaliation, in which instances of police brutality were reported. The protest was, perhaps inevitably, labeled as the Polish Stonewall by the foreign

press, although it did not culminate in a similar mobilization of activism. Tomasz Miłkowski (2006) argued that Roman Pawłowski's second anthology of plays, *Made in Poland* (2006), should be renamed 'Generation Le Madame.' Whereas the shared themes in the Porn Generation included anxiety around puberty, a desire for independence and a fear of adulthood, the writers in the latter volume share an intense dislike for hypocrisy, provincialism and parochial Catholicism that was at the forefront of the Le Madame protests.

5 Recent films to include gay characters and themes include *Sala samobójców (The Suicide Room)* dir. Jan Komasa (2011), *Płynące wieżowce (Floating Skyscrapers)* dir. Tomasz Wasilewski (2013) and *W imię... (In the Name of...)* dir. Małgorzata Szumowska (2013).

5
Rethinking Polish/Jewish relations

Memorializing the Holocaust was considered a critical factor in assuming a new, globalized and Western-focused identity for Central and Eastern European (CEE) countries joining the European Union in 2004. There existed very little in way of memorials in most CEE countries, and in Poland there has been a tense hierarchy of victims of the twentieth century, at which Polish victims of communism or Stalinism were often seen as the pinnacle. Notions of tolerance in the West are consubstantiate with studies of and memorials to the Jewish genocide. Western elites saw the refusal to put the Holocaust at the forefront of national memory in postcommunist countries as a 'moral failing or as a sign of their backwardness,' and one that must be remedied if they were to effectively 'return to Europe' (Mark, 2010: xvi). The sociologist and historian Joanna B. Michlic maintains that coming to terms with an anti-Semitic past is a key element in 'the process of democratization of Poland's political and social life after 1989' (2002: 32). This Western stance generated distrust in Polish anti-communists, who viewed this refusal to regard the suffering caused by communism as equivalent to that experienced by the Jews during and after the Second World War as a symptom of Western superiority. As a result, in public debates, a distasteful competition arose for the victims of communism with those of the Holocaust.

In the immediate postwar years, the historian Michael C. Steinlauf claimed that the Holocaust was excluded or marginalized from Polish public discourse as a result of the need for national unification and the Soviet-imposed anti-fascist interpretation of the war as a united worker's front (1997: 63–74). The persecution of the Jews did not appropriately fit the ideological parameters of this politically motivated interpretation. The suppression of public memory around the Holocaust in the late 1940s was later compounded and reworked by Władysław Gomułka in the late 1950s and 1960s. Gomułka was concerned with the 'ethnonationalization of communism when the "Jewish question" resurfaced within the party itself' (Michlic and Melchoir, 2013: 414). Jewish suffering and victimhood was de-emphasized or equated with Polish experiences during the war, and ethnic Polish acts of heroism were particularly celebrated in an effort to legitimize the Communist Party as the 'people's party' (ibid.: 415). The enthnonationalization of communism eventually resulted in the anti-Semitic purges of 1968, a particularly dark chapter in this history of the PRL. The lead-up to these events was precipitated by a number of factors including the censorship of literature, testimonials and other works on the Holocaust, the attempt to equalize suffering between Poles and Jews in WWII, which emphasized Jewish passivism and even complicity in the activities of Nazi extermination, and claims of Jewish anti-Polonism. This combination of factors, as Steinlauf argues, resulted in the almost total expulsion of the Holocaust from public memory by the late 1960s (1997: 75–88). The factual errors, distortions and omissions of such discourses and canons established in relation to the Holocaust, Polish/Jewish relations, genocide and Polish behavior during the Second World War that were elaborated in Poland in the 1950s–60s had a profound impact on public memory and knowledge, and these remained largely unchallenged until the 1980s.[1]

Grzegorz Niziołek argued that the dramatic and shameful events at the end of the 1960s emerged out of social ressentiment, the basic mechanism of which is 'external passivity' combined with the production of 'fictional scenarios of moral superiority over one's oppressors' (2013a: 225). Feelings of ressentiment were manipulated by communist ideologues against enemies of the state such as Germany and, more ambiguously, against Polish Jews, which resulted in the 'effective cooperation of the large part of society with disgraceful actions of the authorities' (ibid.: 226). Niziołek concludes that the more apparent incitement of hostility towards intellectual and literary communities and Germany was sustained by a concomitant 'encoded release of anti-semitic feeling' (ibid.).

Crucial to the discussion of the March 1968 events is Kazimierz Dejmek's 1967 production of *Dziady* at the National Theatre in Warsaw, which remains a reified watershed in Polish theatre history. Czesław Miłosz asserted that Adam Mickieiwcz's *Dziady* became the 'highest test of skill for theatre director' in the twentieth century (Miłosz, 1983: 223), because the play, which juxtaposes action against passivity in relation to spiritual transformation, functioned as the cipher for nation and, importantly, produced a locus around which the Romantic Hero calls for the collectivist action that is engendered through audience attendance, the founding of a Romantic *communitas*. Themes of sacrifice and resurrection in the text produced notions of national messianism that would prove politically motivational in the nineteenth and twentieth centuries. The full perspective of a collective action, however, needs to be read in relationship to the exclusive notion of community founded through political protest.

In Dejmek's production, Gustaw Holoubek played Konrad, *the* paradigmatic Polish Romantic hero who personifies the nation in his struggle against oppressors and through his disillusionment with a god that has abandoned his people. At the conclusion of the performance, Holoubek was seen bound by chains, although his patriotic spirit remained intact and undiminished, which prompted the audience to applaud for more than half an hour while singing the national anthem before some spectators marched to the Warsaw Mickiewicz monument. The closure of Dejmek's production by communist authorities for its outspoken condemnation of tsarist empiricism that the regime rightly interpreted as anti-communist resulted in mass student riots that were violently suppressed. However, while this production is celebrated as a call to action that launched a historical moment of political disobedience, the results of the March 1968 events – later politically instrumentalized by the Solidarity movement – cannot be divorced from the resulting anti-Semitic purge of Polish Jews, who were used as scapegoats to bring closure to the political unrest that coalesced the anti-Semitic leanings of many Polish Catholics and communists.[2]

Kathleen Cioffi attempts to disentangle the March events and the student protests from the 'patriots,' by which she means the interior propagandists, and a group of partisans within the Communist Party, to whom she attributes responsibility for the purges (1996: 95–7). While the partisans, led by General Mieczysław Moczar, were indeed responsible promoting anti-Semitic rhetoric and modifying the memory of the Holocaust, I would argue that we must also focus on the exclusionary understanding of nation that was espoused through the Dejmek production and the ethnically Polish Catholics to whom it was implicitly addressed. I am certainly not suggesting that Dejmek's production was a direct cause of the anti-Semitic purges, nor that it was staging anti-Semitic rhetoric, but the exclusive formation of a national community through the Romantic paradigm articulated cultural identity as a site of very particular Christian values. The broader cultivation of national, cultural and religious communities was ideologically fused with the outcome of the March 1968 events. Undergirding the questioning of Jewish loyalty to the communist cause was parallel to the implicit exclusion of Jews from the Polish national cause. The lines with which the boundaries of cultural identity are drawn by both communists, for whom society was totalized by political ideology, and Polish nationalists, for whom a national and political community could be distinguished from communist society, have the potential to act in radically divergent modes as discursive sources of inequality.

Conversely, Jerzy Grotowski's short-lived 1964 production *Studium o Hamlecie* (Study of Hamlet) directly engaged with the exclusion of Jews from the national community. The choice to make Hamlet a Jew and the courtiers secret police and government informers resulted in a closure of the production by the censors. Magada Romanska argues that Grotowski continued with the same themes around Polish/Jewish relations in *Studium* that he had begun in *Akropolis*, both of which were written by Stanisław Wyspiański and share a 'quest for Polish self-definition within the larger politico-cultural context' (2014: 110). While the latter performance engaged with the role and presence of Auschwitz in the Polish imaginary, the former very specifically dealt with the persecution of Jews under the communist regime.[3]

Memory and repetition

The fall of communism in 1989 meant that a number of suppressed incidents that frame Polish/Jewish relations entered public debate for the first time. These included the 1941 Jedwabne pogrom, a massacre of Jewish partisans in Koniuchy in 1944, postwar anti-Jewish violence with particular reference to the 1946 Kielce pogrom, the events of March 1968 that resulted in mass emigration of Polish Jews, and the Auschwitz cross. While the placement and removal of a Christian cross on the site of the Auschwitz concentration camp caused controversy around legitimate and multi-faith processes of memorialization that dominated public debate in the 1990s, the conflicting historical accounts of the Jedwabne pogrom have incited the most controversy in recent years. On 10 July 1941, in a small village in the northeast of Poland, up to 1,600 local Jews were rounded up by their neighbors, locked inside a small barn and burned to death. Traditional Polish historiography attributed the guilt for the now infamous pogrom to the Nazis, but historian Jan T. Gross' 2000 study, *Neighbors: The Destruction of the Jewish Community in Jedwabne, Poland*,[4] places the responsibility for the massacre firmly with the local community. The publication of Gross' monograph caused mass outrage, provoking Michlic and Melchior to identify the debate around the pogrom as the most important and longstanding in postcommunist Poland (2013: 405). As the Polish literary scholar Leonard Neuger (2009) notes, 'Many Poles have felt deeply wounded by the Jedwabne case.' This included journalists; historians; the Institute of National Remembrance's Commission for the Prosecution of Crimes against the Polish Nation; the Catholic Church, for what has been portrayed as their culpability in Jedwabne and surrounding areas; nationalists, for what has been deemed a lack of emphasis placed on Polish heroism; and the inhabitants of the village itself, who have felt persecuted. As Alicja Zielińska (2008) pointed out in relation to the Jedwabne public debates, 'Perhaps our [Polish] fear of discovering the bad sides of the past shows that for many years we have been buried in the history of martyrdom: the Poles are just the heroes or the victims.' The debates over Jedwabne have been crucial for the recovery of repressed memories, the airing of past crimes and forms of collusion, and a broader interrogation into the structural dynamics of anti-Semitism in Polish culture. These debates incited and have participated in the wider 'process of challenging and deconstructing anti-Jewish idioms and images'; a concrete part of the post-1989 process of 'rebuilding Poland on a model of civic nationalism, which does not define Polishness in a narrow ethno-national sense' (Michlic, 2006: 2).

Alongside and in relation to the Jedwabne controversy, recent events have demonstrated greater tolerance and more open debate on these subjects in Poland. A number of Jewish publications are available in Polish and there are a great many activist organizations today: the Jewish Historical Institute, the Judaica Foundation, The Jewish Theatre (*Teatr Żydowski*) in Warsaw and the Jewish Cultural Center. In 2006, a memorial was erected at the site of the pogrom in Kielce on the sixtieth anniversary of the massacre. In the past few years, many works of literature and a number of plays have been written dealing with Polish/Jewish relations. Important voices supporting tolerance and a more pluralistic notion of Polish identity inclusive of Jews and Jewish culture have included Aleksander

Kwaśniewski, former president of Poland; Leon Kieres, former chairman of the Institute of National Memory (Instytut Pamięci Narodowej, IPN); and public intellectuals such as Father Adam Boniecki, Jan T. Gross, Maria Janion, Father Stanisław Musiał, Hanna Świda-Ziemba and Joanna Tokarska-Bakir. Of enormous significance has been the opening in 2013 of POLIN, the Museum of the History of Polish Jews, in Warsaw. The fact that the main exhibition was designed under the guidance of a performance-studies scholar Barbara Kirshenblatt-Gimblett also opens new possibilities and forms of memorialization between museums and/ as performance spaces and new lines of inquiry into the performativity of memorialization.[5]

Michlic and Melchoir recently compared 'renewal' and 'rejection' as two contrasting modes of internalizing and espousing Holocaust memory in Poland, which they argue were characterized by interviews from leading scholars in the newspaper *Rzeczpospolita* in 2009. While Alina Cała of the Jewish Historical Institute in Warsaw recognizes a degree of Polish culpability for the Holocaust as a result of the ethno-nationalist movement National Democracy and the Catholic Church's dissemination of anti-Semitic propaganda prior to 1939, as well as the broader mistreatment of Jews in Polish society, the historian and politician Władysław Bartoszewski posited that denunciators of Jews were largely restricted to the margins of Polish society. Michlic and Melchior observe:

> While Cała's position stands for and expresses the current intellectual and moral desire for renewal of the memory of the Holocaust, including even the most uncomfortable aspects of Polish/Jewish relations, Bartoszewski's stance demonstrates the difficulty with which this renewal might be fully accepted and absorbed even by those members of Polish society who are not only far from militant nationalism and antisemitism but also have a noble record in helping Jews. (Michlic and Melchior, 2013: 405)

Bartoszewski's position is then linked with what the historian Jerzy Jedlicki has theorized as the 'bezradność' ('powerlessness') of the renewal process across the generational spectrum. Michlic and Melchior claim that the tension between renewal through social and cultural integration of eclipsed or painful histories that have the power to overshadow national narratives of heroism, victimhood and martyrdom and the ongoing rejection of such narratives is the primary concern of memory politics today.

In his groundbreaking study *Polski teatr Zagłady* (Polish Holocaust Theatre, 2013), Grzegorz Niziołek describes an irrefutable need to accept the existence of the social memory of specific events that revive the community of witnesses of the Holocaust after 1945, which includes the extermination of Jewish communities, the formation and liquidation of the ghettos, experiences of hiding and scenes of public humiliation and death (2013b: 58). Niziołek unpacks the modes in which Polish society denied the public memory of its own indifference to the witnessing of the suffering of others in the Holocaust, and contends that this denial has been decided through, and influenced by, tensions throughout the whole of postwar Polish culture (*ibid.*: 33). Polish culture (pre and postwar) was co-created by assimilated Jews and Poles with Jewish roots, which means capturing a single historical viewpoint is not possible. Therefore, denial of the past is multifarious. One has to take into account various factors, not just the question of the culpability of passive observers, but also, for example, the potential need to overcome the memory of the spectator's own humiliation (*ibid.*: 54).

'Theatre in this history of repression should be given a special role,' Niziołek claims, 'as it participated in the process of supporting state repression, as well as attempts to break it' (*ibid.*: 33). Both deliberately and unconsciously, theatre became a crucial place of repetition – 'the constant recall of repressed events' that were not direct and readable representations of trauma, but rather symptoms of broader social denial (*ibid.*). Niziołek elucidates a profound transformation in the medium of Polish theater 'as a result of widespread social experience of being a witness to the suffering of others, and a general denial of that experience' (*ibid.*: 34). Clear or easily graspable pictures of the traumatic past were undesirable or difficult to articulate for various reasons at different historical moments. When unambiguous forms of representation fail, Niziołek maintains, the theatre has at its disposal a repetition mechanism that operates in the space of taboo by repeating concealed experience in a symptomatic and affective dimension, reproducing in 'ever new variations the situation of repression and the violation of defense mechanisms' that place the viewer in the uncomfortable position of neutral observer (*ibid.*).[6] This position produces feelings of shock, aggression, compassion, paralysis, anxiety or fear for the spectator.

Ultimately, Niziołek reads the theatre space as a 'libidinal economy,' in which the production of affects release the power of unpredictable consequences (*ibid.*: 36). As a result, he is more invested in the excesses produced in theatre, rather than the theatre's staging of loss or ritualistic role in mourning. While I agree with Niziołek's claim that the theatre is not a place to seek a totalizing or naïve sense of closure,[7] I am also invested in the relationships between historical loss and foundational absence in the staging of traumatic events and narratives that can affect structural transformation and are part of a process of working through trauma that do not rely on notions of secular salvation or a sociopolitical return to a 'pure' or whole community.

The examples I spend time over in this chapter have been carefully selected for their participation in puncturing received histories of Polish/Jewish relations and the realignment of the position of the audience as witness to historical and structural trauma. I side with Saul Friedländer, one of the pre-eminent historians of the Holocaust, who suggests that the narrative structure of written histories should be mediated by commentary that should 'disrupt the facile linear progression of the narration, introduce alternative interpretations, question any partial conclusion, withstand the need for closure' (1992: 52–3). Such commentaries in the theatre function as a return of the repressed, offering openings in historical narratives that are diachronic and not conclusive or absolute, but that testify to the trauma of such events. I am equally attentive to Dominick LaCapra's cogent warning against the production of a clear-cut binary between history and memory or their unmitigated conflation. The first tendency fails to register the affects of memory on the construction of historical narratives, and posits history as fact and analysis in opposition to the uncriticality, and even potential myth making, of memory. The second tendency simply moots the question of nuanced distinctions between history and memory, thus reducing history to personal anecdote or autobiographical sketches. LaCapra concludes,

> Memory is a crucial source for history and has complicated relations to documentary sources. Even if in its falsifications, repressions, displacements, and denials, memory may nonetheless be informative – not in terms of an accurate empirical representation of its object but in terms of that object's often anxiety-ridden reception and assimilation by both participants in events and those born later. (LaCapra, 1998: 19)

Memory, therefore, should remain in a dynamic tension or relation with history that is mutually questioning.

Precisely this drive towards renewal, the concomitant struggle against final closure and a generative tension between history and memory are at work in the performance examples I have chosen to concentrate on in this chapter. I position these as examples of what LaCapra calls 'working through,' a term he takes from Freudian psychoanalysis and applies to the historian and theorist, as well as wider sociopolitical contexts. 'Working through' a traumatic history can be distinguished from, although not diametrically opposed to, 'acting out.' While the former indicates a 'desirable process' that allows individuals and collectives to 'gain critical distance on a problem and to distinguish between past, present and future,' a process by which one 'acquires the possibility of being an ethical and political agent,' 'acting out' is defined by a tendency to relive the past – to be haunted by its ghosts, caught up in its nightmares – in a repetitive, compulsive or uncritical manner (La Capra, 2001: 142–4). As the performances I analyze suggest, 'working through' is not a linear, totalizing or teleological process that ultimately transcends or annuls 'acting out.' Rather, these performances, in effect, make visible the scars and residues from the past that continue to shape the present without attempting to either valorize or conceal trauma in the cultural and political landscape. With regards to counterpublics, these new productions offer visibility to those excluded from national histories, thus enabling theatre to 'restore citizenship to those who have been excluded in history' (Pawłowski, 2010), so that, as Maria Janion famously extolled, Jews will be included among 'our' (no longer homogenous) dead as part of the work of producing a Polish/Jewish community of memory (2000: 243–58).

LaCapra has distinguished two modes of using theory in relation to the representation of the Holocaust. The first mode involves the denial or repression in a redemptive narrative that excludes or devalues trauma, presenting values and ideas as viably realized in facts. The second problematic method aggravates trauma, insisting there is no alternative to 'symptomatic acting-out' beyond a purely imaginary hope for totalization of full disclosure. However, following Jacques Derrida, LaCapra offers a third potential, proposing a use of theory that coalesces criticism with self-criticism without recourse to narratives of redemption or salvation (1996: 192–4). The productions I have singled out attempt this latter process, performing discourses that are critical of revisionist histories as well as being self-conscious of their own constructed forms, while refusing to find closure through fetishistic or redemptive narratives that valorize heroism and sacrifice at the cost of all other discourses. These theatre-makers have resisted the false or disavowed forms of closure that Jan T. Gross and Joanna B. Michlic have fought against in self-assured or biased attempts in Polish historiography to revise Polish/Jewish relations in exclusively Polish nationalistic terms. For these scholars and artists, the unbearable excesses of the past are neither disguised nor banished, and the symptomatic acting-out of repetition compulsions is openly staged in order to foreground the responsibility of working through traumatic and repressed histories shared by Poles and Jews.

Who is our class?

Theatre critic and dramaturge Roman Pawłowski (2010) noted that new forms of drama appearing on Polish stages after 2000 dealt primarily with the realities of capitalism and the free market, portraying the negative consequences of radical reforms, social pathologies and class inequality. At the end of the decade, however, a new preoccupation emerged among theatre-makers to explore national histories including the legacies of the Second World War, the Holocaust, the Katyń massacre, a series of mass executions of Polish nationals by the NKVD in 1940, the SB (Służba Bezpieczeństwa, the Communist secret police), KOR (*Komitet Obrony Robotników*, the Workers' Defense Committee) and the Solidarity movement. Pawłowski convincingly argues that this shift in focus was a reaction to the historical policies pursued by the main political parties in their competition for power and control over the national symbols of memory. Unlike an institution such as the Muzeum Powstania Warszawskiego (Warsaw Uprising Museum), opened in 2004, that openly celebrates patriotic spirit while marginalizing non-ethnic Polish suffering, the new historical dramas have overtly challenged 'official' versions of the past, offering a recalibration of national histories rather than their veneration.

One of the most significant examples of this new historical drama was Tadeusz Słobodzianek's play *Nasza klasa* (*Our Class*, 2009), which evokes the Jedwabne pogrom and its repercussions.[8] Covering a period of 80 years of Polish/Jewish relations, Słobodzianek's text addresses a number of the main topics in this chapter. Significantly, *Nasza klasa* was the first play to win the Nike Prize, the highest achievement for a literary work in Poland. Barbara Gruszka-Zych (2010) wrote that the choice of this drama was another example of the very fashionable literary trend to force Poles to apologize for the sins against the Jews, which undermined the significance of the award. On the other hand, Grażyna Borkowska (2010), the head of the Nike jury, stated that Słobodzianek was awarded for his ability to paint the story of the executioners and victims – of murderers and the murdered – in shockingly simple language. The decision to give a Nike award to *Nasza klasa* has significant political connotations, as it is a public acknowledgment of Polish anti-Semitism and culpability in the Holocaust and subsequent pogroms and mass emigrations.[9]

The material for the play derived from divergent sources. Although Słobodzianek read Gross' study, he cites a school photograph from Jedwabne, showing both victims and perpetrators of the massacre, as the original inspiration for the play. However, the playwright pointedly leaves out any mention of either Jedwabne or nearby Radziłów, so that the diegetic village is not isolated to one geographical position, but rather functions as 'somewhere' in Poland. The narrative follows the lives of ten classmates, born between 1918 and 1920. Catholics are firmly identified as Poles, although this national status is less stable for the Jewish students. Over the course of the twentieth century, a number of violent acts and personal sacrifices are legitimized in the name of the community. Słobodzianek's project is profoundly pluralist and the play purposefully fails to incite patriotic fervor. The ethical tension at the heart of Słobodzianek's interrogation of community stems from the particular relationship between the bonds of a community and the identity of the individual under particular and shifting conditions of nationhood through multiple occupations and regimes. The class comes to represent the Polish population at large, calling attention to the very concept of 'nation' itself, which is rendered an ambivalent notion in the staging of the debate between nationalism and Enlightenment discourses. In these biographies, the abstraction of nation is emphasized over its perceived particularities. The geographies of physical and psychic borders are constantly traversed, redrawn or overrun. The Polish nation comes to form an imaginary space that is predicated on its internal divisions and differences, and the interactions between Poles and Jews break down the boundaries famously drawn by the American historian Raul Hilberg (1993) in a discrete triad of perpetrators, victims, and bystanders without reverting to apologist or revisionary strategies.

The Polish production premiered at the Teatr na Woli in 2010, staged by the Slovakian director Ondrej Spišák, a longtime collaborator of Słobodzianek.[10] While the critical response to the Polish premiere was largely positive, and the production was generally hailed as a wise lesson in ethics and Polish history, the designation 'our class' provoked a variety of responses from the Polish press. Joanna Szczęsna wrote in *Gazeta Wyborcza* that '*Our Class* opens questions about crime and punishment, guilt and condemnation, suffering and forgiveness from history that moves straight into the scene of *our life*' (2010, emphasis added). One defensive review in *Gość Niedzielny*, a nationalistic Catholic magazine, entitled 'To nie "nasza klasa"' ('It's not "our class"'), claimed that Poles were shown as villains while the Jews were treated as victims (Gruszka-Zych, 2010).

Polish novelist Izabela Filipiak (2011) argued that the elite urban audience felt alienated from the text and failed to empathize with characters from a rural village, and that for cosmopolitan intellectuals the Polish peasantry represented in the play also did not appear to be 'our class.' As these reviews indicate, particular notions of culture and ethnicity and productions of history and remembering are key to the concrete experience of nations, and prevent them from becoming purely arbitrary concepts.

Spišák had sought to emphasize the story's versatility: its pertinence to inter-ethnic conflicts across the world today, and its universal message that private lives often give way to politics. Resisting the impulse towards nationalism, and favoring psychological truth over historical authenticity, Spišák sought to reconstruct a simple story of people without placing any emphasis on geographical location or time period. The set was confined to a wooden floor, a wall with a door and four rows of school desks with chairs. Changes in tone and action were indicated by the physical gestures and voices of the actors, who appeared to age over the course of the play. Spišák used a proscenium stage broken into two separate spaces, downstage reserved for the living and upstage for the dead. The placement of the dead behind the living stressed the immensity of suffering and the enormous burden of guilt overwhelming the narrative, serving as a reminder that it takes several generations to heal the trauma of ancestors. By the end, the school furniture of childhood is empty and the doorway is like a dark mouth stuffed with the dead. Spišák staged Polish history as a procession of occupying regimes through symbols affixed above the door: the cross gave way to the swastika, which was replaced by the sickle and hammer, 'compounding dangerous divisions' between Poles forced to choose sides during political occupations (Derkaczew, 2010a).

Marcin Kościelniak (2010) argued that Słobodzianek allowed for too much intimate detail of the characters' private thoughts, as their reported memories left no room for ambivalence or mystery. As a result, the critic contends that reported memory is experienced as absolute. Claims such as Kościelniak's raise questions about the status of trauma in language. For if the actors can lucidly report their desire, guilt, or regret, is the experience of trauma itself not lost – that which has not yet been circumscribed or mitigated by language and abridged by memory?

Here it is useful to recall that 'ghosts that cannot be assuaged or placated' (Kurkiewicz, 2010) are a staple of the Polish dramatic canon, and for Słobodzianek, the ghosts of the classmates link his play with Tadeusz Kantor's *Umarła klasa* (*The Dead Class*, 1975) specifically and his 'Theatre of Death' series more broadly. However, while for both artists working on memory is crucial for establishing agency, there is a significant distinction between their stagings of the dead. If Kantor's 'Wielopole' is suspended between historical biography and geographical specificity and the more ambiguous and unlocatable territory of cultural and personal memories, Słobodzianek produces distance between historical events and memories through his refusal to directly locate the play's action in Jedwabne. Neither revert to a purely illusionary 'nowhere' that might etherealize rather than address historical problems. Kantor does indeed stage memories in order to account for historical loss, but his interrogations into memory and trauma as mediums are radically unstable, constantly shifting and redirected, which calls attention to transhistorical absences; namely, the inability of society to be wholly unified or the individual to be self-identical. It is not only that Kantor was 'aware of power as a central factor in mediating the public appearance of collective memories in communist Poland,' it was also important that he 'challenged the frames of intelligibility' by providing access to 'silenced, suppressed and disavowed experiences' (Gluhovic, 2013: 102). Performance theorist Milija Gluhovic connects this theatre practice with 'countermemory,' attending to that which has been 'negated, deemed unrepresentable on account of its traumatic nature, or silenced' (*ibid.*: 103), a process that could also be attributed to Słobodzianek's project. There is, of course, always the risk that repetition itself, or the compulsive turn to repetition, can result in a melancholic fixation on paradox or impasse (LaCapra, 2001: 49). However, Kantor's 'Theatre of Death' remained fluid, distinguishing between absence and loss in an effort to work through trauma and, at the same time, to remain open to the excesses generated in each live experience in the theatre.

As I will demonstrate in the next section, Słobodzianek does not enter into a distasteful balancing of accounts between victims and perpetrators, but rather is attempting to find a way to 'viably come to terms with (without every fully healing or overcoming) the divided legacies, open wounds, and unspeakable losses of a dire past' (LaCapra, 2001: 45). His ghosts enact events not in attempt to foreclose investigations into the past, or to produce an absolute and final historical account, but rather as part of an acute need to accept the existence of the cultural memory of particular, traumatic events.

Collusion and guilt

Allusions in *Nasza klasa* to Marshal Piłsudski (1867–1935), a leader who opposed anti-Semitism and judged citizens not on their ethnicity but on their loyalty to the state, allowed for the elaboration of a political program that adapted, rather than vilified, internal difference. Both the Depression and the increase in support for the National Democracy, or Endecja party (which supported the Polonization of non-ethnic Poles such as German, Ukrainian, and Belorussian populations living in the country and feared Jewish economic supremacy) amplified anti-Semitism in Poland in the 1930s. Piłsudski's death marked a negative turn in Polish/Jewish relations – much of the Jewish population saw him as their protector.

The play also brings to the fore the lure of victimhood embedded within Polish national tropes. The Polish historian Andrzej Nowak has focused in his writing on the positive role monumental national history plays in a society. Michlic argues that Nowak's position 'subscribes to the traditional model going back to the nineteenth century, wherein defending national honor and creating "a good feeling within the community to which the historian belongs" form the basis of conceptualization' (2002: 28). Within this 'monumental history,' Poles are depicted as heroes and/or victims, and this collective image places Poles above culpability. Jan Błoński critiqued this position in his controversial 1987 article, 'Biedni Polacy patrzą na getto' ('The Poor Poles look at the ghetto'), contending that Poles 'want to be also – and only – victims' (Błoński, 1987: 321). Gross vehemently asserts that Poland must shed such identifications if it is to retell its history to itself (cited in Michlic, 2002: 9).

The inclusion of Zygmunt in the biography of Poland presented in *Nasza klasa*, however, troubles the characterization of Poles as solely (passive) victims or even as bystanders. Zygmunt betrays his country time and again, spying for Soviets and Nazis alike while informing on his fellow ethnic Poles, which contradicts popular Romantic and nationalist narratives that stereotype Poles solely as victims and never as perpetrators. Zygmunt instigates the gang rape of his Jewish classmate, Dora, and after the Soviets are replaced by the occupying Nazis, he recounts his fear that the Amskommandent would find a letter he had written to Stalin, testifying to his loyalty to the NKVD. The letter is not found and the Amskommandent takes Zygmunt by the hand after hearing that his father was murdered by the Soviets and tells him that he will be complicit in the ethnic cleansing. Later, Zygmunt is one of the villagers who helps round up the local Jews and forces them into the barn. He describes the bodies, piled one on top of the other, so tangled that he has to take an axe to cut the charred corpses into smaller pieces in order to bury them. What makes Zygmunt's behavior even more reprehensible is a letter he writes to a former Jewish classmate who immigrated to America in the mid-1930s, in which he casts the blame for the pogrom on the Nazis. Here, Słobodzianek evokes two primary themes in the defensive Polish-nationalist approach – the focus on German culpability or the conflation of Jewish and Communist identity, both of which have at times served as justifications for crimes committed by ethnic Poles.

By allowing Zygmunt equivalent stage time to draw out his biography, Słobodzianek undermined uncomplicated binaries between bystander and perpetrator. What's more, neither Jews nor ethnic Poles display behavior that produce a consistent national or ethnic identity, and categories such as protagonist and antagonist are built up only to be destabilized or subverted. This was also the case for Menachem, a Jew who survives the Holocaust and then tortures and murders former classmates as a UB officer for the Soviets in order to take revenge for the death of his wife and child. Portrayed by Przemysław Sadowski, Menachem's 'victimhood' was undermined by the actor's athletic and imposing physicality. Słobodzianek maintained that he was not interested in identifying whether the Jews or the Poles informed more to the NKVD; rather he wished to show the mechanism of evil that leads to certain actions (cited in Zielińska, 2008). The pretence of innocence is more often than not predicated on the blurring of past crimes.

While in the West those who hid Jews during the war were exonerated or praised, the opposite was often true in Poland. It was common practice for Poles who gave Jews shelter to keep it secret from their neighbors (Gross, 2006: 252). Zocha hides Menachem during the war, in which a sexual relationship develops between them. Decades later, when Abram tells Zocha that Menachem has arranged from Israel for her to receive the Righteous Among the Nations medal, she is alarmed rather than honored. Abram, who is now fully Americanized, cannot understand her reaction. Zocha recounts how her new husband in the US is furious when he finds out she hid a Jew. Many Poles who won the Righteous Among the Nations medal were socially ostracized as a result (*ibid.*: 260), and as Ewa Uniejewska (2011) observed, the play suggests that it is easier to be announced 'Righteous Among Nations' than to be called a good classmate. Słobodzianek does not confine this shame for harboring Jews to a distant past, but addresses it again when Zocha comes back to visit the village in the 1980s. Wishing to see the graveyard where the Jews were buried after the burning of the barn, she invites Rachelka to join her. Despite the fact that Rachelka's entire family is buried at the site, she refuses, keeping the past at a distance in order to securely maintain her life among her ethnically Polish neighbors.

Gross identifies the Soviet occupation of Poland in September 1939 as a trope for anti-Semitism in much Polish historiography, noting that the Jewish people of eastern Poland are often seen as having enthusiastically welcomed the Soviet army (2006: 185). The underlying premise of this assertion links Jews with communism, and this prejudice is reflected through a number of incidents enacted in the performance. Heniek, a Catholic, claims that Jews erected an arch to welcome the Red Army. Władek, a fellow classmate, acknowledges that both Jews and Poles hung red flags outside their houses. These remarks reflect an embedded notion of segregation, in which a Jew is not identified as Polish; yet Władek's account also refers to a specific actual historical incident. In Jedwabne, there were only three Polish houses that did not hang the red flag, but as Słobodzianek (2009b) commented when conducting research for the play, today every long-time inhabitant of the village claims to have lived in one of those three houses.

Reviewers were attentive to the hierarchy of suffering presented by the contrast between Nazi and Soviet occupations of eastern Poland. The pogrom takes place during the former's occupation, which places particular emphasis on this historical moment. However, given that performance covers a period of more than 80 years in just three hours, the Soviet occupation in 1939 is given relatively significant treatment. In the span of just a few moments, three separate perspectives are articulated. On one hand, Władek at first enjoys the occupation because the Soviet communists seemingly break down social hierarchies and attempt to erase differences between rich or poor, Jew and Catholic, although he later changes his mind and decides that the Soviets are an enemy to stand against in defense of the motherland. Rysiek, a Catholic, details a violent beating he suffers at the hands of Soviet guards, clearly exposing the abuse the Poles suffered under the occupation.

Yet perhaps most important for this discussion is the perspective of Jewish classmate Jakub Katz, who describes how people had to queue for hours for basic supplies and castigates the 'Soviet paradise,' thus subverting the assertion found in standard history textbooks that the Jews enthusiastically welcomed the Red Army. The different perspectives on the Soviet occupation presented in the play bring to mind a claim Gross makes that many Polish scholars find contentious even today: 'One wonders whether the persistent collective memory of alleged Jewish collaboration with the Soviets does not function here as a displacement of the collaboration with the Nazis of Polish peasants and residents of small towns' (Gross, 2006: 185). As the action unfolds, the manner in which anti-communism becomes indelibly linked to anti-Semitism intensifies, a conflation that was one of the primary excuses for anti-Semitism in the twentieth century. Gross has written extensively on the notion of *żydokomuna* (Judeo-communism), a conflation of Jew and communist in Polish society, which became particularly troubling after the Kielce pogrom when Catholic bishops refused to speak against postwar violence directed against Jews for fear that they would be seen to be supporting the Soviets by proxy. The ideology supporting *żydokomuna* is typically paradoxical. The Jews were accused of supporting both Zionist and communist agendas simultaneously, despite the obvious fact that such agendas were in direct conflict. The examples of *żydokomuna* are pervasive in *Nasza klasa*. After the Jews are brought to the barn to be murdered, Heniek tells the others to get a nice big bat and help to lay Comrade Lenin to rest; Zygmunt says to the assembled Jews that they will be taken to the ghetto in Łomża where they will see for themselves the consequences of collaborating with the Soviets.

Zygmunt's argument correlates anti-Semitism to Polish nationalism, as if the latter is somehow dependent upon the former. A similar attitude was prevalent during the years immediately following WWII. A perverse morality guided anti-Semitic violence, differentiating between killing Jews and robbing their corpses and households. A thief was, in general, frowned upon, although murder was not only tolerated, it was vindicated as an act of nationalist loyalty. The pillaging of dead Jews recurs throughout the performance. After murdering Katz, for instance, Zygmunt checks his pockets. Władek remembers that in the aftermath of the Jewish massacre in the barn outside of the village, the corpses' mouths were searched for gold fillings. The Amskommendant asks the Poles cleaning up the bodies to strip, and those who pillaged the bodies are punished. Władek indicates that they deserve this 'nasty shock' from the German commander and the brutal beating that follows. Gross has suggested that while killing Jews was 'a behavior that could be appreciated by fellow citizens,' plundering merely 'generated envy' (Gross, 2006: 109).[11]

When the critic Gruszka-Zych (2010) criticized Słobodzianek for not representing Germans onstage although they were an active force on the scene, she failed, first, to see the purpose of the performance as an interrogation of Polish identity, and, second, to conceive of the way in which presence is conjured through absence. The Germans gave the order on July 10, 1941 that all the Jews be destroyed. Although Gross observes, 'It is also clear that had Jedwabne not been occupied by the Germans, the Jews of Jedwabne would not have been murdered by their neighbors' (2001: 47), this is not an attempt to legitimize the position that attributes full responsibility for the pogrom to the Nazis. Gross argues:

> If all evidence about what took place between Poles and Jews during the war had disappeared, and even if we only knew the particulars of the Nazi crimes, we would still be able to tell the broad strata of Polish society took advantage of Nazi policies and joined in the spoliation of the Jewish neighbors. (Gross, 2006: 260)

Gruszka-Zych's position mirrors that of the Polish historian Tomasz Szarota (2002), who expressed his hope in one interview that historical evidence would be found to show that the Germans and not the Poles were responsible for the massacre in Jedwabne, which Michlic claims 'shows the psychological need to see the Polish community as virtuous' (2002: 29).

The play reflects this mode of thinking in its reference to the unveiling of the memorial to the murdered Jews erected in the fictional village, which mirrored the real-life event in Jedwabne, a ceremony that was attended by the president, the ambassador, the mayor, MPs, senators, people from the arts, but in which the villagers themselves refused to participate. When Zocha visits the site of the pogrom, she finds a plaque that attributes guilt for the pogrom to the Nazis, a reference to the Jedwabne marker that was not changed to include Polish collaboration in the pogrom until 2001. The then president of Poland, Aleksander Kwaśniewski, and other Catholic and political Polish luminaries attended the commemorative ceremony at which the new plaque was revealed. Controversially, Kwaśniewski apologized to the Jews on behalf of the nation. The villagers boycotted the event and, in response, founded the Komitet Obrony Dobrego Imienia Jedwabne (Committee to Defend the Good Name of Jedwabne), a group that Słobodzianek (2009b) compared to the Ku Klux Klan in the newspaper *Gazeta Wyborcza*.

There were two primary reactions to the president's apology: it was welcomed as both proof of the new democratic process, deferential to the country's multiethnic past; yet at the same time, it was condemned as 'a national scandal defiling the good name of Poland' (Czajkowski, 2001: 5). This symptomatic reaction from the defensive camp came from the academic cleric Michał Czajkowski, who reflected, 'Those who really love Poland and serve her "good name" in the world are those who are labeled as traitors, oppressors of the Polish nation, servants of Zionism [...] communists, moral relativists' (*ibid.*). In the center of Jedwabne, a monument was then erected to commemorate those Poles deported to Siberia by the

Soviets, which Słobodzianek insists was an act of defiance against the Jewish memorial on the outskirts of the town (cited in Nathan, 2009).

From the late 1940s until the end of communism in 1989, the violence and anti-Semitism experienced by Jews in Poland was largely left out of public discourse. Gross maintains that as long as Poland is unable to mourn the deaths of its Jewish neighbors, the country will live in infamy (2006: 258). Likewise, Słobodzianek insists that if the Poles do not take on this subject others will do it for them:

> We [Poles] need to face it, because it is a fundamental obligation of our consciousness, both individual rights in general regardless of where a person lives, and also awareness [...] I will still have a sense of guilt, and that – as seen today in various example in Poland – causes hatred and aggression. (cited in Zielińska, 2008)

Nasza klasa has roused political debate through its examination of traumatic events, unresolved culpability, totalitarianism and its effects on individuals, and as a result it has contributed to a serious debate about Polish official historical memory.

Dybbuks

Hanna Krall observed that Krzysztof Warlikowski's theatre is based on four pillars: antiquity, the Bible, Shakespeare and the Holocaust. In response to Krall's observation, Warlikowski argued that the Holocaust must at some point come to any Polish artist, given that it is the most Polish topic, and the most important part of Polish history (cited in Pawłowski, 2009). The director further observed that 'if we [Poles] do not rethink the situation of the Jews in Poland in a different way, we will never be [at peace] with ourselves. Our words will not be sincere. Our theatre will not be sincere' (Warlikowski, 2015: 93–94). I will now turn to a further undercutting of binary oppositions between memory and history, interrogation of internal differences in Polish national identities, critique of Polish heroism and victimhood and the cultivation of alternative Polish/Jewish histories in two of Warlikowski's productions, *Dybuk* (2003) and *(A)pollonia* (2009).

It was in Warlikowski's staging of *Burza* (*The Tempest*, 2003) at Warsaw's Teatr Rozmaitości that publicity explicitly highlighted a focus on Polish/Jewish relations in the director's work. The confrontation between culprits and victims in the play was linked to the then raging debate around Polish anti-Semitism and collusion with the Nazis sparked by the publication of Gross' *Neighbors*. Although no direct reference was made to Jedwabne, scenographer Małgorzata Szczęśniak's design included a back wall with temple windows that was intended as a memorial to the Jews of Jedwabne. Warlikowski compared the final act of *The Tempest* to the highly controversial televised ceremony in which Kwaśniewski publicly apologized to the Jewish community and accepted Polish responsibility for the Jedwabne massacre (cited in Gruszczyński, 2003). On a thematic level, Warlikowski saw the marriage between Miranda and Ferdinand, whose father wanted to exterminate Prospero, as analogous to a generation of Poles and Jews creating a 'brave new world' through admissions of culpability and attempts at forgiveness.

It was not until his 2003 production *Dybuk. Między dwoma światami* (*Dybbuk. Between Two Worlds*, TR Warszawa) that Warlikowski very explicitly interrogated the absence of Jewish culture in postwar Poland. The production had a two-part structure that seamlessly fit together Szymon Ansky's 1920 Yiddish-language play and Hanna Krall's eponymous contemporary short story from her 1995 collection *Dowody na istnienie* (*Evidence for Existence*), and used the dybbuk, a wandering soul in Jewish mysticism that possess a living person and controls their conduct, as an ambivalent metaphor for cultural memory. Ansky's play, which absorbed the atmosphere and superstitions of the Jewish shtetl, was developed as part of his ethnographic studies that involved three years of documentation of the folkloric traditions of Jewish communities in, among other places, the Podolia and Volhynia regions. The plot centers around a young Yeshiva student, Chanan, who falls in love with Lea, the daughter of a wealthy merchant. When Lea is contracted by her father Hejnech to marry a man of her own social class, Chanan commits suicide. His spirit returns as a dybbuk that possesses Lea's body and prevents her from participating in the wedding. To exorcise the dybbuk, Hejnech hires a tzaddik, the 'righteous one,' a leader and teacher of a generation that devote themselves to the study of the Torah and its commandments, who reminds him of the marriage arrangement contracted with Chanan's father when the children were in infancy. By forsaking this sacred agreement, Hejnech has produced a dybbuk, and the play closes with the transcendental restitution of the rightful lovers in eternity (death).

There is a scant production history of Ansky's *Dybuk* in postwar Poland. After the death of Stalin, productions with Jewish themes could be produced again and *Dybuk* appeared twice at Warsaw's Teatr

Żydowski (Jewish Theatre; directed by Abraham Morewski in 1957 and by Chewel Buzgan in 1970). Both productions placed scenographic emphasis on Jewish folkloric traditions and rituals. While Jewish mysticism was crucial for productions in the 1920s and 30s, the postwar stagings attempted to portray the relics of Jewish culture decimated by the Holocaust (Pawłowski and Węgrzyniak, 2003). These elements were again emphasized in Andrzej Wajda's revival of the play at Kraków's Stary Teatr in 1988. Wajda placed a screen of semi-transparent black tulle across the front of the stage, which produced a historical blurring of the scenic action and imagery that was comparable to fuzzy black-and-white archival photographs. There appear to be two possible readings of this staging decision: either the landscape of death in the form of a cemetery and an eerie synagogue evoked a lost world that reinforced the ghettoization of the history of Polish Jewry or, despite the apparent interest in reconstructing Ansky's ethnographically informed studies of Jewish life, Wajda's production suggested a mythical non-reality more than a historical recreation. Both of these interpretations seem to indicate Wajda's unconscious disavowal of the complex processes of displacement of Jewish memory and culture in Poland. Although Krzysztof Kopka claimed the impulse behind Wajda's production was to 'expand our [Poles'] knowledge of the Jewish nation' in the aftermath of the Second World War (1988b: 4) – significantly, the production opened a year after the controversial publication in January 1987 of Jan Błoński's essay and was consequently read as a theatrical response to the article and its provocations – these scenographic conventions only served to increase sentimentality rather than critical awareness about Jewish otherness within Polish culture.

Warlikowski, on the other hand, removed almost all direct references to Jewish folkloric traditions from his production. Unlike Wajda's staging, Warlikowski did not play Klezmer music, men did not have fake beards or robes, although they did wear yarmulkes, suggestive of contemporary religious identity and cultural belonging. Rather than try to ignore or eschew the particularities of Jewish traditions and identities, this provocative staging decision was rooted in a desire to rethink the philosophical questions within Ansky's text that were broadly inclusive of transnational contemporary European, Israeli and American Jewish cultures and emphasized the ongoing relevance of the play instead of its historical distinctiveness or cultural alterity.

Krall's text, which makes up the second half of Warlikowski's production, focuses on an American Jew, Adam S., possessed by the dybbuk of his half-brother, who was murdered as a child in the Warsaw ghetto.

Adam S. is unable to find the totalizing transcendental closure equivalent to Ansky's lovers through his recourse to contemporary strategies such as psychoanalysis, Buddhism or yoga. Warlikowski did not put an interval between the two texts, which might have reinforced the bifurcation implied in the subtitle 'między dwoma światami' ('between two worlds'). Instead, the Holocaust, which chronologically separates these two worlds, fails to offer a bounded temporality, equally contaminating both the historical before and after, just as the dybbuk infects and permeates both the living and the dead. As a result, it is not that in Warlikowski's adaptation Ansky simply stands in for a distant past, a 'where we were' that can be easily contrasted with Krall's present 'where we are.' Rather, in a disorientating and uncanny manner, this confrontation and comingling of past and present brings attention to the complex configurations of cultural memory and historiography, tied to the notion of the *dybuk* that is derived from Hebrew, meaning 'union' or 'to cleave to.' While a clear historical duality is at first accentuated through scenic elements, such as the centrality of a mirror and the division of the stage into two distinct sections (sacred and secular), Warlikowski's double casting of Ansky's Lea and Chanan as Krall's Adam S. and his wife (Andrzej Chyra and Magdalena Cielecka, respectively) formally deconstructs this duality, indicating a return of the repressed through the diachronic circulation of bodies and identity positions, as well as spirits and memories, related by meaning rather than historical telos or causation.

The performance is framed by a prologue in which the actors recount Hasidic myths and stories on the front of the stage. These tales are played at the level of metaphor, nostalgia or amusing anecdote, with the actors consciously distancing themselves from the material by laughing or gently mocking any excesses of superstition and religious belief. Although these stories have lost their initial connotations, they nevertheless function as a significant reminder of the absences of Jewish culture in contemporary Poland. Jacek Poniedziałek as Hejnech winces and offers a cynical smile when the tzaddik suggests the Court of the Torah be invoked in order to resolve the problem of his daughter's dybbuk. However, Hejnech's shock is apparent when the tzaddik knows – through apparently mystical means – about the marriage agreement he had made with Chanan's father. This tension between religious faith, mysticism and secular rationality was concomitant with Warlikowski's interest in producing a theatrical language that is less sentimental and more balanced in order to free Poles from the embroiled 'emotions of their fathers and grandfathers [...] so as not to repeat their mistakes' (cited in Basara, 2004). Such a focus on rationality was well coupled with Krall's literary form, a cool, emotionally reserved reportage that directly confronts and outlines traumatic events.

Attempting a rational and conscious discussion of traumatic themes opened up by the Holocaust requires a break with earlier literary and theatrical forms. Warlikowski's intermingling of forms and genres provokes a critically self-reflective approach to the past that is not easily reliant on claims to the supremacy of either religious faith or historical accuracy. Warlikowski stages neither a hypostatized past nor a transparent teleology. Rather, these historical, ethnographic, biographical and fictional texts are all submitted to a critique of existing explanatory or interpretive molds, which brings to light the mode in which these various genres make particular claims on spectators. In this sense, Warlikowski offers a critique of safely conventionalized narrative forms, canonicity and historiography that becomes even more pronounced in his use of diverse textual forms in his later adaptations.

In a related manner, Warlikowski did not directly stage the dybbuks as ghosts. Their manifestation was only insinuated by the actors' movements and gestures, and the absence of Jewish life in Poland was only intimated through carefully selected objects, including prewar furniture and lace curtains. Images of paintings that had been inside the now destroyed seventeenth-century Zabłudów Synagogue, a wooden synagogue unique to the Polish–Lithuanian Commonwealth, were projected behind the naked couple of Chanan and Lea (a clear allusion to Adam and Eve and the Old Testament), thus foregrounding a link 'between two worlds,' that of the Jews of the early and late twentieth century who are mediated by the circulation of cultural memories (dybbuks) that refuse to be suppressed. When Adam S.'s dybbuk attempts to take possession of his newborn son, he forbids the exchange. Banging his fist on the table, Chyra as Adam S. declares, 'No ghetto! No Holocaust! You are not going to inhabit my child!' However, when the opportunity arises, Adam S. refuses to allow his dybbuk to leave his body once and for all. The inability to renounce or abandon the ghetto and the Holocaust is thus paired with an equally adamant refusal to pass the burden of these memories onto the next generation. The anxiety that that the living will be forsaken by the dead, the inversion of the familiar Romantic trope that the living will forsake the dead, signals a radical pluralistic vision of two nations, two spirits and two histories sharing the same body. While the dybbuk appears to be a curse that requires an exorcism in Ansky's play (although it is unclear whether the tzaddik is unable to exorcise the spirit or if, like Adam S., Lea is simply unwilling to renounce it), in Krall's text this spirit re-emerges as an integral, emancipatory connection to the past that establishes identity in the present. What's more, Warlikowski's movement from Ansky to Krall does not attempt to resolve or draw a line under the ongoing tensions of Polish/Jewish relations, but rather signals a mandate to work through the inherited trauma of the Holocaust and live with – rather than deny or disavow – incongruity and multiculturalism. After the Holocaust, the dybbuk is not only 'the personification of memory' (Warlikowski cited in Gruszczyński, 2003), it is the ethical imperative to remember and to confront one's own commitment to difference and plurality. When critics such as Marcin Kościelniak assert that the two-part structure of *Dybuk* communicates the loneliness and singularity within communities today (2003: 17), this confrontation with cultural pluralism and tolerance – the centuries-old notion of Poles and Jews sharing the same land – is eclipsed.

Another recurrent tendency in Polish criticism also requires analysis. A number of affinities have been drawn between Adam Mickiewicz's *Dziady* (*Forefathers' Eve*, completed 1832) and Ansky's *Dybuk*, originally noted by the early twentieth-century Polish writer and critic Tadeusz Boy-Żeleński and later by Adolf Rudnicki (1987), which have been equally obfuscating. More recently Pawłowski claimed that Warlikowski extended this likeness with the inclusion of Krall's short story (Pawłowski and Węgrzyniak, 2003). Structurally, the second part of *Dziady* focuses on supernatural encounters, tragic love and suicide, while the third part depicts a Romantic hero's metaphysical transformation as he takes up the burden of suffering for his nation. I would suggest there is a symbolic price to pay for such a comparison that implicitly assimilates *Dybuk* into the Polish Romantic canon, and thereby inadvertently endows it with a comparable set of cultural values. As opposed to drawing attention to structural or thematic parallels between the texts, Warlikowski's intervention seems to propose precisely the opposite commitment. Rather than shoring up well-trodden notions of the Polish national identity, which in Polish Romantic literature are deeply embedded in rhetoric of heroism and victimhood, Warlikowski's *Dybuk* helps to place spectators in a position to critically confront the dissonances performed between Romantic thought and Ansky and Krall's texts. While Pawłowski qualifies *Dybuk*'s cultural resonance, themes and structures through Mickiewicz by calling it the 'Polsko-żydowskie *Dziady*' ('Polish-Jewish *Dziady*'), one would be surprised to encounter the inverse qualification of Polish literature in relation to Jewish culture; for example, a critic referring to a new production of *Dziady* as the 'Polish *Dybuk*.' This qualification through Polish Romanticism, and *Dziady* in particular, obscures an unconscious attempt to reinscribe into the Jewish play precisely the values that Warlikowski critiques.

Postmemory

Of the twenty-first century works dealing with the theme of postmemory, productions of the Polish/Jewish writer Bożena Umińska Keff's short novel *Utwór o matce i ojczyźnie* (*Song of the Mother and the Fatherland*, 2009) deserve particular attention. The novel was first adapted for the stage by Marcin Liber at the Teatr Współczesny in Szczecin in 2010, and then by Jan Klata at Wrocław's Teatr Polski the following year as part of the theatre's sixty-fifth anniversary celebrations. As well as encouraging a concept of the nation as a *matczyzna* (motherland) rather than *ojczyzna* (fatherland), given that women in the novel function as carriers and inheritors of history, Umińska Keff highlights xenophobic attitudes and ongoing experiences of anti-Semitism in Poland. Similar to Warlikowski's productions, one of the most significant aspects of this novel and its subsequent stagings is in the inclusion of Jews in the conception of the Polish homeland. The central tension in the narrative is focused around the competitive, combative and suffocating relationship between two Jewish women, Meter, a Holocaust survivor, and her daughter Usi, who came to adulthood in the oppressive political atmosphere of the PRL. While the characters' conflicting worldviews are pitted against one another, mother and daughter are connected by an unbreakable bond that has its symbolic context marked in the title (*matce i ojczyźnie*), extending the metaphor of the filial relationship between the individual and the nation. Meter lists the traumas of her life, which include her experience of forced migration, starvation and typhus, the events of the Second World War and the Holocaust, and finally as the widow of a communist who commits suicide in reaction to an anti-Semitic smear campaign orchestrated by the Party. Given that Usi has not suffered the same trauma, the mother refuses to treat her as a social equal. In separate reviews in *Teatr*, both Inga Iwasiów (2010) and Jolanta Kowalska (2011) foreground the commonality of the mother's sacrificial passive-aggressive attitude in Poland and observe that this fits within the narrative of symbolic matricide synonymous with physical and emotional emancipation in second-wave feminism. The Matka Polka myth reinforces the notion that women are only granted full social recognition when they become mothers. Therefore, not only does Usi's suffering fail to match the epic scale of her mother's, it can be inferred that her childlessness further distances her from the guarantee of adulthood or maturity and, by association, full citizenship or accepted belonging in the national community. While the toxicity of mother–daughter relationships has also been explored by Polish novelists such as Izabela Filipiak, Anna Janko, Ewa Madeyska and Joanna Bator, the complexity of this relationship is redoubled by Umińska Keff's confrontation with taboos around anti-Semitism and the Holocaust.

In Liber's production, the presence of a copy of Art Spiegelman's comic *Maus* provides a direct reference to what Marianne Hirsch has termed 'postmemory,' which is defined in relation to those whose memory narratives are dominated by traumatic events that preceded their births. Children of Holocaust survivors are the most visible example of a postmemory generation, although Hirsch concedes that this concept can be extended to other postmemories, given their intense relationship to the traumatic memory of the past that is modified by both generational and historical distance (1997: 22). As a result of this distancing from actual experience, postmemory does not connote recollection but rather imaginative investment and creation, and, in particular, to collective memory full of gaps, blanks and uncertainties (Eaglestone, 2004: 80). Significantly, Iwasiów noted that for the first time in Polish literature, Umińska Keff subjected inherited trauma to such open contestation, a significant development in the process by which identification takes place and then is worked through. Umińska Keff cleverly calls up precisely the traumatic narratives that can neither be fully understood by Usi nor adequately represented on stage for the audience. In performance, the daughter and spectator are drawn together in their mutual inability to fully grasp the mother's experience. Usi's autobiographical memories are evacuated in favor of the mother's inherited memories, which resonates with Holocaust theorist Robert Eaglestone's argument that the experience of postmemory 'represents the unhappy truth of sins against the parents being visited upon the children,' who are 'obliged to accept the burden of history and assume the task of sustaining it' (*ibid.*). Given that only suffering endows a subject with the legitimacy of existence, Usi is reduced to the role of listener rather than historical agent, a blank, voiceless presence that records her mother's life. The daughter is forced to listen without a corresponding opportunity to respond to, debate or contest the complex narratives imposed by the mother. This unidirectional communication produces an unfamiliar discursive battleground in which any attempt at resolution in the narrative structure is rendered untenable. Umińska Keff attempts a reversal of this logic in her recuperation of the daughter's silenced voice, the embodiment of Usi's own biography, and in the revision of the myth of motherhood.

The negative portrayal of the mother was contentious given the sublime status of mothers in Polish literature and, by association, the implicit critique of the 'homeland' (*ojczyzna*) this suggested, thus confronting a redoubled taboo. 'Mother' represents a spectrum of identity positions and tropes, from despot to guardian, rendering 'homeland' a symbolic space of symbolic violence, trauma and blackmail (Kowalska, 2011). However, Umińska Keff's most controversial decision was to produce an unlikeable and tyrannical portrayal of a Holocaust survivor, a victim who becomes an oppressor. As a result, in order not to collapse boundaries between the presence of anti-Semitism in Poland, stagings of the text had to walk a fine line between forms of social critique and nuanced, sensitive representations of Jewishness. This concern was underlined in reviews that used the unfortunate metaphor of the mother as vampire, comparing her unrestrained critical energy to 'feeding' on her daughter's vitality, which too easily calls to mind anti-Semitic rhetoric that posits Jews as bloodsuckers feeding off of the moral health, energy and integrity of the Christian nation.[12]

Beyond the confinement and tension of their own relationship, both mother and daughter are acutely conscious of a more pervasive and suffocating pressure of anti-Semitism in the Polish public sphere. Joanna Derkaczew (2010b) interpreted Liber's production as connecting the particular forms of anti-Semitism bred under communism that attested to social frustrations and xenophobia in contemporary society. This is perspicaciously highlighted in a deliberate reworking of the Solidarity myth. When Usi attempts to join one of the movement's political campaigns in the early 1980s, a fellow demonstrator shouts an anti-Semitic slogan directly at her. The promises of freedom and solidarity are thus framed by anti-Semitic threats. This was further reinforced by Liber's choir, Poles dressed in colorful folk costumes displayed on video projections hurling paranoid anti-Semitic insults taken directly from online forums. While in Liber's production these choral voices function as a sonic space of confinement, in which the voices break down barriers between the privacy of the women's apartment and the threat of their social world, Klata constructed actual prisons in the form of portable metal containers as a multivalent symbol of this containment and surveillance, suggestive of SB police file cabinets, train compartments, prison cells and confessionals. This signified not only the anti-Semitism both characters endure, but also the mode in which roles of hostage-prisoner are dually inhabited in the family home and the public sphere.

Known for his anti-clerical views and critical focus on the intersections of the Polish holy trinity of family-religion-nation, Klata was primarily interested in teasing out what he views as an anachronistic aspect of Polish national identity, a perceived hierarchy of suffering that is not predicated on citizenship but rather a 'tribal' mentality grounded in a founding myth of slavery that defined the relationship between the Polish nobility and the peasantry (cited in Derkaczew, 2011). This notion of tribalism is developed through a number of aesthetic elements: members of the chorus wear dreadlocks and African wooden jewelry, and their make-up is suggestive of ritual masks. While Liber's production focused on the characters very specifically as Polish Jews, Klata was concerned with a more generalized critique of national myths founded upon victimhood, Christian morality and heroism, which marginalized the specificity of the Jewish narrative. The universalization of mother–daughter relationships was most forcefully portrayed through a thickly conjoined plait connecting Meter and Usi, a symbol, somewhere between a rope and an umbilical cord, which at once suggests bondage, interdependence, nourishment and solidarity. Replacing Umińska Keff's narrative linearity with a series of diachronic vignettes that foregrounded replication and reiteration, Klata also exchanged roles between performers, mothers become daughters and vice versa, and the ensemble included one male performer in drag that further implied gender as another category of cultural construction. Just as the chorus chant 'wieczna skarga' ('the eternal complaint'), emphasizing the recurrence of Polish victimhood, this fluid swapping of roles indicated a broader circulation of troubling gendered discourses and a repetition of social roles, duties and subject positions. The particularity of Jewish identity was only tangentially recovered in the concluding scene, in which the chorus sing the Rastafarian song 'Rivers of Babylon' with lyrics adapted from Psalm 137, signifying Jewish longing for a lost homeland after the Babylonian conquest of Jerusalem in the sixth century BC. Klata's production ultimately places postmemory outside of Jewish and Holocaust narratives, and the nature of anti-Semitism is largely left out of the generative (and problematic) metaphors of tribalism that conflate race with notions of slavery.

In Warlikowski's *Dybuk* and Umińska Keff's *Utwór o matce i ojczyźnie*, postmemory functions as an obligation to accept the burden of history and to undertake the task of its sustainment. Within the context of Niziołek's writing, it is interesting to note how the rejection of witnessing in the postwar generation re-emerges for directors of the generation born in the 1960s–70s, who attempt to configure these memories, giving them form and finding their provocative potential. In these stage productions there are clear indications of a move away from the transcendental guarantee of Romanticism in the exposure of conflicting dimensions of history and Polish/Jewish relations. Mixing document with myth and tragedy to complicate empirical events and cultural values, these concerns would again appear in an even more complex account in Warlikowski's inaugural production for his own company, Nowy Teatr.

Polin/Polonia

Warlikowski's original adaptation *(A)pollonia* interrogates Poland's suppressed past, weaving together ancient (Euripides and Aeschylus) and contemporary (Hanna Krall and J.M. Coetzee) material, to critique elevated notions of victimhood and sacrifice deeply embedded in the Polish psyche.[13] 'By questioning the meaning of sacrifice as an ethical imperative,' Krystyna Duniec and Joanna Krakowska argued, Warlikowski 'struck a blow at Polish identity and provided a critical insight into the Christian and Mediterranean mythology in which it is rooted' (2014: xxii). Three victims are staged: Iphigenia, whose father demands the sacrifice of her life for her country; Alcestis, who lays down her life so that her husband might live; and Apolonia Machczyńska, a mother of three who hid 25 Jews during the Nazi occupation. When confronted by an SS officer who offers her the choice to condemn her father for the crime or to denounce herself, Apolonia takes responsibility although it is clear that execution will be the punishment. Apolonia's father, who allows his daughter to make this sacrifice on his behalf, is ultimately unable to bear the burden of guilt and dies four months later, thus rendering her sacrifice doubly superfluous and ineffectual. The adaptation of Greek tragedies also undermines the value of sacrifice. Iphigenia's infantile naivety was emphasized by the adult actor Magdalena Popławska, who wore a young girl's dress and pranced childishly around the stage, ingenuously celebrating a sacrifice that reveals nothing more than her own immaturity and ignorance. Magdalena Cielecka was double cast as Alcestis and Apolonia. Heavily pregnant in both roles, the characters' sacrifices are multiplied by the cost of two lives. This doubling of the sacrifice pushes against familiar narratives in Polish culture that sublimate personal sacrifice and position it as a natural human reflex or national obligation (Ruda, 2009). Warlikowski thus inverts the values traditionally associated with personal sacrifice, rendering selflessness as selfishness, and humility as vanity.

The title, *(A)pollonia*, has a number of overlapping significations. Most obviously, this indexes two characters within the production, the god Apollo and the victim-martyr Apolonia. Drawing parallels between divine and material sublimes, 'Polonia' also refers to Poland as an imagined (sublime) national community during Partitions and periods of occupation and subjugation. Duniec and Krakowska have argued that as a shared fantasy of national identity, 'Polonia' only gained a real body after independence in 1989. This body came at the cost of 'heartbreak, the burden of unfulfilled expectations, and the onus of settling historical accounts and identity dilemmas' (2014: xiv–xv). They contrast 'Polonia' with 'Polin,' the name for Poland in Hebrew and Yiddish. According to legend, Jews forced to migrate as a result of religious intolerance from other parts of Europe read this as '*Po lin*,' or 'stay here,' which was interpreted as a good omen. Polin thus also has mythical resonances, representing the place where for centuries the Jews could feel at home, either by protecting their cultural distinctiveness or through assimilation practices (*ibid.*: xix–xx). Jacek Kopciński suggested that the use of parentheses – (A) – at once suggests and negates the double referent of the title, and this attempt to simultaneously construct and deconstruct is the defining gesture of Warlikowski's production (2009: 8).

In a number of ways, *(A)pollonia* sits in the liminal space between the two parts of *Dybuk*, the historical lacuna separating Ansky and Krall's texts. While *Dybuk* was constructed through metaphor, insinuation, the haunting of the past, *(A)pollonia* directly engages the audience in a dialogic exchange over the Holocaust. Warlikowski remains careful never to fix the limits of contextualization of history and attempts to interrogate rather than facilely undo binaries such as guilt/innocence, justice/injustice, victim/perpetrator and hero/villain that have historical traction in Poland. As opposed to reinforcing these binaries, or simply dissolving them, Warlikowski places them against one another in an unresolved and mutually generative tension. In so doing, the director again uses multiple textual sources and genres without giving priority to a single form of literature, biography, philosophy or historiography. Not only does this give rise to hybrid modes of thinking about Polish/Jewish histories, this further interferes with the renewal or reinforcement of national narratives that disavow culpability or seek easy or definitive solutions to questions of guilt and innocence, remembering and forgetting.

There are some important distinctions between *Dybuk* and *(A)pollonia* that demonstrate the artist's continued dynamic interrogation of Polish/Jewish relations. While *Dybuk* retained a linear plot and narrative across the two sections, *(A)pollonia* makes atemporal leaps across

Figure 4 *(A)pollonia*, directed by Krzysztof Warlikowski. Andrzej Chyra as Hercules. Photo by Magda Hueckel, © Nowy Teatr.

different forms and foundational texts that are loosely juxtaposed without the dramatic guarantee of linearity, which Marta Bryś claimed leaves 'the viewer with a sense of helplessness in the face of such a number of topics and radical theses' (2009: 19). What's more, the withdrawal from excessive emotion in *Dybuk* is replaced by an impassioned and heated incitement against participants in anti-Semitic violence. Bryś suggests that the two prologues offer a distinct change in Warlikowski's thinking about audience and performance function. While *Dybuk* began with stories intimately told by actors no more than a few feet from the edge of the stage that eased spectators into the world of Ansky's play without recourse to the exoticized apparatus of Jewish mysticism and folklore, *(A)pollonia* prevented this kind of participation or identification by violently confronting audiences with the liquidation of the Warsaw ghetto. The latter's opening scene introduces three child mannequins who remain on stage throughout the performance, appearing first as the orphans under the care of Janusz Korczak in the Jewish Orphan's Home in the Warsaw ghetto who are transported to Treblinka, and subsequently as the children of Agamemnon and Clytemnestra, Admetus and Alcestis and Apolonia. These are silent witnesses who will either be sacrificed or will return to offer testimony as interpreters and/or revisionists of the past. The recycling of the mannequins presents the spectator with a peculiar asymmetry in relation to genre and historical specificity. This reoccurrence of the child-mannequins does not suggest the positive actualization of cultural values over time – they never come to adulthood – nor does it reinforce a fatalistic dimension to the narrative, which the double casting of a human actor might more readily suggest. The spectator is given space to imagine their potential destinies as bystanders, victims, heroes or perpetrators. Therefore, the effect of the recycled presence of the mannequins draws the spectator's attention to their own ability to neutralize or frustrate fatalistic repetition compulsions in an effort to conceive of responsible agency or choice.

Not only are victims put on trial, perpetrators are given space to defend their actions. Agamemnon returns from war and is greeted by Clytemnestra in the Polish tradition with bread and salt. Refusing the mantel of heroism, however, Agamemnon desires punishment and wishes to be seen as a murderer despite the fact that as king he is entitled to absolve himself of past crimes and revise the historical record. Maciej Stuhr as Agamemnon confronted the audience with direct address, suggesting that spectators are not morally superior to him simply because they were fortunate enough not to have encountered the same ethical dilemmas. Warlikowski employs this rhetorical convention not in a facile attempt to level the historical playing field by including the excluded voices of perpetrators, but rather to critique the deployment of dubious ethical relativism that underpins revisionist histories and criminal testimonies, such as Adolf Eichmann's testimony in his 1961 trial for crimes against humanity.

The accountability and reliability of discourse is further tested in a long monologue adapted from J.M. Coetzee's 2003 novel *Elizabeth Costello* that draws a parallel between the contemporary treatment of animals for the production of meat and the Jewish genocide. In delivering this speech, Maja Ostaszewska moves between dry academic rhetoric and highly emotive pleas, both of which compete to register as truth claims. On a discursive level Warlikowski offers a critique of the modes in which such claims are produced and circulated; academic rhetoric is privileged at the expense of emotional oratory that is perceived as hysterical or reactive.

These discursive acts are paired with a Righteous Among the Nations ceremony, in which Apolonia is posthumously awarded for saving the lives of Polish Jews. Although this medal signals a heroic act, Ryfka Goldfinger explains in her testimony that Apolonia decided to save her as a young girl only because, unlike her sisters, she had Aryan features. The judge who hears the case for Apolonia's application was played by Andrzej Chyra, whose face was painted with the devilish clown make-up of the Joker from *Batman* comics. Chyra produced a hypocritical spectacle of the historically viable role of this commemorative ritual in determining exoneration. In the background of this scene of judgment, Apolonia is raped and murdered by the SS officer. Overlapping past and present enhances the paradoxes of memory and testimony and the horror of her sacrifice. This is further complicated by the fact that Ryfka's grandson is a soldier in the Israeli army who is willing to kill Palestinians. Warlikowski does not attempt to relativize Holocaust narratives or make a comparison with the Israeli–Palestine conflict. Rather, the director draws attention to the paradoxes of historical trajectories and fates. Saving the life of one person can result in the loss of different lives. Apolonia's son also refuses to forgive Ryfka for placing his mother in a position where she had to sacrifice her life for the Jews she saved. Both in tragic narratives and performative acts of commemoration, the rituals set up to evaluate history fail to reflect the nuanced ethical tensions that mediate collective memory and historical fact, which are embedded in these difficult and multiple discourses of guilt and innocence.

Warlikowski thus not only reveals the inadequacy of such rituals that construct heroism, he also demonstrates how seemingly heroic acts are later rendered ambivalent by the future crimes they engender. It is through these aims – the desublimation of the hero and the ethical paradoxes of fate – that one finds a link to Słobodzianek's project. The gods are not reified, but tempestuous, naughty, selfish and cruel, which is emphasized through the use of internet nicknames (e.g., :pollo:) and Herkules666) and dialogue dominated by sexual innuendo and gallows humor. Projections of filmed close-ups of the actors offer a cinematic contrast to the expansive scale of the stage tragedies, portraying characters as neurotic, ordinary and, ultimately, unheroic. Recording the performance on camera is another mode of documentation open to emotional manipulation. Pairing projected close-ups with offers and refusals of sacrifice, Warlikowski resists uncomplicated empathetic identification with the characters and foregrounds the ideological problem of sacrifice in Polish culture that arises from Christian theology and nineteenth-century Romanticism and martyrology, both of which continue to have widespread currency. The director thus brings to inquiry and places at risk viewers' national and religious commitments.

In the concluding scene, Warlikowski again attempts to place pressure on clear distinctions that bifurcate social and symbolic space. Having spent most of the performance trapped within brightly lit glass and metal cages, the Nowy Teatr actors emerge from these oppressive spaces to sit on the stage to listen to Renatte Jett, a German singer-performer whose music in turn provides relief from and adds tension to the multiple storylines. This is a moment of communion between performer and audience, which Warlikowski later reinvented at the conclusion of *Opowieści afrykańskie według Szekspira* (*The African Tales by Shakespeare*, 2011), when the actors and audience are taught a salsa lesson by Stanisława Celińska. In both examples, the music retains a formal autonomy that has no direct correlation to the preceding action. Warlikowski does not construct a moment of catharsis that relies on the individual's identification with the plot and character, but rather uses music as a means of collective sharing that supplements rather than overrides or disavows memory and provides a measure of critical distance that can form a basis for coalitional responsible action.

What is at stake in this debate over Polish culpability and anti-Semitism is the notion of a collective identity of a people. Nationalism has traditionally been constructed around Romantic motifs that framed Poles as heroic fighters for independence or as victim-martyrs. Pogroms such as the one that occurred in Jedwabne were a break with the Romantic ethos that framed Poland as a savior among nations, a defender of the weak, a mythology that has sustained Polish solidarity through extensive and cruel occupations. Słobodzianek and Warlikowski have tested the elasticity of this mythology, although in dramatically different registers. Both have asked, explicitly and implicitly, whether traditional forms of nationalism acknowledge the guilt of Polish collusion in pogroms, purges and anti-Semitic violence. While Słobodzianek focused on experiences of historical loss that are embedded in specific memories of particular events, Warlikowski draws the viewer's attention to the absence that structures society and is disavowed through sacrifice.

There is always the danger that performance strategies that open up historical questions that are embedded in nuanced social and political specificities to universalized paradigms will end up everywhere and nowhere at once. Universalization of historical specificity can also lend itself all too easily to justifying defense mechanisms, denial strategies and apologetic uses. As opposed to inhibiting genuine critiques of problematic, nationally inflected or distorted historiographies, Słobodzianek and Warlikowski's productions have variously attempted to mitigate the tensions between the particular of the Polish with the more general European or even global in forms that are argumentative and open-ended rather than apodictic.

Notes

1 I choose, along with Paul Vickers (2013), to repeat Halina Filipowicz's gesture of replacing the hyphen that normally connects Polish and Jewish (e.g., Polish-Jewish relations) with a slash (Polish/Jewish). Filipowicz argues that allowing a space to remain between the terms denies the 'possibility for productive interaction,' while the hyphen 'drives a wedge between the two terms.' Alternatively, the slash, she concludes, 'functions as a paradoxical metaphor of both wound and suture' (2001: 3).

2 In 2009, the theatre journal *Notatnik Teatralny* published an issue dedicated to the anti-Semitic events of 1968, which included four new plays. The anniversary of these purges sparked an important political debate and today the government is beginning the process of allowing expelled Jews to recover citizenship. Recent plays dealing with the Polish persecution of Jews that are not analyzed in this chapter, but are worthy of further study, include *Żyd* (*The Jew*, 2008) by Artur Pałyga, staged in Bielsko-Biała, which received the main prize at the festival of Polish contemporary drama in Gdynia in 2008; *Nic co ludzkie* (*Nothing Human*, 2008), produced at In Vitro Theatre in Lublin; Piotr Rowicki's *Przylgnięcie* (Clinging, 2009); an adaptation of *Iwona, księżniczka Burgunda* (*Ivona, Princess of Burgundy*) by Witold Gombrowicz set in the Warsaw Ghetto, staged at the Teatr Dramatyczny in Warsaw (2007). Habima, the National Theatre in Israel, and Teatr Współczesny in Wrocław coproduced *Bat Yam/Tykocin* (2008), which interrogated the complex postwar relations between Jews and Poles. There have also been a number of non-theatre artworks dealing with this subject matter, such as Zofia Lipecka's *After Jedwabne* (2008), a video installation responding to Jan Gross, which has been staged in a number of art galleries.

3 See Romanska (2014) for detailed analyses of Jerzy Grotowski's *Akropolis* and Tadeusz Kantor's *Dead Class* in relation to broader themes and contexts on the Holocaust and Polish culture.

4 First published in Polish in 2000, the English translation was released the following year, 2001.

5 For an excellent overview on the cultural significance of this museum see Stemplowska (2014).

6 Niziołek also expresses his surprise at the marginalization of theatre practices in the study of memory of the Holocaust, especially given the abundance of studies on literature, cinema, visual arts, monuments and museum studies. He also confronts the problem of using terms of theatricality in relation to the Holocaust that treats the theatre as if it were a culturally stable and ahistorical practice (2013b: 34).

7 For a particularly problematic example of such an attempt at closure, see Thompson (2011: 221–35).

8 Another significant play to deal with the Jedwabne debates is *Burmistrz* (*The Mayor*) by Małgorzata Sikorska-Miszczuk (Part 1, 2009; Part 2,

2011). Although Part 1 was given a public reading at the Teatr na Woli in Warsaw in 2009, and in 2011 both parts were produced for Polish State Radio, at the time of publication the play has not been professionally staged.

9 Anna Bikont had also been nominated for the Nike in 2004 for *My z Jedwabnego* (*We from Jedwabne*), the most thorough, well-documented and balanced study of the village. However, Bikont did not win the prize, which might reflect the prevalent apprehension about praising or rewarding a study of Jedwabne at that time.

10 For further discussions of Polish, UK and Lithuanian production histories of *Nasza klasa* see Lease (2012, 2015).

11 It is important to note that it was not until 1997 that a law was passed in Poland entitling Jews to recover property stolen during the war (Gerstenfeld, 2003: 192).

12 See, for example, Sieradzki (2010).

13 The full range of texts adapted for *(A)pollonia* include: Aeschylus' *Oresteia*; Hans Christian Andersen's 'The Story of a Mother'; J.M. Coetzee's *Elizabeth Costello*; Andrzej Czajkowski's 'Mamo, gdzie jesteś?'; Euripides' *Iphigenia in Aulis*, *Heracles* and *Alcestis*; Hanna Krall's 'Pola' in *Tam już nie ma żadnej rzeki* and 'Narożny dom z wieżyczką' in *Żal*; Jonathan Littell's *The Kindly Ones*; Marcin Świetlicki's 'Pobojowisko' in *Zimne kraje. Wiersze 1980–1990*; and Rabindranath Tagore's 'The Post Office.' The production was produced by a number of European theatres and festivals, including Nowy Teatr, the Festival D'Avignon, Narodowy Stary Teatr Kraków, Comédie de Genève, Théâtre Royal de la Monnaie (Brussels), Théâtre National de Chaillot (Paris), Théâtre de Liège and Wiener Festwochen. This international funding also has implications for the universalization of themes on Polish/Jewish relations.

6

Equivalencies of exclusion

Conceptualizing the Polish other has been complicated by the complex coincidence of the country's colonial histories, rebellions and attendant narratives of Polish suffering, marytrdom and victimhood alongside an identification with Western Europe that produces a sense of cultural elitism that distinguishes Poland from Russia. A number of scholars have detected an overlap between the colonizing experiences of language, political economies, labor, resistance and emancipation between postcolonial nations in the Global South and countries formerly governed by or under Russia and later the Soviet Union. One of the earliest and most often cited articles to theorize Poland as a postcolonial space, by literary scholar Clare Cavanagh, took issue with Frederic Jameson's omission of the 'second world' – which Cavanagh refers to as the 'blank spot on the map of modern theory' (2004: 92) – from his definition of modernism and imperialism, the internal dynamics of which are limited to the first and third worlds. Cavanagh recuperates this cultural lacuna by directly addressing Soviet Russia's colonizing policies. In *Niesamowita Słowiańszczyzna* (*Uncanny Slavdom*, 2007) Maria Janion (2007) attempted to think through the silence on postcolonialism for Poland in particular, which has reversed the standard logic of colonial mimicry. Homi K. Bhabha (1994) theorized mimicry as the ambiguous and contradictory intersection in which colonized subjects are pressured to emulate the value system of the colonizing force while simultaneously being denied the agency to fully engage in those identifications, thus insulating hegemonic social relations from contestation. Traditionally, Poland has seen itself as superior to its former colonizer, Russia, identifying instead with Western Europe in a struggle against Russia's perceived cultural inferiority that is framed as a less-civilized 'Asian barbarism' (Janion, 2007: 328). Janion posits this as a longstanding resistance to cultural identification with Slavic nations during the Partitions that was later reinscribed through texts such as Adam Mickiewicz's *Dziady* as a point of mystical enunciation. This evasion of postcolonialism, according to literary theorist David Chioni Moore, is also a response to the Marxist theoretical underpinning of most postcolonial scholars, who have been 'reluctant to make the Soviet Union a French- or British-style villain' (2001: 117). Conversely, the contentiousness of Marxist theory in postcommunist Poland, compounded by an embedded sense of cultural superiority against Russia and a concomitant desire not to be equated with the 'third world' – a hierarchical term that is itself deeply problematic – has certainly forestalled the use of this form of critique (see Korek, 2007: 8). Unsurprisingly, there is some anxiety from scholars who fear that framing East Central European countries as postcolonial implies that these spaces are 'not yet European' (Kuss, 2004: 477). In his essay on anxiety in Polish nationalist rhetoric, Andrew Kier Wise picks up on Ewa Thompson's interpretation of the 'resentment in nationalist commentary about Poland's past' and the ongoing concern regarding threatened sovereignty – which sparked paranoiac debates over eastward EU expansion as another form of Marxist historical determinism – as symptoms of the centrality of colonialism in contemporary Polish discourse (Wise, 2010: 286).

Postcolonial readings of European postcommunist countries are opening up new debates about disempowered subjectivities that offer further challenges to East–West binaries, which can be productively aligned with leftist critiques of class hierarchies. Troubling the congruence of terms in relation to Poland, Moore has proposed the postcolonial category as too narrow and the post-Soviet as too parochial (2001: 112). In addressing the question of whether the postcommunist nations – the former 'second world' in the three-world model made popular during the Cold War – are in fact postcolonial, Gayatri Spivak suggests that the terms 'colonizer' and 'colonized' can be used when 'an alien nation-state establishes itself as ruler, impressing its own laws and systems of education and rearranging modes of production for its own economic benefit' (2006: 828). What makes this particularly difficult in its application to the PRL is the misleading postulation proliferated by Soviet propaganda that East and Central European countries were *voluntarily* taking up and participating in communist ideology. The point is that if research communities assemble themselves around postcolonial theory and identify national culture *as* postcolonial then this has an impact on the way the nation will perceive itself. Janion has argued that the use of the signifier 'postcolonial' will help shift the focus away from the cultural superiority embedded in dominant national-Catholic discourses, that refuse to renounce restrictive understandings of Polishness in relation to the megalomania of national messianism predicated on a disdain for the other that will actualize a more multicultural, multiethnic and pluralistic country (2007: 329).

The Polish-literature scholar Stanley Bill has critiqued the ethnic essentialism that lies at the heart of the debates around postcolonialism in Poland. Scholars such as Ewa Thompson and Dariusz Skórczewski have argued that hybridity and deferential mimicry are negative factors in Polish society today, which can be particularly detected in the cosmopolitan elite who slavishly imitate Western Europe and the US as cultural models. These arguments are inconsistent and find dubious means to justify why Russia, the most recent occupier, failed to assert its cultural hegemony and, thereby, does not function as a model for imitation. Bill (2014) observes that postcolonial theory has been useful for Polish conservatives because of its essentializing tendencies, which have allowed for the defense of traditional Catholic values, an inherent, ethnic Polishness, and a '"primordialist" understanding of nation against new multiculturalist, individualist and civic models of identity.' Often using Polish Romanticism alongside postcolonial theory, an opposition between authentic and inauthentic identity is modeled by conservatives on a distinction between 'creoles,' the leftist intellectual urban elite, and 'natives,' everyone else. Bill is also sensitive to the mode in which conservative Polish thinkers attempt to abandon or disavow the leftist and Marxist roots of much postcolonial theory in order to turn their critique on the remnants of Soviet-enforced communism in current political structures rather than on problematic forms of capitalism. On the opposite side of the political spectrum, Janion strongly advocates for a conception of Polishness that is rooted in pre-Christian Slavic origins, perceiving the original colonial encounter with Latin civilization and enforced conversion to Christianity as the most crucial legacy in postcolonial arguments. In both cases, Polishness continues to be perceived and constructed through purely ethnic terms, so that on neither side of the polarized political spectrum is the conception of Polishness opened up to non-ethnic Poles. While Polish culture is something ethnic others might participate in, the ethnic Pole is involuntarily tied to the national community. As a result, Bill observes, even 'the most inclusive models imply that Polish culture – though it should seek to welcome members of other ethnic groups – is above all the inheritance of ethnic Poles' (*ibid.*).

The postcolonial turn in Poland has been taken up in the theatre in modes that challenge the applicability of the nation's status under this rubric. I will consider two productions that offer exacting challenges to a postcolonial Poland through their assertion of the nation's co-opting of European colonial fantasies with particular reference to Africa: Weronika Szczawińska's *W pustyni I w puszczy z Sienkiewicza I innych* (*In Desert and Wilderness with Sienkiewicz and Others*, 2011) and Krzysztof Warlikowski's *Opowieści afrykańskie według Szekspira* (*The African Tales by Shakespeare*, 2011). What I intend to unpack is the lack of a critical vocabulary and methodology in an approach to cross-racial casting that undermines the democratic project of postcolonial critique and problematizes pluralistic notions of community and national identification that cloak strong ethnic underpinnings.

I rely on Katrin Sieg's excellent study on ethnic drag in the former West Germany to explicate the use of blackface in these productions as a means of producing new discourses around race. Sieg defines ethnic drag as the performance of race as masquerade, which 'erases and redraws boundaries posturing as ancient and immutable,' facilitating 'the exercise and exchange of power' that is not reducible to a single referent, but that 'mediates a range of social conflicts in modernity' inclusive of the clash between socialism and democracy after 1989 (2009: 2–3). Sieg supports the notion that mimetic styles of representation reproduce 'the operations of racial ideology, whereas cross-racial masquerade contests or even transforms social relations organized around race' (*ibid.*: 5). While it is certainly true that critical discourses on any form of cross-racial performance must be self-conscious of the 'ideological operations and social effects organized around race' (*ibid.*), Sieg also enjoins performers to consider the dramaturgical forms in which masquerades are embedded and furthermore to be sensitive to the political projects such forms of denaturalization of identity support. Therefore, just as drag for Judith Butler requires context for its political effect, Sieg does not defend masquerade as intrinsically subversive. In the analysis of the following productions, I will demonstrate how – despite a determined effort on the part of some leftist theatre-makers to denaturalize race in an attempt to combat the ethnic underpinnings of nationalist constructions of Polish cultural identity and exclusionism – the lack of theorization on racial discourses in Poland and the concomitant absence of a postcolonial performance history that engages with multiethnic perspectives through casting have resulted in the arrogation of racial critique exclusively to white bodies in a mode that invalidates that critique and redoubles the exceptionalism of whiteness as the founding basis of representation that relegates other racial and ethnic subjectivities to the background.

In Desert and Wilderness

Weronika Szczawińska's *W pustyni i w puszczy z Sienkiewicza i innych* was directed by Bartosz Frąckowiak at the Teatr Dramatyczny in Wałbrzych in 2011. In preparation for the production, Szczawińska and Frąckowiak spent more than a year gathering material from cultural texts on Africa and postcolonialism, which was uploaded on a blog that functioned as an interactive seminar, archiving comments and discussions, literary tropes, and the accidental 'hits' and discoveries from online searches. The performance is organized around Henryk Sienkiewicz's 1912 novel *W pustyni i w puszczy* (*In Desert and Wilderness*), which follows the African adventures of European children of engineers supervising the maintenance of the Suez Canal, a Polish 14-year-old boy, Staś, and an eight-year-old English girl, Nell, during the Mahdist War of 1881–99. The plot of the novel follows the kidnapping of Staś and Nell after an anti-British insurrection in Port Said by a group of Arabs hoping to exchange the children for Fatima, a relative of the Muslim preacher Mahdi, who led the rebellion. Having survived a treacherous voyage through the desert and jungle, the Arabs, incapable of wielding the weapon themselves, give Staś a shotgun to kill a dangerous lion. After the boy shoots the animal he turns the gun on his captors. After murdering the Arabs, the children escape and again make their way across wilderness and desert with the help of two faithful slaves, Kali and Mea. As a means of producing a postcolonial backwards reading of Sienkiewicz's base text, Szczawińska interwove quotations from authors such as Ryszard Kapuściński, a Polish journalist and travel writer whose colonial leanings have only recently been fully debated; Joseph Conrad's *Heart of Darkness*, the vexed novel of colonial encounter that posits the ostensible impenetrability of the Congo for the European; and J.M. Coetzee's *Elizabeth Costello*. Historian of philosophy Stefan Swieżawski argued that while Sienkiewicz was undoubtedly a talented writer, the prototypes he espoused, which are 'full of contempt and hatred for other nations' (2000: 144) that many generations of Poles have been raised to read in a non-critical light, are deeply troubling. Sienkiewicz not only fully subscribed to colonial fantasies of African inferiority and exoticism, he also supported the Polish claim to the Borderlands that are consonant with the articulation of cultural superiority in Polish national identity. Swieżawski suggests that by adopting such ideals, 'we [Poles] will never become a nation that is open, tolerant, ecumenical' (*ibid.*). Janion similarly asserted that the division between a Sienkiewicz and post-Sienkiewicz mentality reveals drastic forms of tension between national-religious social *cohesion* and the increasing cultural *diversity* of contemporary societies (2007: 327–8).

While Poland does not have a direct history as a colonizer, a subject that is destabilized by Polish colonizing claims to territories in the northeastern Borderlands and parts of western Ukraine, Szczawińska and Frąckowiak highlight the accountability of a history of national fantasies of establishing African colonies that privilege Christian moral values over a perceived African primitivism. This builds on a much older perception of Russia as a bastion of Asian barbarism in opposition to civilized European culture, a binary that, as I mentioned earlier, complicates Poles' identification as Slavs. Frąckowiak placed particular emphasis on the concluding section from Sienkiewicz's novel in which Staś, having safely returned to Europe, fantasizes about a return to the heart of black Africa, where he dreams of establishing a Polish colonial outpost. Frąckowiak argues that this passage refers directly to the colonial phantasm, which he and Szczawińska used as a starting point for the construction of the performance. This phantasm is grounded in a 'very extensive collection of stereotypes of otherness and alienation' that ascribe masculine virtue to the oppression of the 'savage' whose vulgar existence hinges upon cultural hypocrisy and intellectual naivety. Against this, Staś is portrayed in the novel as courageous and quick-witted, the ultimate survivor, while femininity is articulated through Nell as the apotheosis of noble European lineage and gentile manners (cited in Gruszczyński, 2012). The theatre-makers detected within these fantasies a culturally bounded synthesis of martyrdom and heroism and the neo-imperial aspirations of a postcolonial country. In a perverse twist, Staś – whose gender and race articulate the elevation of the white, heterosexual Catholic Pole in mainstream Polish culture – imagines assembling African legions that would liberate partitioned Poland and restore the nation's autonomy, while retaining its own colonial presence in Africa. Reviewing the production, Piotr Grzymisławski (2012) aligned Staś' colonial fantasy as a 'necessary fiction' (Homi Bhabha) that serves to uplift the Polish spirit as a compensation for the humiliation suffered by colonialism. Grzymisławski further suggests that the presence of Sienkiewicz's novel in school curricula in Poland attests to the imperialist fantasies that still lie dormant in Polish culture, which makes it a potent case study for postcolonial critique. As Jolanta Kowalska observed in *Teatr*, Szczawińska and Frąckowiak 'invest in Staś' imperial visions in a the broader context of Polish dreams of a superpower' (2012: 39), which in the production refers to the pre-WWII claims of the Liga Morska i Kolonialna (Maritime and Colonial League), who petitioned the creation of Polish settlements in Brazil, Peru, Liberia, Mozambique and French territories in Africa. The League is represented on stage by a band of delusional and patriotic Polish Scouts, a bigoted militia intent on building a replica of Wawel Castle in the Saharan desert. Kali, Staś' devoted African servant, played by a white actor, produces a homage to the Scouts, beating out the incantation from Part II of Mickiewicz's *Dziady* on a tam-tam drum. Although Staś' aspirations for colonial domination are neither innocent nor without historical context, Kowalska argued that this hero (killing in the name of the honor and the fatherland) does not fit into any contemporary canons of patriotic education. While this claim may be justifiable, the antagonism established between the Polish Scouts and Kali produces two discursive bodies that are at first pitched against one another and then coalesced through the reference to Mickiewicz that places emphasis on the existence of current racialized structures of national identification. Frąckowiak is interested in the way that racism is disavowed and embedded in Polish cultural discourse, which 'exercises discreet, invisible power over our perceptions, behaviors and choices' (cited in Gruszczyński, 2012). Essentially, Frąckowiak is suggesting a disjuncture between understandings of power in the cultural and social field. While a literal reading of the performance might focus on the enforcement of power through coercion and violence, Frąckowiak sides with a Foucauldian theorization of power as generatively normative. Kowalska misses the point in her singular focus on the style of the Scouts' fervent patriotism, which is indeed reliant on outdated Romantic paradigms of insurgence and revolutionary zeal, rather than the form of Polish patriotism that cannot be divorced from the presence of ethnic drag.

In establishing a critique of essentialist notions of race and ethnicity, Frąckowiak used a Brechtian distancing effect, in which actors ostentatiously show character rather than mimetically inhabiting their theatrical roles. Wojciech Niemczyk makes no more claim to an authentic, mimetic representation of Staś than Andrzej Kłak does in his racial masquerade as Kali. However, despite this dramaturgical structure, the performance does not corroborate a concern for mutual recognition of Kali's racial difference. Although Szczawińska and Frąckowiak oppose the European colonization of Africa and the Polish claim to the Borderlands from the double perspective of Staś and the Scouts, this juxtaposition does not offer a place from which the subaltern (Kali or Mea) is given a voice outside of the texts written for them by white authors. Rather, the African other is caricatured through and ventriloquized by white Polish actors, whose white bodies are assumed to be blank canvases onto which Polish-European fantasies of African primitivism can be directly projected. Even if this is intended as a self-consciously anti-racist gesture – that is, a reflexive critique of exclusionary claims to Polish national identity built on a dangerous notion of cultural superiority and ethnic purity – reproducing racist fantasies on white bodies implicitly favors and privileges those bodies.

This problem is not resolved through the staging of Africa (Ewelina Zak) and Europe (Agnieszka Kwietniewska) as two central meta-theatrical figures that comment directly on the geographical positioning of these spaces in the Polish cultural imagination. Piled around the set, fragrant mounds of coffee connote Western consumption and exploitation of the Global South's resources. At the beginning of the performance, the character Africa appears as an amorphous form of writhing blankets with recognizably 'ethnic' patterns. While the scenographic depiction of Africa remains deliberately artificial, signifying 'expropriation and dispossession' (Kowalska, 2012), the character Africa moors this referent to a particular body, a white body in black greasepaint. Ewelina Zak first exposes her darkened arms before revealing that her entire body has been covered in dark brown make-up, accompanied by an 'afro' wig, bright red lipstick and tight black leggings. One Polish critic celebrated this figure as a 'fantastic, ambivalent creation' (Szpecht, 2011). While Africa is intended to be perceived as allegorical, the fact of the dark paint on the actor's body and the assertion of her gender as female is far from ambivalent, although it is indeed fantastical. Europe, who remains visibly unmarked by make-up, is staged as a prim white woman with a parasol to shield her from the damaging rays of the sun. While the ambivalence of Africa was unanimously noted by critics, the semiotic transparency of Europe remained overlooked or unrecognized. The privilege of mimesis is thus unintentionally arrogated to the European body, even if the production efficiently stages national fantasies of otherness embodied by Africa and the African native. In conceiving whether an anti-naturalist staging escapes racist ideologies, it is enough to consider how Europe's white dress does not perform whiteness under the same conditions that the white actor's painted body as Africa performs blackness. This equivalency is undermined by the direct relationship that prevails between a symbolic practice and its social effect. Rather than simply detaching the referent from its sign, Sieg argues that the use of racial masquerade often assumes the universal performativity of whiteness. What is at stake is not an attempt to give voice to the African other, whose subjectivity is blanked out in its reduction to the racist content of Sienkiewicz's text, cultural associations and literary tropes. The white body functions as a universal background, 'an uncritical, unmarked notion of whiteness' (Sieg, 2009: 185), onto which racist fantasies are displayed and made explicit without any attempt to portray the subjective position, attitude or voice of the racialized outsider. This is more than a simple plea for biologically accurate casting, which if used in this performance would quite possibly reproduce a mimetic representation of race that thinly masks an essentialist notion of cultural purity that would only enhance the naturalization of the master–slave hierarchy in colonial power structures. The point is rather that the capacity to erode, rather than simply reproduce, racist ideologies relies on a place for the voice of the subaltern to be heard, a point of subjective identification beyond objective demonstration for the purposes of (white) self-critique. When the Scouts use paint to mark the female slave Mea's white body, turning it 'black' through the violence of their blows that leaves dark handprints, which, when conjoined, become the masquerade of the actress' ethnic drag, the category of whiteness remains uncontested, essentialist rather than constructed, while blackness is seen as an *effect* of colonization. Appropriating these discursive bodies unwarrantably claims both the means and the ends of representation, thus favoring the colonization of African subjectivity over an understanding of cross-racial relations. What's more, as the Scouts paint Mea into 'blackness,' they unleash a stream of linguistic associations such as black mamba, Black Madonna (whose shrine in Częstochowa is the most popular site of Catholic pilgrimage in Poland), soot, ebony and asphalt. This attempt to produce wider resonances through language as a means of making explicit the production of social discourse and the way in which meaning is inflected through unconscious or unintended associations is again reliant on an overdetermined blackness that belies the more benign presence of whiteness on stage. While the associations with blackness are largely pejorative, whiteness remains morally pure or salutary, as demonstrated by Europe's pristine dress and the (white) quinine that saves Nell's life from (black) malaria.

In the binaries that are elaborated, one side is explicitly undervalued (female/male, black/white, Africa/Europe) in several modes that disavow the ongoing marginalization of racial others. At one point, Staś demands that Kali don a starched white collar, which is intended to contrast comically with this mud-splashed skin and colorful rags, in order to communicate with him on a rational, ostensibly 'equal' level, although this mutuality remains conditional and one-sidedly predetermined. While the postcolonial strategy here is clear, the processes of representation are confused. In this exchange, the intention to foreground colonial mimicry, which is later extended to Catholicism and nationalism when a crucifix and Polish flags are imposed upon Kali, is successfully elaborated by the parody of Staś as an archetypal colonial hero. Kali, however, disrupts the intended parody through a type of 'double mimicry,' that is, a white actor assuming the role of the subaltern who attempts to assimilate and reproduce the values of the white colonizer. The explicit parody of Staś is diverted in Kali's 'double mimicry,' which restricts the analysis of race to those identified as other in Polish nationalism. In a corresponding mode, racist fantasies are depicted ambiguously when Nell cedes to her sexual desire for an eroticized 'savage,' named Ostatni Czarny (Last Black Man), played by an athletic white actor in black greasepaint. The appeal of Ostatni Czarny for Nell resides in his unimpeded access to virile masculinity, not conditioned or emasculated by European civilization. Nell expresses her lust for this mythical figure through moans, grunts and sexually explicit movements. While this offers a critique on the fantasy that equates racial difference with sexual difference, the effect of the subversion is reversed when Nell paints her own skin with black make-up and declares, 'Woman is the nigger of the world.' The critic Magda Szpecht asserted that the gender message in this representation, in which 'Africa is a woman, and the woman – Africa,' articulates a broader idea expressed within the infamous phrase coined by Yoko Ono that later became the eponymous duet with John Lennon, yoking women's oppression in patriarchy to racial subjugation. This unfortunate comparison inadvertently reinforces precisely the racism it seeks to indict. As Sieg has argued in a different context, the 'adding on of "race" to other categories of difference, such as class and gender, does not move towards a social dialectic, but stalls it' (2009: 185). Ono's song was attacked for collapsing experiences of gender and racial subjugation into an equivalent and self-identical category, while signifying the racist term of abuse as the ultimate position of subjective indignity. Similarly, Nell's performance not only fails to excavate the song's latent racism, marking the female body with black paint redoubles the political investment in the positioning of blackness as a universal category of exclusion and oppression equivalent to uneven gender relations.

While the production offers a critique of Polish martyrology and heroism, the use of racial masquerade is arrogated to white Polish bodies and there is no alternative parallel performance from actors of color. Is this a refuge from 'raging Eurocentrism,' as suggested by Szpecht, or merely a distorted picture of Europe's self-image through its racist fantasies? Ultimately, the space for the co-presence of the abject African subjects (Kali and Mea) alongside the implied marginalization of the Polish Scouts, whose bigoted patriotism may be read as an indirect response to their own painful experience of colonial oppression, does offer a vantage point on traditional representations of Polish suffering, which is conferred a sublimated position in Polish culture. Unlike the Romantic Polish hero or his female counterpart, Matka Polka, the suffering and humiliation suffered by the black Africans is a standard and unremarkable aspect of their reality that offers no salvationary future in return. While Polish nationalism is challenged, there is not an equal contestation of the foundational whiteness on which it is predicated that would open up new opportunities for cross-racial relations, which is precisely what a postcolonial intervention into Sienkiewicz requires in a multiethnic Poland. As a result, the searing critique of white Polish patriotism and Eurocentrism is undermined by the absence of a concomitant position for the subaltern, which implies an inclination for the white leftist intellectual to intercede into race discourses that favor her.

Phallic divestiture

Similar concerns over the presumed reversal – and potential preservation – of discourses that link racial purity, enforced masculinity and Polish ethnicity were played out in Krzysztof Warlikowski's *Opowieści afrykańskie według Szekspira* for the Nowy Teatr. Crucially, the production was preceded by a public controversy over its advertisement poster, designed by Zbigniew Libera, one of the most significant contemporary Polish visual artists, who is considered to be a precursor of 'sztuka krytyczna' (critical art).[1] The poster depicted two naked white European men painted with bright mock-African patterns that call to mind Kali in *W pustyni i w puszczy z Sienkiewicza i innych*, posing for a female Japanese tourist in blue jeans and an American army sweatshirt with a large camera.

The picture attempts to reverse the current logic of global tourism that positions Europeans as the archetypal tourists who take pleasure in an appreciation of exoticized, abject cultures that simultaneously affirm her superiority while demanding her pity. Libera explained that the 'Africa' he attempted to depict in the poster is located in the obscure phantasmatical region wedged between the standard photographs of African refugee camps that portray emaciated children covered in flies and Leni Riefenstahl's erotically charged photographs of the Nuba tribe in Sudan (cited in Urbaniak, 2011). Poland is here rendered as a tourist site for the Japanese who will ogle Polish 'natives,' thus putting them in the position of Riefenstahl's Nuba tribesmen, whose exotic presence is displayed for the pleasure of Asian consumption. In an interview, Libera claimed that the poster addressed his anxiety about the future of 'white Europe.' Liege, the Belgian city where the production premiered, was mourned by Libera as a space where 'whites no longer rule,' where one finds more people of color on the street than the 'native' white European. Libera sums up the intention of the poster: while the 'whites go wild,' the 'yellow woman goes white.' Not only is this language glaringly racist, it also implicitly propagates the paranoid myth of Polish victimization that much of Warlikowski's work seeks to deconstruct. The status of Riefenstahl's photographs far from being compromised in Libera's poster is rather redoubled, revealing a foundational and unquestioned allegiance to white subjectivity. The body is not shown 'dispassionately' as Libera claims, but, as a result of its circulation through reference to Riefenstahl's photographs that reinvigorates an eroticized reading of the Nuba tribe, again articulates racial difference as sexual difference. Beyond the obvious problem of the ideological task of placing white Polish men as abject objects in the economies of global tourism, which requires the displacement of a racist phantasm of 'Africa' with a dystopic post-white Europe, is the obvious failure of the artist to offer a critique of the European imaginary of 'Africa,' which is confined to a refugee camp and Riefenstahl's problematic aggregation of racial and sexual difference. Libera defended himself against accusations of pornography (the exposure of penises on a public poster) by explaining that he had interpreted Warlikowski's production as the 'story of a dying white man and his fear of the "murzyn chuj"' ('negro dick'). However, the Polish media's preoccupation with the controversy over the public exposure of male genitalia was not only misguided, it deflected the discussion from addressing the deeply racist vision underpinning the poster, which blatantly betrays a real anxiety about the end of the current world order predicated on white privilege and domination through the portrayal of the European as an alienated 'Orientalist.'

This debate cannot be divorced from Warlikowski's production, even if Warlikowski attempts to combat the central ambivalences offered by the poster. *Opowieści afrykańskie* was a large-budget adaptation of three Shakespeare texts, *Merchant of Venice*, *Othello* and *King Lear*. Not constricted to Polish cultural intelligibility, the production was intended to be accessible in various European festivals and on global tours. The adaptation is dramaturgically crafted around the casting of a single actor, Adam Ferency, in the roles of Lear, Shylock and Othello in the interweaving and intertextual editing of the three plays. Originally billed as *Trylogia wykluczonych* (*Trilogy of Exclusion*), the title was later amended to *The African Tales by Shakespeare*, which prompted the critic Aleksander Pyrkosz to ask, 'Where is Africa?' Warlikowski claimed that the 'Africa' in his production was as abstract as the 'Poland' in Alfred Jarry's *Ubu Roi* (1896) (cited in Goźliński, 2011). However, while Poland might be a nebulous and metaphorical presence in Jarry's early absurdist drama, it nevertheless directly figures in the plot. Africa, on the other hand, in Warlikowski's adaptation is not directly invoked in either *King Lear* nor *The Merchant of Venice*. Just as with Libera's poster, in which the abject colonized figure is a stand-in for the African other, the Africa in the performance's title is the basic referent for exclusion of all foreigners. Africa is thus both at once indefinable and overdetermined. Polish critics went to some lengths to theorize the performance, although their attempts are limited by the lack of critical discourses on race and racial masquerade in the Polish cultural field. Drewniak (2012) observed that by using the categories of 'Jew', 'Old Man' and 'Black', Warlikowski tested these categories of exclusion to detect whether those excluded by the community are automatically carriers of virtue and goodness, or whether the stigma of otherness is simply an excuse for arrogance or usurpation. Marcin Kościelniak (2011), on the other hand, argued that despite the production being billed as the 'Trilogy of Exclusion,' Warlikowski used his standard method of deconstructive textual intrusion to tease out concealed motivations and power relations, with the structure of scenes operating above the level of Shakespeare's plots, an experiment that was not overtly concerned with exclusion. Małgorzata Grzegorzewska (2012) maintained that the production was ultimately about 'existential loneliness,' while Aleksander Pyrkosz (2012) called it 'an existential concept of human frailty' in which Warlikowski takes on the role of the anatomist of human misery. This focus on the interiority of the characters diverts attention away from the ideological function of the normative discourses in operation. Ferency does not attempt to show the audience the 'secret depths' of Othello and, equally, the community does not simply fail to include Othello, rather his exclusion is its constitutive feature. That is to say, as opposed to a character produced through psychological depth, Othello is the object of exclusion on which the community finds its material grounds. As these three characters (Lear/Shylock/Othello) have little in common, thematically or otherwise, the specificity of European fantasies of Africa suggested by the title becomes the synecdoche for universal cultural exclusion that is coalesced through the conglomerate anti-hero, *the* universalist, humanist subject. The intention of the adaptation is not to read these three characters exclusively or individually, rather as a new complex, multifaceted figure; an intention that requires an equalizing of each position of exclusion that is compounded by the casting of a single actor, Adam Ferency, to embody all three roles. Interestingly, only one critic, Dorota Wyżyńska (2011), pointed out the decidedly different status of Ferency playing Othello, as opposed to Shylock and Lear.

Taken on their own, Warlikowski's interrogation of each play and character offers a range of social critiques. However, the collapsing of the three into a single, multivalent but coherent referent indicates that although each experience of exclusion has its own cultural particularities, exclusion itself is framed as a universal category. What is left out of this adaptation that conjoins Lear/Shylock/Othello is the historical weight of representation that each particularity conveys, alongside the attendant questions of agency embedded within these categories of representation. Although Warlikowski rejects traditional theatre practices based on mimetic naturalism and unified characterization, it is particularly suggestive that Lear and Shylock were not physically distinguished with any attributes to mark their social exclusion. Alternatively, Ferency painted his head and hands black in order to play Othello. The figure of the Jew on the Polish stage, which I give attention throughout Chapter 5, is differently configured from Lear, primarily here the mental and physical breakdown of an ageing monarch, both of which are divorced from the 'black face' Othello and the ethical questions of racial masquerade this form prompts. The painting of Othello's face and hands makes his 'blacking up' complete when he wears his military uniform, the only parts of his body that are visible in the public sphere. As Othello, Ferency exposes his white body beneath the military uniform as he slowly undresses down to his underwear, thus foregrounding the constructedness of the black make-up on his hands and head. This directly opposes the role of Belize in Warlikowski's production of *Angels in America* (2007), in which spectators were meant to be suspend their disbelief when the white actor (Rafał Maćkowiak) wore brown make-up to signify his differentiated ethnicity.[2]

Figure 5 Equivalencies of exclusion, drag and black face in *Opowieści afrykańskie według Szekspira* (*The African Tales by Shakespeare*), directed by Krzysztof Warlikowski. Photo by Magda Hueckel, © Nowy Teatr.

If Othello is publicly black and privately white, it is not enough to simply draw attention to the scenic constructions of race that are intended to highlight the problems of Shakespeare's text and its production histories as well as the paranoid and racist energies fueling Polish nationalism. As in *W pustyni i w puszczy*, black skin is thus not only excessively and unduly determined as a sign of foreignness, as always-already excluded, but also as the totalizing referent of oppression, which indicates in the Polish cultural sphere there is no black that is integrated, assimilated, unmarked or liberated. As a result, while there is an attempt to deconstruct fantasies of the black other that underwrite ethnically produced Polish nationalism, there is no recourse to equally deconstruct current formations of Polish whiteness.

The problem of uneven equivalencies is equally exposed in the treatment of gender. Warlikowski commissioned new speeches for Desdemona, Portia and Cordelia by the Canadian-Lebanese writer Wajdi Mouawad, as well as additional text edited from J.M. Coetzee, particularly from his novel *Summertime* (2010) that attempt to focus the spectator's attention on the patriarchal structure of Shakespeare's texts. While Warlikowski offers the prerogative of speech to the female characters, he does not extend the same opening of racist discourse to

Othello. Lear's loss of an authoritative voice is coupled with the restitution of the lost or marginalized voices of these injured or ill-treated women, who reject patriarchal models of family, obedience and care. While the women are offered roles beyond 'the schematic position as victims of tradition, discrimination and violence' (Szpecht, 2012), Othello remains singularly embedded within discourses that emblematize white paranoia around racial others. The adaptation does not offer a Butlerian critique of the performativity of gender roles, as Warlikowski attempted in his 2001 production of Sarah Kane's *Cleansed*, but is instead invested in the ethics of representation of silenced female characters in Shakespeare's plays that casts women performers to make space for women's voices. The racial masquerade required for Ferency's embodiment of Othello on the other hand *does* appear to engage with a critique of racist discourse that puts pressure on assumptions of biological essentialism by divorcing the referent of race from the actor's body. Gender and race are therefore treated to opposing dramaturgical structures that variously rely on mimesis and masquerade, empathy and analytical distancing. It may be that in both cases the conventionality of social roles are emphasized, the economic dependencies of the traditional family unit exposed, but Othello's social role is configured through a white body while women's social roles are ascribed to women's bodies. Racial ascription performed by ethnic Poles carries profound ideological weight. Polish nationality is not depicted as an aggregation of disparate ethnicities and races, nor is whiteness detached from understandings of national identity, and the world of male domination in the plays is not synonymous with the postcolonial questions of racial superiority. To subsume them under the same category is to deny the racial privilege attributed to the female characters, even if they are radically subjugated on the basis of their gender.

Unsurprisingly, the phallus becomes a key signifier of racial difference, social power and the construction of community, which requires the symbolic castration of Ferency's transmutable character. The trope of the phallus and castration returns through each section of the production. Castration determined through Othello's racial masquerade, however, evokes a very different history of oppression and subject formation than through Lear and Shylock. For Lear, the phallus loses its discursive power in the penultimate scene when Cordelia has to wash her father's old and flaccid penis while he lays supine in a hospital bed after a tracheal surgery that leaves him speechless. Shylock's public castration is figured through the trial of Bassanio, which culminates in the Jew's loss of all his worldly possessions. The homosexual relationship between Antonio and Bassanio is displayed through erotic foreplay that includes fellatio and Antonio later displays his penis for Portia as a sign that she may claim his body only, but never his heart. The phallus thus belongs solely to the Christian male and Shylock's attempts to co-opt it (the pound of flesh) only testify to his constitutive impotency. Although Shylock has to tolerate the humiliation of the unrestrained anti-Semitism that surrounds him, Othello is always removed from the directly racist jokes that frame white paranoia about his sexual and, by association, political power, largely characterized through obscene references to his penis.

While Lear is castrated through the loss of his voice and physical power and Shylock is castrated by the letter of the (Christian) law, Warlikowski constructed a new scene for Othello that specifically highlights white paranoia around black sexual potency. Set in a gentleman's club, in which Iago, Lodovico and Cassio tell racist jokes and objectify and humiliate Emilia and Desdemona – who arrives at the club dressed in a turban, print dress, clunky gold earrings and a large necklace – Cassio attempts to wrest back masculine power, which he interprets as the improper domain of the black general, whose political power is seen by his white subordinates to be predicated on his sexual power, depicted through paranoid black-penis jokes. Desdemona as the carrier of racial purity must first be humiliated for transgressing racial boundaries by having a black husband and wearing 'African' clothing before ultimately being recuperated as a fellow white European. First Cassio masturbates as he openly fantasizes about Desdemona's ideal feminine beauty before he and the other men provoke her into dancing in a sexualized pseudo-tribal style that escalates in her impersonation of a chimpanzee. The ritual humiliation of Desdemona plays the double role of punishing her as Othello's disobedient wife and undermining Othello's sexual prowess, while also indicting white women who consort with black men. When Othello arrives and finds Desdemona exhausted and upset on the floor in the aftermath of this dance he does not understand what has occurred and incorrectly interprets the event as a sexual provocation, which stokes his violent jealousy. The theme of marital jealousy is reversed and becomes of secondary importance. Rather, as Aleksandra Spilkowska (2013) argues, the subcutaneously palpable jealousy is transferred onto a white society, who become the collective personification of a jealous husband that cannot tolerate the intrusion of the racial other into their space. Differently read, Othello's all-consuming jealousy could be understood as an expression of his lack of agency, which is registered as castration in this scene.

This is evidenced by a new monologue written for Othello, in which he explains that white men cuckold and castrate black men in an effort to control the phallus, demonstrating Othello's own investment in white paranoia. It is no coincidence that his death immediately follows this scene. This phallic divestiture suggests the inevitability of Othello surrendering/being deprived of his virility by the normative structure of racist white supremacy. Othello's death, which only strengthens rather than subdues his phallic power, provokes Iago's fear of miscegenation: 'Since you have ignored my nakedness, your grandsons will have kinked hair, and their mouths will swell up. They will walk in the nude, and their genitals will hang indecently long.' Phallic divestiture is thus tied to the loss of racial purity. Libera's inadvertent misinterpretation of this scene resulted in his unfortunate poster that sided directly with Iago's racist paranoia rather than its critique, which signals the fraught discourse around race in Poland that continues to be perilously undertheorized. Warlikowski works against the poster, but is nevertheless guilty of universalizing race in a mode that can be opposed to Brecht, who problematically understood race as the one referent that remains firmly connected to the natural world. Unlike Warlikowski's important work in the establishment of gay and queer counterpublics that establish historical trajectories of gay identities, new modes of feminism and the opening out of constrained and fragmented Polish/Jewish relations, race is dehistoricized in *African Tales* and used as a means to express a universal social marginalization of otherness that required more nuanced adjustments to notions of positionality.

Many critics were baffled by the final scene of the adaptation, in which Shakespeare's diegetic world is left behind and Stanisława Celińska leads a salsa lesson for performers and audience members. Perhaps one way of interpreting this conceptually obtuse ending is to consider the dance lesson as signifying the ruins of the paternal function. The death of Lear that immediately precedes this scene does not make the experience of community redundant, rather the salsa lesson attempts a different master signifier around which community is organized and understood. Constructing power horizontally rather than vertically (Lear), the salsa lesson is seen to usher in a new horizon of community embodied by joy and amusement in a shared space that is transnational and feminist. Szymon Spichalski (2012) compared this ending with the final scene of *Angels in America*, the optimism of which signals the establishment of a new sensibility, the positive affirmation of life in the face of death that is open-ended and inclusive. There is also no injunction here to produce 'community' per se, but rather an invitation for a temporally limited interaction that does away with the exclusionary demands of community-building.

Trans-European migration

Equally crucial to this discussion is a consideration of the recent phenomenon of immigration into Poland that have produced attendant xenophobic discourses. Aneta Kyzioł (2008) suggested that Dorota Masłowska's *Dwoje biednych Rumunów mówiących po polsku* (*A Couple of Poor, Polish-Speaking Romanians*) flawlessly addressed contemporary national complexes around economic migrants. Controversial for her direct style and use of street vernacular, Masłowska was commissioned to write the play as part of the 2006 TR/PL festival at the TR Warszawa designed to diagnose new social, political and moral challenges for Poland in the wake of EU accession. The action follows two young Poles (Parcha, a television actor, and Dżina, an unemployed single mother) pretending to be Romanian migrants on an all-night drug-fueled road trip. In Warsaw, the play was initially given a staged reading, starring Masłowska herself as the teenage mother, and directed by Przemysław Wojcieszek, who saw the text as a manifesto for the dispossessed generation born in the 1980s. Roman Pawłowski (2006), a strong proponent of Masłowska, saluted the inexhaustible deposits of humor in her work, which allows an audience 'to look deep into the psyche of an average Pole, shaped by television, the Church and the Catholic family.' The young novelist's celebrity attracted a large and enthusiastic crowd at the reading, and the play was formally produced at the TR later that year, and at the Teatr Studio in Warsaw in 2013, directed by Agnieszka Glińska.

At many turns in the play, the plausibility of the existence of 'Polish-speaking Romanians' is called into question. Rather than remarking on a scarcity of economic migrants in Poland, the 'Polish-speaking Romanian' functions as a structural social fantasy through which Masłowska critiques a deeply embedded intolerance towards heterogeneity. 'Romanian' thus stands in for an imaginary figure that is the opposite of a refined or middle-class ethnic Pole who is unconcerned with social etiquette, obsessed with material wealth and defined by an ability to live by wits alone. When Parcha grumbles that 'We're Polish-speaking Romanians, we're lesbians, queers, Jews, we work in an advertising agency' (Masłowska, 2008: 47), it becomes clear how the Romanian is a metonym for prejudice and misplaced social anxiety. Similar to her award-winning novel *Wojna polsko-ruska pod flagą biało-czerwoną* (*Snow White and Russian Red*, 2002), Pawłowski (2006) seems to delight in the way Polish insecurity complexes are compensated for by stereotypes in Masłowska's writing. Embracing the theme of the fancy-dress party ('dirt, stench and disease'), Parcha dresses in a filthy shell-suit and blackens his teeth with a marker, while Dżina disguises herself as a pregnant teenager. When referring to their lives back in Romania, a number of ridiculous and farfetched details are invented, from living in huts and gathering grain from the fields to working in a dog and monkey factory and surviving solely on scraps of meat. The Romanian language is equally trivialized. Parcha speaks in a patois made up of fragments of Latin-derived terminology associated with alcohol and drugs ('aspirina,' 'caffeina,' 'martini,' 'codeinea'), cheap Italian cars ('seicento') and sex ('fellatio'). The pair leaves the party early, ending up stranded on a rural highway without a means to travel back to Warsaw, the ultimate point of geographical identification. The capital city is a respite from the travails of traveling through the countryside, which is inscribed in the setting and dialogue as mystifying, dark and, ultimately, dangerous. After unsuccessfully begging for a lift at a petrol station, Parcha breaks down and takes a man hostage. The drive that ensues is punctuated by sudden outbursts of violence. Under the influence of narcotics, Parcha and Dżina fully assume the identity of the mythical 'Romanians,' a murderer and a thief, temporarily capable of committing transgressions that are precluded in their normal, law-abiding lives (as Poles). The scene oscillates between pleas for help and threats of aggression and brutality, drawing attention to the various configurations of victimhood the West places on the subaltern, epitomized here by the Romanian.

This is matched by a temporary loss of linguistic ability through flawed, repetitive syntax, indicating that socialization and politeness values are entrenched in the Polish language. Masłowska is known for her dismantling of the Polish language through the deliberate misuse of grammatical structures, the appropriation of slang, club culture and television jargon, as well as the invention of neologisms, puns and other linguistic tricks, all of which makes her writing notoriously difficult to stage and to translate. Most of the characters the protagonists meet on their nighttime escapade are taken in by the illusion that they are migrants, which grows out of Parcha and Dżina's refusal or inability to function as normal members of society. Masłowska plays masterfully with expectation – it is only in the second scene that the audience is made aware that they have been equally deceived, that the pair are Poles and not Romanian migrants – thus placing spectators on an equal footing with the characters Parcha and Dżina encounter.

Amy Robinson organizes a theory of racial representation in relation to two oppositional positions of spectating. Robinson's theory revolves around a central triangulation of passing, in which a 'passer' is allowed access into white society through her skin tone and the 'dupe', a white person who misidentifies her skin color as a mimetic sign of racial identity. This interaction is formalized by the presence of an in-group witness who belongs to the same racial group as the passer. In Masłowska, with the absence of an in-group witness to decode the successful ethnic-drag performance, the audience is first positioned as the 'dupe'; the hallucinating characters are presented as Romanians, which allows spectators to identify the characters' dirty clothing, poor personal hygiene and drug-taking as an authentic expression of ethnic Romanian identity. This misperception is only later reversed and the seeming 'ethnic truth' is displayed as a simulacrum, a masquerade that exposes the social privilege granted to ethnic Poles.

The British critic Paul Taylor (2008) noted that Masłowska's depiction of postcommunist Poland presents 'a world where new wealth fails to take notice of destitution and where identity is established by differentiation from undesirable strangers.' Role-playing itself becomes a central preoccupation when Parcha admits that he is not a Polish-speaking Romanian, but a Pole on a comedown who plays a priest on a popular television soap opera, *Plebania* (*Vicarage*). His role as Father Grzegorz is as real to him in the second half of the play as his role as a Romanian in the first two scenes was under the influence of drugs and alcohol. The anti-essentialist diagnosis offered by Masłowska is twofold: not only is the constructedness of national identity a subject for circumspection, the stability of the ego is overshadowed by a compulsion to both act out *and be conditioned by* a 'theatrical' role. The guilt Parcha experiences for his illicit behavior is directly attributable to the fact that he plays a respectable and well-loved Catholic priest on TV; although, it should be stressed, Catholicism itself does not provide an adequate communal fabric but rather stands as an adversary for Parcha, who is plagued by its dogmas, confessions and fasts.

There are a number of insightful conclusions that can be drawn from this performance, not least of which is the inversion of the typical question: to what extent does the host culture shape the migrant? This can be reformulated as: how far is the host culture's self-identity reliant on its determination of the figure of the migrant other? Rather than soliciting empathy with the protagonists that absolves them of responsibility, Masłowska challenges spectators to consider how emerging trends in cosmopolitan Polish life have produced a generation that is self-centered, materially driven and immature. Recalling that Łukasz Drewniak (2006) claimed that foreigners in Poland have been traditionally depicted in art as evil or threatening perpetrators in contrast to Polish innocence, bravery or victimization, I want to highlight the mode in which Masłowska takes part in corresponding processes of national examination that do not seek to conform to conventional unifying doctrines but reveal the ways in which the embodiment of foreigners has been shaped by stereotypes in national discourses. On the other hand, in light of my critique of Frąckowiak and Warlikowski's productions, it is difficult not to see some of the same concerns I expressed earlier appear in the use of ethnic drag. However, one cannot equate equivalence between Polish postcolonial fantasies of 'Africa,' blackness as a sign of oppression and Masłowska's interrogation of pejorative cultural framings of economic migrants. Masłowska's critique is, however, catalyzed by the ethnic other from within the bounds of Polish cultural experience that is predicated on the elision of the foreigner's subjectivity. These are still Poles dressed as Romanians. And, what's more, the concern is with the universal category of exclusion, i.e. Polishness as articulated through otherness, finding its external boundaries through conservative Catholic-nationalist definitions of Polish cultural identity and, obversely, its internal boundaries through liberal claims to tolerance and inclusion that fail to take into account the economic exclusions of capitalism and migration. Once the mantel of the Romanian 'roles' has been dropped, the concerns they provoke are never returned to; rather, once again, the standard questions of Polish identity that are linked to Polish ethnicity and Catholicism are carefully articulated and become the exclusive concern of the play, leaving the binary between Pole and 'Romanian' ultimately in place.

In all three productions, the theatre-makers feel empowered to articulate a critique of Polish values through the lens of race and ethnicity that begs the question whether it is possible to tie a critique of ethnic nationalism purely and singularly to the ethnically Polish body. It is true that Masłowska attempts to combat the representation of foreigners as evil or threatening, but the privilege of speech nevertheless falls to the Polish actors that excludes the political agency and material bodies of the ethnic other, in this case the Romanian migrant, a category that is 'open' to gays and Jews. In the productions under consideration, ascribing racial difference to the foreigner's body constitutes them in opposition to the European, which fails to attend to the constructedness of whiteness (as opposed to the obvious construction of blackness) while confining the analysis of race to those perceived as other to Polishness. While the performances attempt to disarticulate biology from culturally constructed notions of racial character, they do not purport to resolve social contradictions in the confrontations they stage between ethnically Polish bodies and other cultures. Although *W pustyni i w puszczy z Sienkiewicza i innych* offers a counternarrative to Poland as a postcolonial space, Africa is presented as an undifferentiated, unknowable and ultimately impenetrable reality, in which Staś, as the proto-European colonizer, attempts to impose his civilization through language and Christian morality. Poland is thus subsumed under the referent of colonial Europe, not its attendant marginalized subaltern, with a full capacity to reproduce colonial discourses. The attempts to 'play' the subaltern challenges Poland's status as postcolonial by the distancing produced through approximation and masquerade. If Frąckowiak's production offered little variation on current critical postcolonial discourses while obscuring or disavowing some of the real political potentials of staging race in Poland on the contemporary stage, Warlikowski attempted to produce equivalences of exclusion without properly attending to the ethics of representation produced by the particularities of ethnicity, race and gender in the Polish cultural context. Employing actors of color, for instance, might have actually challenged facile or easily won arguments for postcolonial equivalences in postcommunist Europe and the Global South. Such casting choices are not a call for biological essentialism, but rather suggest an opportunity for visibility, dialogue and exchange, which are foreclosed through cross-racial casting that in effect colonizes non-ethnically Polish bodies and ventriloquizes their voices. Throughout this chapter, I have attempted to challenge the equivalencies of exclusion that move across the political spectrum on race and ethnicity, demonstrating that the universalization of exclusivity as a category fails to take into account the particularities of oppression that are systemically linked to the prerogative of whiteness, as well as the postcolonial imperative to allow for a speaking position that does not render the subaltern invisible and silenced, which is the ethical work of theatrical representation. The problem for the subaltern is not necessarily that she is unable to articulate her position, but rather that such articulations are not heard or attended to in dominant social discourses, nor in the appraisal and subversion of those discourses in political theatre practice.

Notes

1 'Sztuka krytyczna' is term introduced by the art critic and theorist Ryszard Kluszczyński, which signifies a grouping of visual arts in Poland in the 1990s that provided a critical commentary on culture, politics and economy in the post-1989 environment.
2 In this production, Belize was figured as an Indian rather than African American character. Not wishing to fully participate in the 'blackface' that would have been required of making Rafał Maćkowiak an African American, the director attempted to downplay the racist potentials of this racial masquerade, while simultaneously eliding the historical and political interrogation of African American identities that is so crucial to Tony Kushner's text.

Conclusion

I will conclude with three performance examples that produced effects in and across Polish public spheres that embody many of the main arguments I have set out in this book. The first relates to national negotiations of ethnic visibility and the policing of collective memory, the second to the inclusion of ethnic others, while the third concerns critiques of public decency that resulted in mass demonstrations. In each case, the theatre as a producer of discourse and (counter)publics, an arbiter of cultural identity and morality and a space for visibility reveal the ongoing significance of this artistic form *as* a political act and generator of dissensus.

When it was announced in 2006 that the *enfant terrible* of Polish theatre, Jan Klata, would attempt a cultural rapprochement between Poland and Germany by staging the body of the other in a postdramatic performance that contrasted the political elite responsible for the Treaty of Yalta with the testimonies of ethnic Poles and Germans impacted by the forced migrations produced by the treaty, the Polish government responded. Prior to the production's opening at Wrocław's Teatr Współczesny, the mass of media attention around the performance was in part due to Dorota Arciszewska-Mielewczyk, a senator from the Law and Justice Party in Gdynia, who requested a copy of the script before the premiere to ascertain whether a subject of such national importance was being treated with appropriate sensitivity. In her letter, Arciszewska-Mielewczyk argued that cultural institutions have the imperative to promote Polish culture and referred to the theatre as a 'temple,' thus associating theatregoing with practices of worship and nation-building.¹ Krystyna Meissner, artistic director of the Teatr Współczesny, categorically rejected this request on grounds that political censorship of the theatre in Poland had formally ended after 1989. Marek Mutor, director of the National Cultural Centre in the Ministry of Culture, defended the senator's letter, at once denying claims of censorship while simultaneously suggesting that there are political narratives in the creative field that the state has the right to evaluate. In an effort to support this claim, Mutor conjured the tenuous and unsubstantiated example of grassroots organizations in the US who write letters of protest when 'a work of art offends Christian values' (cited in Wysocki 2006a), thus aligning religious and national ethics and implying that censorship is allowable at the level of the audience if not the state.

Benedykt Wietrzykowski, president of the anti-German Stowarzyszenie Gdynian Wysiedlonych (Association of Displaced Gdynia Inhabitants) who also sent a letter of protest, lamented the exclusion of Gdynia residents from the cast of real-life expellees, which was split between five ethnic Poles who had been moved from the recovered territories (Ziemie Odzyskane) in Lower Silesia to Wrocław (formerly Breslau) and five ethnic Germans who were deported to West Germany. The most obvious exclusion, however, was not the residents of Gydnia who had also been expelled at the outset of the war, but the Jewish residents, whose absence from postwar Central and East European populations was signified only at one moment in the performance by feathers falling from the flies when one women recalls Jewish homes being looted by their neighbors after deportations during the German extermination campaign in Podolia. Although he admittedly knew little about the content of the performance, Wietrzykowski maintained that the suffering of displaced Poles during the Second World War, a theme that is subsumed under the rubric of historical accuracy, should be the starting point of any discussion on the topic (cited in Wysocki, 2006b).

While Klata's production opened up longstanding discussions around the change of national borders at the end of Second World War that led to the expulsion of Polish and German populations, which Aneta Kyzioł championed as an astute social diagnosis, I argue that the production provoked a contentious and crucial debate around the inclusions and exclusions of non-Polish subjects, bodies and voices on Polish national stages as part of the ongoing production of interpretive communities of national culture in political theatre practice. What is crucial to point out in the Law and Justice Party's deliberate and highly popular attack on *Transfer!* was the anxiety supporting unfounded claims that Klata, an infamous provocateur and flaunter of national values, would produce an inaccurate depiction of the past. In opposition to this investment in theatre as a site for the legitimization of a particular interpretation of the past, one might recall Freddie Rokem's discussion of 'performing history' wherein the theatrical space serves as a forum for the dialectical tensions that underpin the relationship between historical events and social discourse (2000: 1–25). What this production offered audiences was contradictory, disconnected and transnational accounts of these expulsions that resisted conventional narratives that privilege Polish suffering. Giving the prerogative of speech to both Polish and German subjects and attending to the questions raised by the mass transfer of populations across east and central Europe at the conclusion of the Second World War, *Transfer!* marks an important milestone in the effort to include those traditionally excluded from nationalist understandings of Polishness.[2]

Although Klata challenges this tradition, his singular inclusion of ethnic Poles and Germans in the highly ethnically diverse area of southwest Poland, and the absence of Jews in the particular context of Second World War narrative testimonies, nevertheless demonstrates that the prerogative of staging and producing history, even if disjointed, contingent, personal and without claim to objectivity, is reliant not only on a concrete choice of themes and narratives but, crucially, on the political force of *representation*; that is to say, on the inclusion of bodies and voices of ethnic others. The political drive of theatre cannot be reduced simply to the inclusion of marginalized subjects; rather it is the *means* of the representation of the oppressed that makes the theatre a political act. I close this book with this production as the conservative reaction from the Law and Justice Party so evidently highlights the degree to which such political acts, and the inclusion of non-ethnic Poles on the Polish stage in particular, have been regulated.

Political theatre in Poland has accounted for and embodied the contradictions and inequalities engendered by the development of liberal democracy and the free market in the current nation-state. As I have observed, the generations of theatre-makers to produce work after the demise of communism have emphasized a concern with the fate of the individual over the collective that was markedly absent in previous generations. Maria Janion has argued that this generation represents the conclusion of the Polish Romantic paradigm, comprised of common values, fears and passions around which cultural identity was constituted during the Partitions and occupations of the country in nineteenth and twentieth centuries. These generations of directors and playwrights can be defined by a certain exhaustion with the promises of neoliberalism and the free market, and an adamant refusal to speak with a united voice. Roman Pawłowski has pointed out that pre-1989 'generational theatre' in the country traditionally functioned as a site of solidarity in its resistance to the totalitarian political system.

While many critics have lamented this breakdown of social cohesion, I have demonstrated the ways in which nascent pluralism and the cultivation of distinctive and personalized attitudes to national character, accepted morality and public discourse have led to striking innovations in contemporary theatre that condition and reshape the public sphere. Certainly the opening up of European borders and the prospect of easy emigration have been major contributors to changes in artistic output and recent shifts in inter-EU migration have radically impacted Polish culture and have led to an increasing trend to identify between, rather than with, nations.[3] This phenomenon has drawn attention to the problematic theorizations across the political spectrum that posit Poland as postcolonial and Polishness as ethnically bound. And as the labor market continues to diversify and expand both in the European Union and globally, it has become increasingly difficult to conceive of Polish national identity and culture in purely ethnic terms.

This final chapter focuses broadly on the equivalencies of exclusion in the public sphere because I believe the most profoundly imminent task for Polish theatre today is a coalitional engagement with and representation of a multiethnic Poland that includes a systemic interrogation of xenophobia and an embrace of xenophilia. Moving discourse on race, ethnicity and postcolonial theory in a new self-critical direction, Frąckowiak's first production as deputy artistic director at the Teatr Polski Bydgoszcz (TPB) is a solid example of this political commitment, offering a radical rethinking of otherness that I have critiqued in this chapter.[4] Devised with the ensemble, *Afryka* (*Africa*, 2015) proposed a more sophisticated understanding of the discursive body, retreating from ethnic drag in the pursuit of a critique of whiteness in an attempt to raise a critical consciousness outside of dominant ideologies on race that exacerbate and stabilize social differences. Rather than attempting to embody the racialized other, the actors parody and critique the subject positions enabled through the privileging and visibility of their own bodies, and put at risk problematic transhistorical certainties on European superiority.

In a surprising number of reviews, Polish critics asked why it was relevant for Poles to think about Africa. In response, Frąckowiak articulated the multiple and nuanced modes in which contemporary cultural identities and lifestyles are not restricted by national or ethnic borders but are predicated on transnational flows of capital and labor, religious teaching and AIDS. As I have argued throughout this book, one of the most crucial elements of political theatre practice in the development of publics and counterpublics has been the effort to rethink Polish identity outside of a narrowly defined ethnic category, and to demonstrate the greater social relevance of what is perceived to be limited to the private sphere. In this way, audiences may come to understand the modes in which their subjectivity has profound and immediate resonance with others. Judith Butler argued that a 'constitutive or relative outside is, of course, composed of a set of exclusions that are nevertheless *internal* to that system as its own nonthematizable necessity. It emerges within the system as incoherence, disruption, a threat to its own systematicity' (1993: 39, emphasis in original). Feminist performance scholar Geraldine Harris added nuance to this argument, asserting that:

> any invocation of an identity category is performed in such a way as to foreground the processes of production, the exclusions, the dis-identifications and abjections on which that category is based. The idea is not to name or try to include all these excluded 'others' within the category but to demonstrate the category's incapacity to include or summarise the field of social relations, hence creating a space for future rearticulations and resignigifications. (Harris, 1999: 71)

A production like *Afryka* that foregrounds the inclusion of racial and ethnic minorities has a triple purpose: not only will this make those excluded or marginalized visible in the public sphere, this political act will at the same time bring into focus the exclusionary limitations of society's assumed shared values and collective ideals and, finally, offer a crucial opportunity to signify Polishness, citizenship and cultural identities differently.

As I argued in the introduction, political theatre, as a site and form of public debate, does not propose to bracket inequalities, but rather to emphasize them, thus challenging the very social prejudices that are disavowed through attempts to neutralize them. Rancière has offered theorists a productive critical vocabulary to articulate the aesthetics of politics, making visible that which was unknown or invisible, or producing subject positions on the part of those with no part. By interrogating the Romantic hero, I demonstrated how directors critiqued particular and often nostalgic and nationalistic claims to the public sphere and collective identity and memory in the wake of political transformation. After 1989, it becomes clear how the very same repressed and marginalized public in critical ways returned in its obverse form, as the exclusive community that legitimates its own interests and articulations of nationhood and nationality. In considering the visibility and representation of women, gays and lesbians, Polish/Jewish relations and non-ethnic Poles I have shown how the assertion of a particular public constitutes culture as autonomous and singular, rather than multivalent, fluid and multiethnic. For this reason, I have drawn attention to theatre-makers who produce and champion rival publics and counterpublics that challenge the assertion of a self-identical Polish public built upon received and highly restrictive understandings of cultural identity, and which seek to coalesce inter- and intrapublics.

This positioning of the theatre as a crucial space in the public sphere is a concrete move away from the one-way relationship between theatre, audiences and critics, which renders the former as a passive object to be interpreted by the latter. As Paweł Mościcki has argued, political theatre today is not, contrary to a widespread opinion, an empty word. 'You just need to fill it with new content, discarding old habits and unnecessary nostalgia. Activating new interactive forms of engagement' (2008: 9). Jacques Rancière claimed that 'politics is, above all, an intervention into what is visible and sayable' (2010: 37). In this sense, political theatre functions as dissensus, which is not a 'conflict of interests, opinions or values,' but is rather 'a division inserted into "common sense": a dispute over what is given and about the frame within which we see something as given' (*ibid.*: 69). Just as notions of the political are in flux, so are artistic practices that not only have resonant social impact, but are manifestations of the political itself, as was evident in the unprecedented scandal produced by the Malta Festival Poznań's commission to stage Rodrigo García's *Golgota Picnic*, which critiques mass consumerism and deconstructs elements of Christianity. Filmmakers, theatre directors, journalists, politicians, cardinals and bishops all participated in the debates around censorship, freedom of expression, the violation of national blasphemy laws and the state of Polish and European democracy sparked in June 2014 when Catholics gathered to protest and block access to selected theatres across the country. Unintentionally, the conservative protests provoked by García's production effectively highlighted the signification of theatre in Poland after 1989 as a site for dissensus rather than as a locus for community spirit or nationalist solidarity. One can no longer simply assume cultural values as givens nor as synonymous with pre-1989 or pre-1939 Polish cultures, which were, of course, not homogenous themselves. The ultimate assessment of a public and a counterpublic is its durability in the circulation of discourse and the activation of its voluntary members. That's what political theatre is.

Notes

1 See quotations from the letter in Wysocki and Sawka (2006).
2 Although one of the strengths of the performance was the scattered or random dramaturgy of the individuals' memories, which included the concurrence of shocking accounts of suffering with comical and nostalgic interludes, one might suggest that the use of testimonial implicitly participates in the construction of historical trajectories, and the inclusion of both Polish and German perspectives gives political legitimacy to a transnational, and therefore conciliatory, expression of these expulsions.
3 For an analysis of recent productions that engage with Polish migration in the EU see Lease (2014).
4 Paweł Wodziński and Bartosz Frąckowiak joined forces in 2014 to lead the Teatr Polski Bydgoszcz in a new direction. Focusing not only on the political impetus and register of the repertoire, the new directors have attempted to repurpose the building itself. The theatre is now open during daytime hours and not only for evening performances in attempt to bring the theatre more forcefully into public life. Alongside the new opening hours, Wodziński and Frąckowiak have scheduled debates on postcolonial theory, democracy and neoliberalism as well as offering workshops for children and adults on related themes and topics. Wodziński and Frąckowiak are demonstrating that theatre-makers need to devise their own rules, demands and goals, and generate original ideas, modes of engagement and publics. This development in Bydgoszcz offers an exciting new model and role for Polish theatre in the twenty-first century that takes up precisely such efforts.

BIBLIOGRAPHY

Aleksandrowicz, Dariusz. 1995. Vom Messianismus zum Nationalismus, in Erich Goldbach (ed.), *Vom Vorurteil zur Vernichtung? 'Erinnern' für morgen*. Muenster: Lit.
Anderson, Benedict. 2006. *Imagined Communities: Reflections on the Origin and Spread of Nationalism*. London: Verso Books.
Antoniewicz, Grażyna. 2005. Słowacki nie tylko dla brunetów. *Dziennik Bałtycki*, October 13.
Aston, Elaine and Geraldine Harris (eds). 2007. *Feminist Futures?* Basingstoke: Palgrave.
Baluch, Wojciech. 2008. Koniec cywilizacji buntu? Trzy dramaty Przemysława Wojcieszka. *Dialog*, May 15.
Baniewicz, Elżbieta. 1990. Hamlet: Gram dla siebie. *Twórczość*, May 1.
Baniewicz, Elżbieta. 1992. The Interhuman Church: Staging Gombrowicz in Post-Communist Poland. *Performing Arts Journal* 14(2), 97–103.
Baniewicz, Elżbieta. 1996. Theatre's Lean Years in Free Poland. *Theatre Journal* 48(4), 461–78.
Baniewicz, Elżbieta. 1999. Współczesność. *Twórczość*, February 1.
Baniewicz, Elżbieta. 2002. Obnażeni. *Twórczość*, July 1.
Baniewicz, Elżbieta. 2007. Kleczewska – warto kibicować. *Twórczość*, March 28.
Baran, Mirosław. 2005. Problemy klasowe na ostrzu noża. *Gazeta Wyborcza – Trójmiasto*, September 29.
Basara, Zbigniew. 2004. Z uznaniem, lecz bez entuzjazmu. *Nowy Dziennik*, November 16.
Bator, Joanna. 1999. Płeć demokracji. *Gazeta Wyborcza*, June 26.
Bhabha, Homi K. 1994. *The Location of Culture*. London and New York: Routledge.
Bierman, Nikołaj. 2013. Kabaret Warszawski. *Gazeta.ru*, December 19.
Bill, Stanley. 2014. Seeking the Authentic: Polish Culture and the Nature of Postcolonial Theory. *nonsite.org* (Online Journal in the Humanities), 12.
Błoński, Jan. 1987. Biedni Polacy patrzą na getto. *Tygodnik Powszechny*, January 11.
Bodio, Tadeusz. 1999. Psychology of Transformation: From Romanticism to Pragmatism, in Konstanty Adam Wojtaszczyk (ed.), *Poland in Transition*. Warsaw: Elipsa.
Borkowska, Grażyna. 2010. Nike 2010: Co się stało z tamtą klasą? *Gazeta Wyborcza*, October 3.

Borowski, Mateusz and Małgorzata Sugiera. 2013. Political Fictions and Fictionalisations: History as Material for Postdramatic Theatre, in Karen Jürs-Munby, Jerome Carroll and Steve Giles (eds), *Postdramatic and the Political*. London: Bloomsbury Methuen Drama.
Bourdieu, Pierre. 2003. *Pascalian Meditations*. Cambridge: Polity.
Bradshaw, Michael J. and Alison Stenning (eds) 2004. *East Central Europe and the Former Soviet Union: The Post-Socialist States*. New York and London: Routledge.
Bryś, Marta. 2007. Wniosek o pozwolenie na ekshumację. *Nowa Siła Krytyczna*, January 15.
Bryś, Marta. 2009. (D)ybuk w (A)polonii: Między dwoma światami. *Didaskalia – Gazeta Teatralna*, August–October.
Burzyńska, Anna R. 2012. Tradycja i profanacja. *Dialog*, December 1.
Butler, Judith. 1990. *Gender Trouble: Feminism and the Subversion of Identity*. New York and London: Routledge.
Cabianka, Marta. 2005. Jak w Polsce grać Polskę. *Foyer*, September 3.
Carlson, Marvin. 2001. *The Haunted Stage: The Theatre as Memory Machine*. Ann Arbor: University of Michigan Press.
Case, Sue-Ellen. 2007. The Screens of Time: Feminist Memories and Hope, in Elaine Aston and Geraldine Harris (eds), *Feminist Futures?* Basingstoke: Palgrave.
Cavanagh, Clare. 2004. Postcolonial Poland. *Common Knowledge* 10(1), 82–92.
Chlasta-Dzięciołowska, Magdalena. 2007. Duchowi memu dali w pysk i poszli… *E-teatr.pl*, January 27.
Chojka, Joanna. 1998. Robaki i bóstwa. *Tygodnik Powszechny*, April 26.
Chowaniec, Urszula. 2012. Feminism Today: Reflections on Politics and Literature, in Urszula Chowaniec and Ursula Phillips (eds), *Women's Voices and Feminism in Polish Cultural Memory*. Newcastle: Cambridge Scholars.
Chowaniec, Urszula and Ursula Phillips (eds). 2012. *Women's Voices and Feminism in Polish Cultural Memory*. Newcastle: Cambridge Scholars.
Cieślak, Jacek. 2002a. Dramaturgia ważniejsza od nagości. *Rzeczpospolita*, February 8.
Cieślak, Jacek. 2002b. Rozbrojony ładunek emocji. *Rzeczpospolita*, February 11.
Cieślak, Jacek. 2004. Tren dla panny S. *Rzeczpospolita*, July 5.
Cieślak, Jacek. 2005a. Klasyka w nowej wersji. *Rzeczpospolita*, October 19.
Cieślak, Jacek. 2005b. Mezalians miłości z pieniędzmi. *Rzeczpospolita*, October 15.
Cieślak, Jacek. 2005c. Miłość na pomnikach historii. *Rzeczpospolita*, October 27.
Cieślak, Jacek. 2007. Współczesne *Dziady*. *Rzeczpospolita*, February 19.
Cioffi, Kathleen. 1996. *Alternative Theatre in Poland, 1954–1989*. London and New York: Routledge.
Corcoran, Steven. 2010. Introduction, in Jacques Rancière. *Dissensus: On Politics and Aesthetics*. London: Continuum.
Cytowska, Magda. 2002. Love story 2002. *Życie*, January 23.
Czajkowski, Michał. 2001. Czysta Nierządnica. *Tygodnik Powszechny*, May 27.
Czerwinski, E.J. 1988. *Contemporary Polish Theatre and Drama (1956–1984)*. New York: Greenwood Press.
Davies, Norman. 2001. *Heart of Europe: The Past in Poland's Present*. Oxford: Oxford University Press.
De Lange, Sarah and Simona Guerra. 2009. The League of Polish Families between East and West, Past and Present. *Communist and Post-Communist Studies* 42(4), 527–49.
Delgado-García, Cristina. 2012. Subversion, Refusal, and Contingency: The Transgression of Liberal-Humanist Subjectivity and Characterization in Sarah Kane's *Cleansed*, *Crave*, and *4.48 Psychosis*. *Modern Drama* 55(2), 230–50.
Derkaczew, Joanna. 2007a. Ekshumacja spod dywanu. *Gazeta Wyborcza*, January 18.
Derkaczew, Joanna. 2007b. Teatr żywych trupów. *Gazeta Wyborcza*, March 29.
Derkaczew, Joanna. 2008. Andy Warhol według Lupy. *Gazeta Wyborcza*, February 12.
Derkaczew, Joanna. 2010a. Nasza osierocona klasa. *Gazeta Wyborcza*, October 20.
Derkaczew, Joanna. 2010b. Czym ta trauma? Mą ojczyzną… *Gazeta Wyborcza*, April 2.

Derkaczew, Joanna. 2011. Wyścig ofiar po współczucie według Jana Klaty. *Gazeta Wyborcza*, January 7.
Derrida, Jacques. 1994. *Specters of Marx: The State of the Debt, the Work of Mourning and the New International*. London and New York: Routledge.
Dmitruczuk, Anita, 2013. Gej zajął miejsce Żyda. *Gazeta Wyborcza – Opole*, March 29.
Dolan, Jill. 2005. *Utopia in the Theatre*. Ann Arbor: University of Michigan Press.
Dolińska, Michalina. 2002. Droga do katharsis, *Gazeta Wyborcza – Poznań*, January 9.
Drewniak, Łukasz. 2002. Tratwa Meduzy. *Przekrój*, January 13.
Drewniak, Łukasz. 2006. Polak, czyli Rumun i Niemiec. *Dziennik*, November 17.
Drewniak, Łukasz. 2007. PRL Revisited. *Tygodnik Powszechny*, June 3.
Drewniak, Łukasz. 2012. Trzy pogłoski i Warlikowski. *Bluszcz*, January 11.
Duniec, Krystyna. 2012. *Ciało w teatrze: Perspektywa antropologiczna*. Warsaw: Instytut Historii PAN.
Duniec, Krystyna and Joanna Krakowska. 2006. Feminiści na scenę: Teatr na lewo. *Res Publica Nowa*, April 7.
Duniec, Krystyna and Joanna Krakowska. 2014. Introduction, in Krystyna Duniec, Joanna Krakowska and Joanna Klass (eds.) *(A)pollonia: Twenty-First Century Polish Drama and Texts for the Stage*. London, New York and Calcutta: Seagull Books.
Dziewulska, Małgorzata. 2006a. *Dlaczego Szekspir?* Warsaw: Polskie Wydawnictwo Audiowizualne.
Dziewulska, Małgorzata. 2006b. Żywy trup. Romantyczność w teatrze Grzegorzewskiego. *Didaskalia*, August 6.
Dziewulska, Małgorzata. 2009. Teatr potrzebuje upiorów. *Dwutygodnik*, June 13.
Eaglestone, Robert. 2004. *The Holocaust and the Postmodern*. Oxford: Oxford University Press.
Edwards, Jason. 2008. *Eve Kosofsky Sedgwick*. London: Routledge.
Epstein, Steven. 1998. Gay and Lesbian Movements in the United States: Dilemmas of Identity, Diversity and Political Strategy, in Barry D. Adam (ed.), *The Global Emergence of Gay and Lesbian Politics: National Imprints of a Worldwide Movement*. Philadelphia: Temple University Press.
Fidelis, Małgorzata. 2014. *Women, Communism, and Industrialization in Postwar Poland*. Cambridge: Cambridge University Press.
Filipiak, Izabela. 2011. *Jewish Themes in Contemporary Polish Literature*, panel at the Polish Literature Since 89 Conference (discussant), University College London, 10 November.
Filipowicz, Halina. 1992. Polish Theatre after Solidarity: A Challenging Test. *The Drama Review* 36(1), 70–89.
Filipowicz, Halina. 2001. Taboo Topics in Polish and Polish/Jewish Cultural Studies. *The Journal of the International Institute* 9(1), 3–8.
Fischer-Lichte, Erika. 2008. Reality and Fiction in Contemporary Theatre. *Theatre Research International* 33(1), 84–96.
Fischer-Lichte, Erika. 2014. *Dionysus Resurrected: Performances of Euripides' The Bacchae in a Globalizing World*. London: Wiley-Blackwell.
Fleche, Anne. 1995. When a Door is a Jar, or Out in the Theatre: Tennessee Williams and Queer Space. *Theatre Journal* 47(2), 253–67.
Fleming, Michael. 2012. The Regime of Violence in Socialist and Postsocialist Poland. *Annals of the Association of American Geographers* 102(2), 482–98.
Fordoński, Krzysztof. 2007. Three Men in Bed. *Polskie Radio*, www2.polskieradio.pl/zagranica/de/news/artykul33520.html (accessed September 15, 2014).
Fraser, Nancy. 1992. Rethinking the Public Sphere: A Contribution to the Critique of Actually Existing Democracy, in Craig Calhoun (ed.), *Habermas and the Public Sphere*. Cambridge, MA: MIT Press.
Fraser, Nancy. 2003. Social Justice in an Age of Identity Politics: Redistribution, Recognition and Participation, in Nancy Fraser and Axel Honneth (eds), *Redistribution or Recognition? A Political-Philosophical Exchange*. London: Verso.

Fraser, Nancy and Axel Honneth (eds) 2003. *Redistribution or Recognition? A Political-Philosophical Exchange*. London: Verso.
Friedländer, Saul. 1992. *Probing the Limits of Representation: Nazism and the 'Final Solution.'* Cambridge, MA: Harvard University Press.
Fukuyama, Francis. 1992. *The End of History and the Last Man*. New York: Free Press.
Gabryk, Marzena. 2007. Plusy: Minusy. *Didaskalia – Gazeta Teatralna*, February 1.
Gerould, Daniel. 1986. Introduction: From Adam Mickiewicz's Lectures on Slavic Literature Given at the Collège de France. *The Drama Review* 30(3), 91–2.
Gerstenfeld, Manfred. 2003. *Europe's Crumbling Myths: The Post-Holocaust Origins of Today's Anti-Semitism*. Jerusalem: Jerusalem Center for Public Affairs, Yad Vashem and World Jewish Congress.
Gill, Graeme. 2002. *Democracy and Post-Communism*. London: Routledge.
Gluhovic, Miljia. 2013. *Performing European Memories: Trauma, Ethics Politics*. Basingstoke: Palgrave Macmillan.
Górny, Maciej. 2007. From the Splendid Past into the Unknown Future: Historical Studies in Poland after 1989, in Balázs Trencsényi and Péter Apor (eds), *Narratives Unbound: Historical Studies in Post-Communist Eastern Europe*. Budapest: Central European University Press.
Gowin, Jarosław. 2001. Naród-ostatni węzeł. *Rzeczpospolita*, January 18.
Goźliński, Paweł. 2011. Pan Lear umiera. *Gazeta Wyborcza*, October 10.
Grabowska, Magdalena. 2012. Bringing the Second World In: Conservative Revolution(s), Socialist Legacies, and Transnational Silences in the Trajectories of Polish Feminism. *Signs* 37(2), 385–411.
Graff, Agnieszka. 1999. Patriarchat po seksmisji. *Gazeta Wyborcza*, June 20.
Graff, Agnieszka. 2006. We Are (Not All) Homophobes: A Report from Poland. *Feminist Studies* 32(2), 434.
Graff, Agnieszka. 2013a. Lost Between the Waves? The Paradoxes of Feminist Chronology and Activism in Contemporary Poland. *Journal of International Women's Studies* 4(2), 100–16.
Graff, Agnieszka. 2013b. Wolność słowa czy wolność władzy. *Gazeta Wyborcza*, May 9.
Graff, Agnieszka. 2014. *Modern talking. O szansach modernizacji społecznej w Polsce*, symposium, Krytyka Polityczna, Warsaw, 8 January.
Gross, Jan T. 2001. *Neighbors: The Destruction of the Jewish Community in Jedwabne, Poland*. Princeton: Princeton University Press.
Gross, Jan T. 2006. *Fear: Anti-Semitism in Poland after Auschwitz*. New York: Random House.
Grossman, Elwira. 2012. Gender Dynamics in Polish Drama, in Urszula Chowaniec and Ursula Phillips (eds), *Women's Voices and Feminism in Polish Cultural Memory*. Newcastle: Cambridge Scholars.
Gruszczyński, Arek. 2012. Pustynie i puszcze polskiego teatru. *Dwutygodnik*, April 4.
Gruszczyński, Piotr. 1995. Lunatycy nowej rzeczowości. *Tygodnik Powszechny*, June 25.
Gruszczyński, Piotr. 1996. Wolność czyli prawdziwy koniec bohatera Polaków. *Teatr*, April 1.
Gruszczyński, Piotr. 1999. Martwe litery. *Tygodnik Powszechny*, July 4.
Gruszczyński, Piotr. 2002a. Kasandra. *Tygodnik Powszechny*, March 3.
Gruszczyński, Piotr. 2002b. Golas. *Dialog*, April 1.
Gruszczyński, Piotr. 2003. Dybuk, czyli Dziady. *Tygodnik Powszechny*, September 21.
Gruszczyński, Piotr. 2006. *Jan Klata's H*. Warsaw: Polskie Wydawnictwo Audiowizualne.
Gruszka-Zych, Barbara. 2010. To nie 'nasza klasa.' *Gość Niedzielny*, November 18.
Grzebałkowska, Magdalena and Dorota Karaś. 2011. Był sobie Polak, Andrzej, czterej pancerni i gej. *Gazeta Wyborcza*, March 5.
Grzegorzewska, Małgorzata. 2012. Cena funta mięsa. *Teatr*, February 1.
Grzymisławski, Piotr. 2012. Gdzie jesteśmy w geografii? *e-tear.pl*, 5 January.
Habermas, Jürgen. 1991. *The Structural Transformation of the Public Sphere: An Inquiry into a Category of Bourgeois Society*. Cambridge, MA: MIT Press.

Habermas, Jürgen. 1999. The European Nation-State and the Pressures of Globalization. *New Left Review*, 235, 46–59.
Habermas, Jürgen. 2002. *The Inclusion of the Other*. London: Polity Press.
Halberstam, Judith. 2005. *In a Queer Time and Place: Transgender Bodies, Subcultural Lives*. New York: NYU Press.
Hann, Christopher M. 2002. Farewell to the Socialist 'Other,' in Christopher M. Hann (ed.), *Postsocialism: Ideals, Ideologies and Practices in Eurasia*. London: Routledge.
Harris, Geraldine. 1999. *Staging Femininities: Performance and Performativity*. Manchester and New York: Manchester University Press.
Harris, Geraldine. 2014. Post-postfeminism? Amelia Bullmore's *Di and Viv and Rose*, April de Angelis' Jumpy and Karin Young's The Awkward Squad. *Contemporary Theatre Review* 24(2), 177–91.
Hilberg, Raul. 1993. *Perpetrators, Victims, Bystanders: The Jewish Catastrophe, 1933–1945*. London: Lime Tree.
Hirsch, Marianne. 1997. *Family Frames: Photographs, Narrative and Postmemory*. London: Harvard University Press.
Iwasiów, Inga. 2010. Tratwą przez Polskę. *Teatr*, June 1.
Jackson, Shannon. 2011. *Social Works: Performing Art, Supporting Publics*. New York and London: Routledge.
Janion, Maria. 1975. *Gorączka romantyczna*. Warsaw: PIW.
Janion, Maria. 1979. Czas formy otwartej. *Życie Literackie*, December 2.
Janion, Maria. 2000. *Do Europy tak, ale razem z naszymi umarłymi*. Warsaw: Sic!.
Janion, Maria. 2007. *Niesamowita Słowiańszczyzna: fantazmaty literatury*. Kraków: Wydawnictwo Literackie.
Janowska, Katarzyna and Piotr Mucharski. 2006. Konserwatywna prowokacja. *Gazeta Wyborcza*, March 1.
Jedlicki, Jerzy. 2009. Polacy wobec Żydów: Bezradność. *Gazeta Wyborcza*, June 26.
Jędrzejczak, Piotr Bogusław. 1986. Pełna snu perła… *Teatr*, February 1.
Joseph, Miranda. 2002. *Against the Romance of Community*. Minneapolis: University of Minnesota Press.
Kalukin, Rafał. 2013. Między nepotyzmem i homofobią. *Newsweek Polska*, April 2.
Karpiński, Maciej. 1989. *The Theater of Andrzej Wajda*. Cambridge: Cambridge University Press.
Katafiasz, Olga. 2006. Skrzydła bez oczu. *Didaskalia – Gazeta Teatralna*, February 1.
Kijowska, Joanna. 2007. Warlikowski rozpęta burzę. *Dziennik*, February 17.
Kłopocka, Iwona. 2004. Dozwolone od lat 18. *Nowa Trybuna Opolska*, December 9.
Kłossowicz, Jan. 1986. Tadeusz Kantor's Journey. *The Drama Review* 30(3), 98–113.
Kobialka, Michal. 1993. *A Journey Through Other Spaces*. Berkeley: University of California Press.
Kobialka, Michal. 2009a. Tadeusz Kantor and Hamed Taheri: Of Political Theatre/Performance. *The Drama Review* 53(4), 78–91.
Kobialka, Michal. 2009b. *Further On, Nothing: Tadeusz Kantor's Theatre*. Minneapolis: University of Minnesota Press.
Konic, Paweł. 1989. 'Marzyciele' – teatr myśli. *Teatr*, March 1.
Kopciński, Jacek. 2000. Reżyserskie solówki. *Życie*, February 28.
Kopciński, Jacek. 2002. Król naprawdę jest nagi. *Rzeczpospolita*, May 9.
Kopciński, Jacek. 2005. Makbet Kleczewskiej i Jarzyny. *Teatr*, September 1.
Kopciński, Jacek. 2009. Melancholia cieni. *Teatr*, August 1.
Kopciński, Jacek. 2013. Trendsetter na urzędzie. *Teatr*, July 1.
Kopka, Krzysztof. 1988a. Głosy umarłych. *Teatr*, March 1.
Kopka, Krzysztof. 1988b. Oni tu żyli. *Teatr*, August 1.
Korek, Janusz. 2007. From Sovietology to Postcoloniality: Poland and Ukraine from a Postcolonial Perspective, in Janusz Korek (ed.), *From Sovietology to Postcoloniality: Poland and Ukraine from a Postcolonial Perspective*. Huddinge: Sodertorns hogskola.

Kornaś, Tadeusz. 1996. Gra w dziady. *Echo Kraków*, January 10.
Kornaś, Tadeusz. 2004. Makbet Wielkiego Miasta. *Didaskalia – Gazeta Teatralna*, December 1.
Kornaś, Tadeusz. 2007. *Between Anthropology and Politics: Two Strands of Polish Alternative Theatre*. Warsaw: Instytut Teatralny im. Zbigniewa Raszewskiego.
Kościelniak, Marcin. 2003. Bóg jest historią. *Didaskalia – Gazeta Teatralna*, October 1.
Kościelniak, Marcin. 2010. Odrobiona lekcja. *Tygodnik Powszechny*, November 23.
Kościelniak, Marcin. 2011. Mała apokalipsa. *Tygodnik Powszechny*, December 6.
Kosiński, Dariusz. 2011. Remember to Forget: Collective Performances of National Grief as an (Anti-)Memory Machine. Unpublished conference paper. Performance Studies international (PSi).
Kowalczyk, Izabela. 2013. *Matki-Polki, Chłopcy i Cyborgi… Sztuka i feminizm w Polsce*. Poznań: Galeria Miejska Arsenał.
Kowalczyk, Janusz. 1999. Nocą nago na strychu. *Rzeczpospolita*, October 27.
Kowalczyk, Janusz. 2002. Oczyszczeni – bulwersujący spektakl teatralny. *Rzeczpospolita*, January 21.
Kowalska, Jolanta. 2007a. Prywatna wojna z Mickiewiczem. *Teatr*, March 1.
Kowalska, Jolanta. 2007b. Polska czyli coś do śmiechu. *Didaskalia – Gazeta Teatralna*, April 1.
Kowalska, Jolanta. 2011. Czarne jest piękne! *Teatr*, March 1.
Kowalska, Jolanta. 2012. Maski inności. *Teatr*, September 1.
Kozłowski, Michał. 2008. What Makes Poland a Post-Communist Country? *Politics and Culture* 4, http://politicsandculture.org/2010/09/19/what-makes-poland-a-post-communist-country (accessed April 24, 2015).
Krajski, Stanisław. 2005. Homoseksualizm i prostactwo. *Nasz Dziennik*, December 1.
Krakowska, Ewa. 2012. Feminism Polish Style: Our Tradition or a Borrowed One? in Urszula Chowaniec and Ursula Phillips (eds), *Women's Voices and Feminism in Polish Cultural Memory*. Newcastle: Cambridge Scholars.
Krakowska, Joanna. 2007. Anioły w Ameryce, czyli ustanawianie uniwersalizm. *Dialog*, September 1.
Kraszewski, Charles S. 1998. *The Romantic Hero and Contemporary Anti-Hero in Polish and Czech Literature: Great Souls and Grey Men*. Lewiston: Edwin Mellen Press.
Kujawińska Courtney, Krystyna and Katarzyna Kwapisz Williams. 2005. *The Polish Prince: Studies in Cultural Appropriation of Shakespeare's Hamlet in Poland*. Łódź: University of Łódź.
Kuhar, Roman. 2011. The Heteronormative Panopticon and the Transparent Closet of the Public Space in Slovenia, in Robert Kulpa and Joanna Mizielińska (eds), *De-Centring Western Sexuality: Central and Eastern European Perspectives*. London: Ashgate.
Kulpa, Robert and Joanna Mizielińska. 2011. *De-Centring Western Sexuality: Central and Eastern European Perspectives*. Farnham: Ashgate.
Kurczewski, Jacek. 1999. The Rule of Law in Poland, in Jiri Přibáň and James Young (eds), *The Rule of Law in Central Europe: The Reconstruction of Legality, Constitutionalism and Civil Society in Post-Communist Countries*. Farnham: Ashgate.
Kurkiewicz, Juliusz. 2010. Chcę komplikować odpowiedzi. *Gazeta Wyborcza*, July 6.
Kuss, Merje. 2004. Europe's Eastern Expansion and the Reinscription of Otherness in East Central Europe. *Progress in Human Geography* 28(4), 472–89.
Kutz, Kazimierz. 2006. In Defense of Common Sense Speech. *e-teatr.pl*, March 6.
Kuźmiński, Michał and Michał Olszewski. 2008. Demirski on the Myth of Wałęsa. *Tygodnik Powszechny*, June 6.
Kyzioł, Aneta. 2007. Trupa wyciąga trupy. *Polityka*, March 29.
Kyzioł, Aneta. 2008. Z perspektywy Obcego. *Polityka*, November 25.
LaCapra, Dominick. 1996. *Representing the Holocaust*. Ithaca: Cornell University Press.
LaCapra, Dominick. 1998. *History and Memory after Auschwitz*. Ithaca and London, Cornell University Press.

LaCapra, Dominick. 2001. *Writing History, Writing Trauma*. Baltimore: John Hopkins University Press.
Laszuk, Anna. 2009. Queer po polsku, czyli nowoczesny closet. *Furia Pierwsza*, December 1.
Lease, Bryce. 2012. Ethnic Identity and Anti-Semitism: Słobodzianek Stages the Polish Taboo. *The Drama Review* 56(2), 81–100.
Lease, Bryce. 2014. Opening Borders, Closing Nations: How 'Generation Nothing' Stages Polish Migration. *Contemporary Theatre Review* 24(1), 6–20.
Lease, Bryce. 2015. Theatre as Action, Dramaturgy as *Streben*: Cultural Confrontations at Lithuania's National Drama Theatre. *The Drama Review* 59(1), 119–35.
Lefort, Claude. 1988. *Democracy and Political Theory*. Minneapolis: University of Minnesota Press.
Lehmann, Hans-Thies. 2002. Co widzieli państwo ostatnio w teatrze? *Didaskalia – Gazeta Teatralna*, April 1.
Lehmann, Hans-Thies. 2006. *Postdramatic Theatre*. London and New York: Routledge.
Lévi-Strauss, Claude. 1987. *Introduction to the Work of Marcel Mauss*. London and New York: Routledge.
Liskowacki, Artur D. 2011. Zygarlicka: Bez czułości. *Dialog*, January 1.
Majchrowski, Zbigniew. 1998. Improwizacja na odejście. *Dialog*, July 1.
Makaruk, Maria. 2012. Do Europy tak, ale razem z naszymi upiorami. *Teatr*, September 1.
Mark, James. 2010. *The Unfinished Revolution: Making Sense of the Communist Past in Central-Eastern Europe*. New Haven: Yale University Press.
Masłowska, Dorota. 2008. *A Couple of Poor, Polish-Speaking Romanians*, trans. Lisa Goldman and Paul Sirett. London: Oberon.
Matynia, Elżbieta. 2009. *Performative Democracy*. Boulder and London: Paradigm.
McNay, Lois. 2008. *Against Recognition*. London: Polity Press.
McRobbie, Angela. 2004. Post-Feminism and Popular Culture. *Feminist Media Studies*, 4(3), 255–64.
Michalska, Julia. 2010. Poland's National Museum Champions Gay Rights. *The Art Newspaper*, June 1.
Michalski, Cezary. 2013. Szczepkowska: Jestem odporna na szyderstwa. *Krytyka Polityczna*, November 8.
Michlic, Joanna Beata. 2002. The Polish Debate about the Jedwabne Massacre, http://sicsa.huji.ac.il/21michlic.pdf (accessed April 24, 2015).
Michlic, Joanna Beata. 2006. *Poland's Threatening Other: The Image of the Jew from 1880 to the Present*. Lincoln: University of Nebraska Press.
Michlic, Joanna Beata and Małgorzata Melchoir. 2013. The Memory of the Holocaust in Post-1989 Poland, in John-Paul Himka and Joanna B. Michlic (eds), *Bringing the Dark Past to Light: The Reception of the Holocaust in Postcommunist Europe*. Lincoln: University of Nebraska Press.
Mickiewicz, Adam. 1986 [1844]. Lectures on Slavic Literature Given at the Collège de France. *The Drama Review* 30(3), 93–7.
Miłkowski, Tomasz. 2006. Pokolenie Le Madame. *Przegląd*, April 23.
Miłkowski, Tomasz. 2007. Anioły w Warszawie. *Przegląd*, May 6.
Miłkowski, Tomasz. 2012. The Theatre Shedding Skin: (A Sketch for a Portrait), in Anna Leszkowska (ed.) *Transformation: The Polish Theatre after 1989*. Warsaw: IATC.
Miłosz, Czesław. 1983. *The History of Polish Literature*. Berkeley: University of California Press.
Mishra, K.P. 2007. Fukuyama's End of History: Triumph of the Liberal State. *The Indian Journal of Political Science* 68(3), 465–74.
Moore, David Chioni. 2001. Is the Post in Postcolonial the Post in Post-Soviet? Toward a Global Postcolonial Critique. *Publications of the Modern Language Association (PMLA)* 116(1), 111–28.
Morawiec, Elżbieta. 1977. Chochole dusze. *Życie Literackie*, July 10.
Morawiec, Elżbieta. 1984. The Theatre of Jerzy Grzegorzewski: Between Theatre and Non-Being. *Performing Arts Journal* 8(2), 75–88.

Morawiec, Elżbieta. 1988. Nie stargam cię – nie! Ja uwydatnię. *Tygodnik Powszechny*, June 12.
Mościcki, Paweł. 2008. *Polityka teatru. Eseje o sztuce angażującej*. Warsaw: Krytyka Polityczna.
Mouffe, Chantal. 1993. *The Return of the Political*. London: Verso.
Muñoz, José Esteban. 1999. *Disidentifications: Queers of Color and the Performance of Politics*. Minneapolis: University of Minnesota Press.
Nathan, John. 2009. Our Class and the Bloody History of Poland that Refuses to Die. *The Times*, September 11.
Neuger, Leonard. 2009. *The Place of Crime: Program Notes for Our Class*. London: Royal National Theatre.
Niziołek, Grzegorz. 1990. Pasja. *Teatr*, June 1.
Niziołek, Grzegorz, 2001. Muzyka 'Bachantek.' *Didaskalia – Gazeta Teatralna*, April 1.
Niziołek, Grzegorz. 2013a. Ressentiment as Experiment: Polish Theatre and Drama after 1989, in Ursula Phillips (ed.), *Polish Literature in Transformation*. Berlin: Lit Verlag.
Niziołek, Grzegorz. 2013b. *Polski teatr Zagłady*. Warsaw: Instytut Teatralny im. Zbigniewa Raszewskiego and Wydawnictwo Krytyki Politycznej.
Niziołek, Grzegorz. 2015. Theatre for Neurotics. *Polish Theatre Perspectives* 1(1), 52–62.
Norval, Aletta J. 1996. *Deconstructing Apartheid Discourse*. London: Verso.
Nowak, Basia. 2010. 'Where Do You Think I Learned How to Style My Own Hair?' Gender and Everyday Lives of Women Activists in Poland's League of Women, in Shana Penn and Jill Massino (eds), *Gender Politics and Everyday Life in State Socialist Eastern and Central Europe*. Basingstoke: Palgrave Macmillan.
Nyc, Iga. 2007. Pojedynek potworów. *Wprost*, February 1.
Olczyk, Agnieszka. 2004. Urodzeni mordercy. *Didaskalia – Gazeta Teatralna*, December 1.
Oliver, Kelly. 2004. Witnessing and Testimony. *Parallax* 10(1), 78–87.
Pankowski, Rafał. 2010. *The Populist Radical Right in Poland: The Patriots*. London and New York: Routledge.
Pawlak, Anna. 2013. Powstało dzieło feministyczn. *Gazeta Opole*, January 14.
Pawłowski, Roman. 1997a. Powstanie w teatrze. *Gazeta Wyborcza*, November 30.
Pawłowski, Roman. 1997b. Konserwa Pandora. *Gazeta Wyborcza*, September 30.
Pawłowski, Roman. 2002. Oddział zamknięty. *Gazeta Wyborcza*, February 25.
Pawłowski, Roman. 2003. Polsko-żydowskie *Dziady*. *Gazeta Wyborcza*, December 6.
Pawłowski, Roman. 2005a. Agata szuka pracy. *Gazeta Wyborcza*, December 23.
Pawłowski, Roman. 2005b. Teatr niemoralnego niepokoju. Gazeta Wyborcza, December 23.
Pawłowski, Roman. 2006. Królowa w rumuńskim przebraniu. *Gazeta Wyborcza*, May 24.
Pawłowski, Roman. 2007. Comédie-Polonaise. *Gazeta Wyborcza*, February 22.
Pawłowski, Roman. 2009. Rzecz, która nie lubi być zabijana. *Gazeta Wyborcza*, May 16.
Pawłowski, Roman. 2010. Polska dramaturgia współczesna już nie taka współczesna. *Gazeta Wyborcza*, November 29.
Pawłowski, Roman and Rafał Węgrzyniak. 2003. Polsko-żydowskie *Dziady*. *Gazeta Wyborcza*, December 6.
Penn, Shana and Jill Massino (eds). 2010. *Gender Politics and Everyday Life in State Socialist Eastern and Central Europe*. Basingstoke: Palgrave Macmillan.
Piekarska, Magda. 2011. Tęczowa trybuna 2012: A to są te koteczki – kibice. *Gazeta Wyborcza – Wrocław*, March 1.
Pietrasik, Zdzisław. 2005. Duma i obrzydzenie. *Polityka*, November 12.
Pilch, Jerzy. 2002. Szekspirówna teledysku. *Polityka*, February 16.
Plata, Tomasz. 2006. *Strategie publiczne, strategie prywatne: Teatr polski 1990–2005*. Warsaw: Świat Literacki.
Plata, Tomasz. 2007. 'Teatr Kleczewskiej: przemoc przekazu,' Rozmowa Joanny Derkaczew, Piotra Gruszczyńskiego, Beaty Guczalskiej i Tomasza Platy, *Dialog*, April 1.
Pleśniarowicz, Krzysztof. 2004. *The Dead Memory Machine: Tadeusz Kantor's 'Theatre of Death.'* Aberystwyth: Black Mountain Press.

Pobiedzińska, Justyna. 2007. Odnowa, czyli od nowa. *Nowa Siła Krytyczna*, January 16.
Pyrkosz, Aleksandra. 2012. Bluźnierstwo sceniczne. *Teatralia*, April 23.
Rancière, Jacques. 2004. *The Politics of Aesthetics*. London and New York: Continuum.
Rancière, Jacques. 2010. *Dissensus: On Politics and Aesthetics*. London and New York: Continuum.
Rancière, Jacques. 2014. *The Emancipated Spectator*. London: Verso Books.
Reading, Anna. 1992. *Polish Women, Solidarity and Feminism*. Basingstoke: Macmillan.
Robinson, Amy. 1994. It Takes One to Know One: Passing and Communities of Common Interest. *Critical Inquiry* 20(4), 715–36.
Rokem, Freddie. 2000. *Performing History: Theatrical Representations of the Past in Contemporary Theatre*. Iowa City: University of Iowa Press.
Romanska, Magda. 2014. *The Post-Traumatic Theatre of Grotowski and Kantor: History and Holocaust in Akropolis and Dead Class*. London: Anthem Press.
Ruda, Małgorzata. 2006. Bywają historie żałośliwsze. *Dekada Literacka*, September 25.
Ruda, Małgorzata. 2009. Daremność ofiary, *Dekada Literacka* 5/6, May 16.
Rudnicki, Adolf. 1987. *Teatr zawsze grany*, Warsaw: Czytelnik.
Salvato, Nick. 2010. *Uncloseting Drama: American Modernism and Queer Performance*. New Haven and London: Yale University Press.
Savran, David. 1995. Ambivalence, Utopia, and a Queer Sort of Materialism: How 'Angels in America' Reconstructs the Nation. *Theatre Journal* 47(2), 207–27.
Saxonberg, Steven and Dorota Szelewa. 2007. The Continuing Legacy of the Communist Legacy? The Development of Family Policies in Poland and the Czech Republic. *Social Politics: International Studies in Gender, State and Society* 14(3), 351–79.
Schmidt, Piotr. 2007. Tabu w teatrze. *G-punkt.pl*, November 17.
Schneider, Rebecca. 1997. *The Explicit Body in Performance*. London and New York: Routledge.
Segel, H.B. 1977. *Polish Romantic Drama: Three Plays in English Translation*. Ithaca: Cornell University Press.
Shields, Stuart. 2007. From Socialist Solidarity to Neo-Populist Neoliberalisation? The Paradoxes of Poland's Post-Communist Transition. *Capital & Class* 31(3), 159–78.
Sieg, Katrin. 2009. *Ethnic Drag: Performing Race, Nation, Sexuality in West Germany*. Ann Arbor: University of Michigan Press.
Sieradzki, Jacek. 1985. Wariacje Grzegorzewskie. *Twórczość*, November 1.
Sieradzki, Jacek. 1991. Gombrowicz sceniczny. *Polityka*, May 25.
Sieradzki, Jacek. 1993. Deficyt uczuć wyższych. *Polityka*, November 6.
Sieradzki, Jacek. 1997. Księżniczka techno. *Polityka*, February 15.
Sieradzki, Jacek. 2010. Ślizg. *Odra*, May 19.
Słobodzianek, Tadeusz. 2009a. *Our Class*, adapted by Ryan Craig, trans. Catherine Grosvenor. London: Oberon Books.
Słobodzianek, Tadeusz. 2009b. *Journal Extracts: Program notes for Our Class*. London: Royal National Theatre.
Smith, Anna Marie. 1998. *Laclau and Mouffe: The Radical Democratic Imaginary*. London and New York: Routledge.
Spichalski, Szymon. 2012. Leśny jarmark szekspirowski. *Teatr dla Was*, February 2.
Spilkowska, Aleksandra. 2013. Opowieści zdeformowane. *Teatralia*, January 30.
Spivak, Gayatri Chakravorty. 2006. Are We Postcolonial? Post-Soviet Space. *Publications of the Modern Language Association (PMLA)* 121(3), 828–36.
Stankiewicz-Podhorecka, Temida. 2005. Bełkot słowa i gimnastyka bioder. *Nasz Dziennik*, November 2.
Staszewski, Wojciech. 2011. Penis na Dworcu Śródmieście. *Gazeta Wyborcza*, December 1.
Stavrakakis, Yannis. 1999. *Lacan and the Political*. London and New York: Routledge.
Steinlauf, Michael C. 1997. *Bondage to the Dead: Poland and the Memory of the Holocaust*. Syracuse: Syracuse University Press.

Stemplowska, Zofia. 2014. Polin: A Wish to Be Remembered. *The Times Literary Supplement* (*TLS*), November 19.
Stokfiszewski, Igor. 2011. Stokfiszewski: W stronę akcji bezpośredniej. *Krytyka Polityczna*, December 27.
Sugiera, Małgorzata. 1988. Kto wspominasz dawne chwile… *Więź*, September 1.
Swieżawski, Stefan. 2000. *Lampa wiary: rozważania na przełomie wieków*. Kraków: Wydawnictwo Znak.
Szacka, Barbara. 2006. *Czas przeszły, pamięć, mit*. Warsaw: Wydawnictwo Naukowe Scholar.
Szacki, Jerzy. 1995. *Liberalism after Communism*. Budapest: Central European University Press.
Szarota, Tomasz. 2002. Jedwabne bez stereotypów. *Tygodnik Powszechny*, May 12.
Szczepkowska, Joanna. 2013. Homo dzieciństwo. *e-teatr.pl*, March 22.
Szczęsna, Joanna. 2010. To jest nasza klasa. *Gazeta Wyborcza*, October 18.
Szpecht, Magda. 2011. Jądro postkolonializmu. www.g-punkt.pl, June 27.
Szpecht, Magda. 2012. Opowieści tęczowe według Sienkiewicza i innych. www.g-punkt.pl, December 29.
Targoń, Joanna. 2002. Wykręcony świat. *Gazeta Wyborcza – Kraków*, May 14.
Targoń, Joanna. 2007. Kręgi piekielne z przewodnikiem. *Gazeta Wyborcza*, April 30.
Taylor, Paul. 2008. A Couple of Poor, Polish-Speaking Romanians. *The Independent*, March 11.
Thompson, Ewa M. 2011. Ways of Remembering, in Tamara Trojanowska (ed.), *New Perspectives on Polish Culture: Personal Encounters, Public Affairs*. New York: PIASA Books.
Thompson, Simon. 2006. *The Political Theory of Recognition: A Critical Introduction*. Cambridge: Polity Press.
Tickell, Adam and Jamie Peck. 2003. Making Global Rules: Globalisation or Neoliberalisation, in Jamie A. Peck and Henry Wai-Chung Yeung (eds), *Remaking the Global Economy: Economic-Geographical Perspectives*. London: Sage.
Turner, Victor. 1995. *The Ritual Process: Structure and Anti-Structure*. New York: Aldine Transaction.
Udalska, Eleonora. 1997. Polish Theatre after 1989. *Canadian Slavonic Papers/Revue Canadienne des Slavistes*, 167–9.
Uniejewska, Ewa. 2011. Zaczęłam mieć odwagę być jaskrawa. *Nowa Siła Krytyczna*, May 30.
Urbaniak, Mike. 2011. Ten teatr jest skandalem. *magazynwaw.com*, November 25.
Urbaniak, Mike. 2013. Warszawa to nie bułka z masłem. *Przekrój*, May 20.
Vickers, Paul. 2013. Constructing a Memory of Polish/Jewish Community in Tadeusz Słobodzianek's Our Class, in Ursula Phillips (ed.), *Polish Literature in Transformation*. Berlin: Lit Verlag.
Wakar, Jacek. 1997. Wysokie koszty nowatorstwa. *Życie Warszawy*, September 30.
Walczewska, Sławomira. 2006. 'Damy, rycerze i feministki.' *Kobiecy dyskurs emancypacyjny w Polsce*. Kraków: eFKa.
Wałęsa, Lech. 2013. Interview for the television channel TVN24, 01 March.
Wanat, Andrzej. 1993. Krok od mizantropii. *Teatr*, December 1.
Warkocki, Błażej. 2004. *Homofobia po polsku*. Warsaw: Sic!.
Warkocki, Błażej. 2013. Homobiographies and Gay Emancipation, in Ursula Phillips (ed.), *Polish Literature in Transformation*. Berlin: Lit Verlag.
Warkocki, Błażej. 2014. *Różowy język: Literatura i polityka kultury na początku wieku*. Warsaw: Krytyka Polityczna.
Warlikowski, Krzysztof. 2015. Life in a Cemetery, Krzysztof Warlikowski talks to Piotr Gruszczyński. *Polish Theatre Perspectives* 1(1), 93–108.
Warner, Michael. 2002. *Publics and Counterpublics*, New York: Zone.
Wąsiewicz, Mirella. 2004. Myślę, że Hamlet jest Polakiem. *Gazeta Wyborcza – Trójmiasto*, July 2.
Węgrzyniak, Rafał. 2009. Pasja. *e-teatr.pl*, April 14.

Węgrzyniak, Rafał. 2011. Teatr na Lewo. *Notatnik Teatralny*, December 1.
Wierzejski, Wojciech. 2006. Wierzejski o gejach: zlać ich pałami! *Życie Warszawy*, May 11.
Winnicka, Bożena. 1988. Z pieśni myśl wysłuchać. *Życie Literackie*, April 24.
Wise, Andrew Kier. 2010. Postcolonial Anxiety in Polish Nationalist Rhetoric. *The Polish Review*, 55(3), 285–305.
Witts, Noel. 2010. *Tadeusz Kantor*. London and New York: Routledge.
Wojciechowska, Ryszarda. 2005. Bohater na miarę Szekspira. *Dziennik Bałtycki* & *Wieczór Wybrzeża*, January 4.
Wolf, Larry. 1994. *Inventing Eastern Europe: The Map of Civilization on the Mind of the Enlightenment*. Stanford: Stanford University Press.
Wysocki, Tomasz. 2006a. Najlepsza jest kontrola oddolna. *Gazeta Wyborcza – Wrocław*, April 27.
Wysocki, Tomasz. 2006b. Kolejny protest Wysiedlonych Gdynian przeciw wrocławskiemu teatrowi. *Gazeta Wyborcza – Wrocław*, June 17.
Wysocki, Tomasz. 2007a. *Dziady* polityczne. *Gazeta Wyborcza – Wrocław*, January 12.
Wysocki, Tomasz. 2007b. Marsz upiorów narodowych. *Gazeta Wyborcza – Wrocław*, January 19.
Wysocki, Tomasz. 2007c. Polak ogląda w lustrze swoje czarne podniebienie. *Gazeta Wyborcza – Wrocław*, April 17.
Wysocki, Tomasz and Jan Sawka. 2006. Pani senator prześwietla teatr. *Gazeta Wyborcza – Wrocław*, April 26.
Wyżyńska, Dorota. 2001a. Greckie *Dziady*. *Gazeta Wyborcza*, February 5.
Wyżyńska, Dorota. 2001b. Zmaganie. Rozmowa z Krystianem Lupą. *Gazeta Wyborcza – Stołeczna*, March 10.
Wyżyńska, Dorota. 2005. TR bez 'Bzika'. *Gazeta Wyborcza*, December 17.
Wyżyńska, Dorota. 2006. Labirynt Rafała Mohra. *Stołeczna*, March 15.
Wyżyńska, Dorota. 2011. Ferency – czarny Otello, Żyd Shylock i Król Lear. *Gazeta Wyborcza*, December 1.
Zadara, Michał. 2010. Solidarność jako wstyd. *Tygodnik Powszechny*, August 24.
Zalewska, Kalina. 2005. Homofobia Romana Pawłowskiego. *Miasto Stołeczne Warszawa*, October 31.
Zarrilli, Phillip. 1995. *Acting (Re)Considered: A Theoretical and Practical Guide*. London and New York: Routledge.
Zielińska, Alicja. 2008. Tadeusz Słobodzianek o 'Naszej klasie'. *Kurier Poranny*, May 30.
Žižek, Salvoj. 2002. *For They Know Not What They Do: Enjoyment as a Political Factor*. London: Verso.
Žižek, Salvoj. 2006. *The Parallax View*, Cambridge, MA: MIT Press.

INDEX

1989 1–9, 15–20, 26–7, 29–33, 36, 42, 44, 46–7, 52n3, 54–5, 58, 62, 65, 74, 76–7, 79, 83–8, 95, 108, 110, 113, 115, 117, 135, 136n1, 138, 141–2, 156, 167, 177, 197n1, 199, 201–3

Althamer, Paweł 11–12
Ansky, Szymon
   Dybuk (The Dybbuk) 157–68
anti-Semitism 13, 15, 18, 24, 38, 66, 111, 113, 136n3, 142, 148, 150–1, 153–4, 156–7, 162–5, 171, 190
Augustynowicz, Anna 24, 88–91, 86
Axel, Erwin 64

Baniewicz, Elżbieta 58, 63, 83, 91, 98
Bartoszewski, Władysław 143
Bator, Joanna 86, 163
Bernhard, Thomas
   Auslöschung (Erasure) 37–8
   Kalkwerk (The Lime Works) 36, 87
   Na szczytach panuje cisza (Over All the Mountain Tops) 41
Bill, Stanley 176–7

bitwa o krzyż (battle for the cross) 72
Błoński, Jan 151, 158
body 25, 40, 87, 89, 90, 95–6, 99, 157, 160, 181–2, 185, 187, 189, 195, 198, 201
   civic 17, 113
   ethnically Polish 25, 195
   exposure 41, 96
   female 93, 95, 100, 107, 183
   male 87, 89, 96, 116
   pathologized 24, 135
   phenomenal versus actor's 99, 189
   social versus national 16, 41–2, 130, 167
Borowski, Mateusz 13–14
Boy-Żeleński, Tadeusz 161
Broch, Hermann
   Lunatycy (The Sleepwalkers) 37, 41
Bryś, Marta 68, 168
Büchner, Georg
   Woyzeck 102
Budzisz-Krzyżanowska, Teresa 83–4
Bulgakov, Mikhail
   Mistrz i Małgorzata (The Master and Margarita) 38–9

Index

Burzyńska, Anna R. 34, 51, 81
Butler, Judith 28n7, 107, 177, 189, 202

Cała, Alina 143
capitalism 4–6, 8, 13, 18–20, 30–2, 34, 44, 73, 78, 80, 84, 120, 122, 132, 147, 176, 195
 anti-capitalism 42
 failure of 123
Carlson, Marvin
 double vision 160
Case, Sue-Ellen 100
Catholic Church
 gay rights 114, 119
 liberalism 27
 nuclear family 129
 Polish/Jewish relations 142–3
 political right 135
 in the PRL 26n2
 public role 45–7, 64, 86–7, 91, 135, 192
 theatre staged in churches 7–8
Cavanagh, Clare 174
Chekhov, Anton 9, 10, 57
Chioni Moore, David 175
Chlasta-Dzięciołowska, Magdalena 65, 67
Cielecka, Magdalena 100–1, 159, 166
Cieślak, Jacek 49, 51, 78, 118
Cieślak, Piotr 37
Cioffi, Kathleen 6–8, 44, 140
Coetzee, J.M. 166, 169, 173n13, 178, 188
communism 4, 6–8, 15, 19–20, 22–4, 32, 39, 42–5, 49, 79–80, 108, 111, 122, 136n1, 139, 150
 anti-Communist 37, 45–6, 52n3, 74, 79, 114, 138, 140, 153
 anti-Semitism 140–1, 156, 164
 collapse of 5–6, 27n3, 29, 34, 73, 85, 135, 141, 200
 ethnonationalization 139
 homosexuality 135
 nationalism 2, 20, 141

postcommunism 5–6, 18, 25, 26n2, 31–3, 35, 39, 42–3, 55, 65, 78, 85–6, 138, 142, 175–6, 194
post-Communist 32, 45, 52n3
pre-Communist Poland 74
resistance to 26, 29–30, 46, 52n1, 82
Soviet-enforced 1, 19, 23, 38–9, 44, 84, 119, 153
theatre 9, 21, 29–30, 35, 41–2, 52, 55, 96, 139–40
 versus capitalism 8, 31–2, 84
 versus democracy 85, 92, 108
 versus socialism 5
 victims of 138
 see also Solidarity
community 3, 14–15, 41, 51, 63, 81–2, 98, 115, 134, 145–6, 148, 151, 155, 189, 191
 exclusive 20, 73, 109, 140, 186–7
 fetishization of 14
 national 2, 9, 15–16, 23, 61, 73, 141, 163, 167, 177, 202–3
 pluralistic 177
 Romantic 23, 41, 61, 63, 66, 68, 81
 spirit 3, 10, 32, 62, 81, 203
 substance 61–2
 of witnesses 144
Czajkowski, Michał 155

Dejmek, Kazimierz 2, 55, 59, 64, 81, 139–40
Demirski, Paweł 23, 47–8, 51, 52n4, 73, 76, 81, 123
 Był sobie POLAK POLAK POLAK i diabeł (There was a Polack, Polack, Polack and the Devil) 69–70
 Dziady. Ekshumacja (Forefathers' Eve. Exhumation) 66–8
 Tęczowa trybuna 2012 (Rainbow Stand 2012) 131–5
 Wałęsa. Historia wesoła, a ogromnie przez to smutna (Wałęsa. A Cheerful Story, and Because of This Enormously Sad) 78–80

democracy 4–6, 9, 16–19, 22, 23, 26, 27n3, 30, 74, 108, 128, 133–4, 200, 203, 204n4
  and gender 86, 88, 123
  'grey democracy' 35
  and homosexuality 110–11, 113
  and multiculturalism 132
  nationalism 2–3
  see also pluralism
dissensus 3, 15–16, 19, 21, 25, 73, 82, 98, 198, 203
Dolan, Jill
  utopian performative 123, 129–30
Dostoyevsky, Fyodor 17, 41, 57
  Bracia Karamazow (The Brothers Karamazov) 35, 37, 87
drag 90, 103, 105–8, 165
  and transvestism 106
Drewniak, Łukasz 43, 98, 108, 186, 195
Duniec, Krystyna 40, 42, 46, 92, 95, 166–7
Dziewulska, Małgorzata 60, 75

Eaglestone, Robert 163
ethnic other 176, 195, 199–200
Euripides 12–13, 166, 173n13
  Bacchae 96–7
Europe
  Central and Eastern Europe 4, 16, 19, 27n5, 29, 32, 74, 113, 126, 138, 175–6, 200
  colonization 181–4, 187, 199
  Eastern Bloc 4
  European Union (EU) 45–6, 54, 91–2, 113, 122, 201
  European values 4, 41, 56, 65, 123, 171, 177, 179
  'return to Europe' 5, 138, 179, 181
  Western Europe 12, 24, 27n5, 47, 54, 88, 131, 174–6
  see also migration
exclusion
  exclusive Polishness 17, 33, 81, 140, 177, 181, 195
  Jews 141, 199

minorities 15, 18, 177, 184, 186–7, 196, 199, 201
social 11, 14, 16, 21, 26, 49, 82, 120, 187, 202
women 81–2, 86, 108, 126
see also community

Feminism
  communism 87
  League of Polish Women 86
  in Poland 2, 24, 85–6, 91–4, 108–9, 191
  postfeminism 93
  second wave 86, 92, 162
  sztuka kobiet (women's art) versus sztuka feministyczna (feminist art) 93
  third wave 42, 91–2
  Western 87
Ferency, Adam 186–7, 189
Fidelis, Małgorzata 86
Filipiak, Izabela 116, 149, 163
Fischer-Lichte, Erika 9, 12
  perceptual multistability 99
Foucault, Michel
  reverse discourse 135
Fraser, Nancy 19–22, 28n7, 131–2
  perspectival dualism 132
  recognition 22, 131

García, Rodrigo
  Golgota Picnic 203
Gardzienice 40, 97, 109n4
gay and lesbian rights and identities 24, 33, 70, 110–16, 119–26, 128–37, 191, 195, 203
  coming-out narrative 126, 129, 136
gender 1–3, 11, 13, 16, 20, 24, 33, 37, 40, 79, 84–6, 88–9, 91, 93–108, 116, 120, 122–3, 125, 128–30, 134, 165, 179, 181, 183–4, 188–9, 196
  communism 85–7
  masculinity 20, 24, 95–6, 102, 107–8, 123, 127–8, 135–6, 183–4

Generation NIC (Generation Nothing) 78
Gierek, Edward 7, 48, 64
Gluhovic, Milija 150
Gogol, Nikolai
  The Government Inspector 48–9
Gombrowicz, Witold 57
  Iwona, księżniczka Burgunda (Ivona, Princess of Burgundy) 89–90, 100, 172n2
  Ślub (The Marriage) 33–4, 52n1
Gomułka, Władysław 44, 139
Grabowska, Magdalena 85–6
Graff, Agnieszka 85–6, 91–3, 112, 114, 127
Gross, Jan T. 25, 38, 112, 142–3, 146, 148, 151–7, 172n2
Grotowski, Jerzy 3, 40, 96, 126, 141, 172n3
Gruszczyński, Piotr 37, 43–4, 77, 81, 101
Grzegorzewski, Jerzy 9–11, 23, 57–66, 73, 80–1
Grzymisławski, Piotr 179–80
Gustowska, Izabella 93

Habermas, Jürgen 16, 19–20, 22
Halberstam, J. Jack 132–3
Hanuszkiewicz, Adam 7, 64, 90
Harris, Geraldine 94, 202
heroism 117, 127, 139, 142–3, 146, 156, 161, 165, 169–70, 179, 184
  see also Romantic hero; Romanticism, Polish
heterosexuality 24, 94, 100, 107–8, 120
Hilberg, Raul 148
Hirsch, Marianne 163
HIV and AIDS 13, 90, 123, 125–2, 202
Holocaust 111–12, 139, 145–8, 152, 156, 158–67, 170, 172n3
  bystander 148, 151–2, 169
  memory and memorialisation 70, 138–40, 143–4, 162–3, 172n6
  perpetrator 148, 150–2, 167, 169
Holoubek, Gustaw 2, 7, 39, 140
homophobia 15, 18, 24, 111, 113, 116, 120–3, 132, 134–5

'homoprawda' (homolobby) 110
Kampania Przeciw Homofobii (KPH, Campaign Against Homophobia) 116
homosexuality *see* queer
Hudziak, Andrzej 39, 97

identity politics 15, 92, 112, 115, 126, 130, 132, 134–5
inscenizator
  versus reżyser 57, 59
Institute of National Remembrance (Instytut Pamięci Narodowej, IPN) 142

Janion, Maria 54, 58, 65, 86, 91, 143, 146, 174–6, 179, 200
Jarocki, Jerzy 7–10, 33–5, 37, 43–4, 52n1, 57, 81
Jarzyna, Grzegorz 12, 27n5, 47, 50, 71, 100–1, 109n1, 114
Jedlicki, Jerzy
  bezradność 143
Jewish Historical Institute (Żydowski Instytut Historyczny, ŻIH) 142–3
Jews and Jewishness 24–5, 38, 112–13, 138–48, 151–71, 172n2, 173n11, 186–7, 189, 191–2, 195, 199, 203
  see also Polish/Jewish relations

Kaczyński, Jarosław and Lech 16, 45–6, 53–5, 67, 69, 78, 113, 118–24
  Fourth Republic 46, 67, 69, 118, 120, 122–3
  Law and Justice Party (Prawo i Sprawiedliwość) 16, 45, 54–5, 67, 78, 120–1, 136n4, 198–9
Kane, Sarah 12–13, 71, 92
  4.48 Psychosis 100–1
  Cleansed (Oczyszczeni) 98–101, 125, 189
Kantor, Tadeusz 3, 7, 23, 40, 55–6, 69, 80–1, 149–50, 172n3
Kapuściński, Ryszard 178
Katyń massacre 53, 147

Klata, Jan 23, 25, 48–51, 52n6, 66, 69, 71, 74–8, 81, 162, 164–5, 198–200
Kleczewska, Maja 24, 101–8, 109n5
Kobialka, Michal 16, 56, 81
Komorowski, Bronisław 72
Kopciński, Jacek 1–2, 11–12, 98, 106, 167
Kopka, Krzysztof 61, 158
KOR (Komitet Obrony Robotników) 147
Kornaś, Tadeusz 59, 105
Kosiński, Dariusz 53–4
Koterski, Marek
  Życie wewnętrzne (Inner Life) 88
Kowalczyk, Izabela 93
Kowalczyk, Janusz 95–6, 98
Kowalewski, Maciej 125
Kowalska, Jolanta 68, 70, 162, 164, 180–1
Kozyra, Katarzyna 40, 93, 100
Krakowska, Ewa 87
Krakowska, Joanna 42, 46, 92, 95, 134, 166–7
Kulawik, Teresa 86
Kulpa, Robert 113, 123
Kushner, Tony
  Angels in America 63, 123–6, 128–9, 134–5, 187, 191, 197n2
Kwaśniewski, Aleksander 45, 142–3, 155, 157

LaCapra, Dominick 145–6, 150
Laclau, Ernesto 18–19
Lefort, Claude 9, 17–18
Lehmann, Hans-Thies 13, 98
Le Madame 136–7n4
Levin, Hanoch
  Krum 97–8
Liber, Marcin 25, 90, 162–5
Libera, Zbigniew 40, 184–6, 191
Lupa, Krystian 9–11, 17, 24, 35–42, 48, 57, 87
Łysak, Paweł 71

Machczyńska, Apolonia 166–70
Makaruk, Maria 65
mannequins 37, 40, 168–9
martyrdom 69, 72, 142–3, 179
Masłowska, Dorota 25
  Dwoje biednych Rumunów mówiących po polsku (A Couple of Poor, Polish-Speaking Romanians) 192–5
  Wojna polsko-ruska pod flagą biało-czerwoną (Snow White and Russian Red) 193
Matka Polka (Mother Pole) 61, 79, 97, 162, 184
Matynia, Elżbieta 6, 61, 94–5, 97
McRobbie, Angela 93
Meissner, Krystyna 199
memory 60, 81, 144, 146, 149–50, 161, 170–1
  collective 74, 79, 153, 163, 170, 198–9
  countermemory 150
  cultural 7, 74, 150, 157, 159
  disorientating force 57
  and history 145, 156
  Inn of Memory 56
  memory politics 45, 143
  national identity 27n3, 46, 52n3, 138, 140, 143, 147, 158, 172n6, 202
  postmemory 162–3, 165
  public 139, 144
  see also Holocaust
Michlic, Joanna B. 25, 138–9, 142–3, 146, 151, 155
Michnik, Adam 35
Mickiewicz, Adam 43, 54–5, 58, 140
  Dziady (Forefathers' Eve) 11, 53–61, 63, 65–9, 71, 75, 161, 175, 180
migration 47, 162, 195, 198, 204n2
  economic migrant 192–5
  emigration 141, 148, 201
  immigration 192
Miłosz, Czesław 140

Index

Mizielińska, Joanna 113, 123
Modzelewski, Marek 109n1
Dotyk (Touch) 115, 120
Morawiec, Elżbieta 57, 59, 61
Mościcki, Paweł 47, 203
Mouffe, Chantal 18–19
Mrożek, Sławomir 43–4, 74
Musil, Robert
  Marzyciele (The Dreamers) 36
Muzeum Powstania Warszawskiego
  (Warsaw Uprising Museum) 147
Mykietyn, Paweł 95

national identity 2, 11, 15, 17, 22–4,
  26, 27n3, 33, 61, 64, 72, 81, 84,
  116, 118, 126, 161, 165, 167, 179,
  181, 189, 194, 201
  and ethnicity 16, 24–5, 33, 131,
    149–51, 180, 184, 195–6, 201
  Polishness 2, 11, 15, 17, 22, 33, 42,
    63, 133, 142, 176, 195–6, 200–2
nationalism 2, 9, 18, 25, 46, 51, 56,
  81, 85, 125, 130, 134–5, 142–3,
  148–9, 154, 171, 183–4, 188, 195
neoliberalism 4, 17, 26, 31–3, 35, 42,
  49, 69, 74, 93, 200, 204n4
New Left 43, 92
  Krytyka Polityczna (KP, Political
    Critique) 47, 52n6
Niziołek, Grzegorz 35, 95, 109n2, 139,
  143–4, 165, 172n6
Nowak, Andrzej 151
Nowak, Basia 86
Nowak, Maciej 1–2, 46–8, 74, 79
nudity 39, 41, 89–90, 95–6

Osterwa, Juliusz 64

Pałyga, Artur 25, 172n2
Pankowski, Rafał 45, 111–13
Paul II, John 40, 49, 70, 87–8, 122
Pawłowski, Roman 11, 40, 63–5, 89,
  94, 100, 115, 119–20, 122, 137n4,
  146–7, 156, 158, 161, 192–3, 201

perversity 24, 96, 102, 106–7, 135
Piłsudski, Józef 56, 76, 150–1
Plata, Tomasz 9–10, 106–7, 109n5
Pleśniarowicz, Krzysztof 56
pluralism 2–3, 9, 16, 18–19, 23, 26, 30,
  41–2, 63, 82, 92, 124, 129, 142,
  148, 160–1, 176–7, 201
  multiethnic 155, 176, 178, 184,
    201, 203
POLIN, the Museum of the History of
  Polish Jews 143
Polish/Jewish relations 25, 139, 141–3,
  145–73, 191, 203
  Auschwitz Cross 141
  Jedwabne 25, 38, 67, 141–2, 147–57,
    171, 172n2, 172n6, 173n9
  Kielce pogrom 141, 154
  March 1968 events 7, 25, 44, 55, 64,
    111, 139–41, 172n2
  Righteous Among the Nations
    152, 169
  żydokomuna
    (Judeo-communism) 152–4
political 2–6, 9, 13–14, 17–22, 26–7,
  31–2, 41, 44–6, 52n3, 52n6, 55,
  73–4, 111–12, 132–3, 141, 176
  act 3, 8, 133, 198–200, 202
  theatre 1–3, 6–10, 13–17, 19–21,
    23–7, 30, 32–4, 37–8, 42–4,
    46–8, 54, 56, 58, 61–2, 64–5,
    68, 70, 80–1, 95–6, 98, 127,
    130–6, 140, 147–8, 156,
    177, 183–4, 192, 195–6,
    198–203
polityka historyczna (historical
  politics) 45
Pollesch, René 47
Polonia 167
Polska Rzeczpospolita Ludowa (PRL)
  4–5, 8, 18, 26n2, 30, 32, 42–4, 48,
  67, 70, 79, 82n3, 122, 139, 162,
  175–6
Poniedziałek, Jacek 95, 99, 125,
  129, 159

postcolonial 25–6, 92, 174–80, 183–4, 189, 195–6, 201, 204n4
   hybridity 176
   Marxist theory 175
   mimicry 175–6, 183
   'second world' 5, 174–5
Prus, Maciej 59
publics
   counterpublics 14, 20–4, 82, 109, 123–30, 133, 136, 146, 191, 202–3
   interpublic versus intrapublic 22, 203
   public sphere 2, 8, 19–23, 26, 47, 54, 85–6, 108, 121, 129, 113, 133, 164, 187, 198, 201–3
   versus private sphere 9, 76, 83, 85, 95, 112, 149, 202

queer 23–4, 99–100, 103–4, 106, 111, 113–17, 122–36, 191–2
   camp aesthetics 92, 98, 112, 116, 125
   communitas 129
   public space 134
   theory 1, 24, 92–3, 113
   time 113

race
   black and blackness 177, 179, 181–4, 186–91, 193, 196, 197n2
   ethnic drag 177, 180, 182, 194–5, 201
   masquerade 177, 180, 182, 184–9, 194–6, 197n2
   mimesis 181, 189
   white and whiteness 11, 19, 26, 128, 178–96, 201
Radical Right Parties (RRP) 45–6
Radio Maryja 70, 121–2, 136n3
Radziwiłowicz, Jerzy 34, 84
Rancière, Jacques 14–15, 18, 20, 28n6, 202–3
Ravenhill, Mark 92
   Shopping and Fucking 114

Robinson, Amy 194
Rokem, Freddie 200
Romanska, Magda 141, 172n3
Romanticism, Polish 23, 27n5, 43, 49, 54–6, 58, 61–82, 97, 126, 161, 166, 170, 176
   communitas 51, 140
   messianism 51, 54, 140, 176
   Romantic hero 23, 35, 41, 53–4, 60–9, 73–82, 96, 140, 143, 141, 161, 184, 202
Round Table Talks 29, 73, 79–80, 83, 110
Różewicz, Tadeusz
   Śmierć w starych dekoracjach (Death in the Old Decorations) 57
Rubin, Wiktor 122
Rydzyk, Tadeusz 122, 136n3

sacrifice 61, 80, 97, 125, 140, 146, 148, 162, 166, 168–71
Schiller, Leon 42, 59, 126
Schneider, Rebecca
   binary terror 99
Schwab, Werner 47, 88
   Moja wątroba jest bez sensu albo zagłada ludu (My Liver is Pointless, or People's Annihilation) 89
   Prezydentki (First Ladies *or* Holy Mothers) 87–8
Second World War 34, 38, 42, 85, 96, 136n1, 138–9, 147, 158, 162, 199–200
secularism 41, 45–7, 63, 87, 105, 126, 145, 159
Shakespeare, William
   Hamlet 69, 74–8, 83–4, 95–6, 108, 136, 141
   Macbeth 50, 104–6
   Midsummer Night's Dream 102–4
   Taming of the Shrew 95
   The Tempest 97–8, 156–7

Index

Sieg, Katrin 177, 182–3
  see also race: ethnic drag
Sienkiewicz, Henryk 177–84, 196
Sierakowski, Sławomir 47, 52n6
Sikorska-Miszczuk, Małgorzata 25, 172–3n8
Skiba, Piotr 38, 41, 87
Słobodzianek, Tadeusz 25
  Nasza klasa (Our Class) 147–56, 170–1
Słowacki, Juliusz 49
  Balladyna 56, 90–1
  Fantazy 49–50
Smoleńsk crash 53–4, 72, 82
socialism 5–7, 19, 42–4, 86, 177
Solidarność (Solidarity) 23, 27n4, 29, 44, 47, 52n, 3, 67, 73–80, 82n3, 85, 87, 110–11, 140, 147, 164
Spivak, Gayatri 175
Stalin, Joseph 7, 43–4, 53, 64, 119, 151, 157
Stalinism 7, 138
Staniewski, Włodzimierz 96–7, 109n4
Stary Teatr (Kraków) 33–41, 51, 59, 83–4, 87, 100, 158, 173n13
Steinlauf, Michael C. 138–9
Stokfiszewski, Igor 132–3
Strzępka, Monika 23, 47–8, 51, 52n4, 66–73, 81, 123, 130–5
suffering 24, 40, 60–1, 97, 103, 138–9, 144, 147–9, 153, 161–3, 165, 174, 179, 184, 199, 200, 204n2
  hierarchy of 138, 153, 165
Sugiera, Małgorzata 13–14, 60–1
Swinarski, Konrad 9, 36, 56–62, 67, 75, 83, 126
Szczepkowska, Joanna 110–12, 114, 136n1
Szczęśniak, Małgorzata 95, 157
Szczawińska, Weronika 25
  W pustyni i w puszczy z Sienkiewicza i innych (In Desert and Wilderness with Sienkiewicz and Others) 177–81

sztuka krytyczna (critical art) 184, 197n1
Szylak, Aneta 74

Teatr Dramatyczny (Warsaw) 7–8, 37, 71, 95, 109n1, 114, 172n2, 178
Teatr Narodowy (National Theatre, Warsaw) 7, 10, 33, 59, 63, 109n1
Teatr Ósmego Dnia (Theatre of the Eight Day) 7, 32
Teatr Pieśń Kozła (Song of the Goat Theatre) 40, 109n4
Teatr Polski Bydgoszcz 71, 109n1, 201, 204n4
Teatr Polski (Poznań) 71
Teatr Polski (Wrocław) 10, 43, 66, 122, 130, 162
Teatr Rozmaitości (TR Warszawa) 12, 47, 51, 52n6, 63, 71, 95–6, 100, 109n1, 116–17, 123, 125, 156–7, 192
Teatr Studio (Warsaw) 59, 192
Teatr Współczesny (Szczecin) 88, 90, 162, 172n2
Teatr Współczesny (Wrocław) 198–9
Teatr Wybrzeże (Gdańsk) 46–9, 59
Teatr ZAR 109n4
Theatre Institute (Instytut Teatralny im. Zbigniewa Raszewskiego) 1–2, 51, 142
Thompson, Ewa 79, 172n7, 175–6
Tomasik, Krzysztof 116–17
trauma 15, 43, 61, 68, 144–7, 149–50, 156, 160–4
  working through versus acting out 145–6
Trela, Jerzy 35

Umińska Keff, Bożena
  Utwór o matce i ojczyźnie (Song of the Mother and the Fatherland) 162–5

Villqist, Ingmar
  Anaerobes 114–15
violence 14, 25, 32–3, 42, 51, 77, 89, 91–2, 95, 98, 100, 105, 113–14, 118, 120–2, 141, 154, 156, 164, 168, 171, 180, 182, 189, 193
visibility 9, 16, 100, 111, 113, 115–16, 120, 124, 126, 146, 196–9, 201–3

Wajda, Andrzej 8–9, 24, 57, 74–7, 79, 82n3, 83–5, 95–6, 108, 158
Wałęsa, Lech 47, 74, 78–80, 110–13
Warkocki, Błażej 111–12, 116–17, 123–4, 131–2, 134–5
Warlikowski, Krzysztof 11–12, 24–5, 27n5, 40, 63, 95–108, 123–36, 156–62, 165–71, 177, 184–91, 194, 196
Warner, Michael 14, 20, 130
Węgrzyniak, Rafał 47, 52n4, 126, 158, 161
Witkiewicz, Stanisław Ignacy (Witkacy) 38, 57
  Szewcy (The Shoemakers) 52n6
Witkowski, Michał
  Lubiewo (Lovetown) 115–16

Wodziński, Paweł 23, 71–3, 81, 204n4
Wojcieszek, Przemysław 192
  Cokolwiek się zdarzy, kocham cię (Whatever Happens, I Love You) 109n1, 117–21
  Darkroom 121–2
Wyspiański, Stanisław 59, 75–6, 83–4, 141
  Klątwa (The Curse) 88
  Noc listopadowa (November Night) 11, 61–4
  Powrót Odysa (Return of Odysseus) 37
  Wesele (The Wedding) 57–8
  Wyzwolenie (Liberation) 62

Zadara, Michał 23, 46, 51, 70, 80, 82n3
Żebrowska, Alicja 40, 93, 100
Ziemie Odzyskane (Recovered Territories) 32, 199
Žižek, Slavoj 15, 18, 28n7, 52n6
Żmijewski, Artur 40, 127
Żurawiecki, Bartosz 116
  Sekstet 115, 119
  Trzech panów w łóżku, nie licząc kota (Three Men in Bed, Not Counting the Cat) 116

EU authorised representative for GPSR:
Easy Access System Europe, Mustamäe tee 50,
10621 Tallinn, Estonia
gpsr.requests@easproject.com

www.ingramcontent.com/pod-product-compliance
Ingram Content Group UK Ltd.
Pitfield, Milton Keynes, MK11 3LW, UK
UKHW021840140426
5217IPUK00022B/1535